Perfect Days

PORTUGAL

Travel with **Insider Tips**

Contents

 TOP 10 4

That Portugal Feeling 6

For chapters: See inside front cover

TOP 10

Not to be missed!

Our TOP 10 hits – from the absolute No. 1 to No. 10 – help you plan your tour of the most important sights.

1 ⭐ PRAIAS DO ALGARVE ► 164

Sandwiched between cliffs and the Atlantic, these Algarve beaches are a mix of tiny bays and long stretches of golden sand (left).

2 ⭐ SAGRES & CABO DE SÃO VICENTE ► 167

Named after Saint Vincent, the *Cabo* ("Cape") pushes dramatically out to sea in the southwestern most corner of the Algarve.

3 ⭐ BELÉM ► 50

The glory of Lisbon's seafaring age is kept alive in this district a short way outside the city centre. Its highlights include the Torre de Belém and the Mosteiro dos Jerónimos.

4 ⭐ SINTRA ► 56

This small town and its surroundings are overflowing with nature and culture. You'll be impressed by its lush green slopes, its magnificent twin palaces and its castle walls from the Moorish era.

5 ⭐ MOSTEIRO DE BATALHA ► 114

This highly decorative stone monastery is unmatched by any edifice in Portugal. It was built as a symbol of the nation's victory over their Spanish neighbours.

6 ⭐ COIMBRA ► 118

Coimbra, the most beautiful university town in the country, is a popular place to study. Spend some time discovering its diverse charms by the Mondego river.

7 ⭐ FÁTIMA ► 122

Even if you're not very religious, you'll find it hard to resist the atmosphere in Fátima, one of the best-known pilgrimage destinations in Christendom.

8 ⭐ SERRA DA ESTRELA ► 124

The "Star Mountains" stand at an altitude of nearly 2,000m (6,562ft). Head there to explore the hiking routes and rock formations of Portugal's highlands.

9 ⭐ CASTELO DE SÃO JORGE ► 61

Lisbon's extensive castle complex is just waiting to be discovered. Visitors are rewarded with some fantastic views out over the beautiful city.

10 ⭐ VILA NOVA DE GAIA ► 88

Wine fans should check out this town on the banks of the Douro opposite Porto, Portugal's second largest metropolis. It's home to some major port wine cellars that are definitely worth a visit.

THAT
PORTUGAL

Find out what makes the country tick and experience its unique flair – just like the Portuguese themselves.

LIFE'S A BEACH

Portugal is full of fantastic beaches. Nowhere is this more true than in the Algarve, the flagship region between **Vila Real de Santo António** and the **Cabo de São Vicente**. If, like many surfers, you prefer wilder seas, travel to the **Costa Vicentina** in the extreme southwest instead.

Head south of Lisbon to find the city dwellers' favourite beach retreats on the **Costa da Caparica**. If you're in central Portugal, explore the sands near **Peniche**, **Nazaré** and **Figueira da Foz**.

PLAYING THE MARKET

The Portuguese love their markets. And why wouldn't they? They sell newly plucked oranges, freshly caught fish, tasty herbs,, vegetables, goat's cheese, sausages, honey from the beekeeper and a great deal more besides. Markets come in all shapes and sizes, ranging from the weekly event in **Olhão's** magnificent market halls to the sale held in **Barcelos** on Thursdays. Check them out for a colourful, vibrant, authentic Portuguese experience!

SAIL AWAY

Portugal is an old seafaring nation, so there's no better way to admire its coast than from the water. Numerous boat trips set off to discover the caves, bays and cliffs of the Algarve, particularly during the summer months. The region around **Lagos** is especially stunning – you'll find plenty of tour operators there who are ready and waiting to show you the sights.

GREEN TOURISM

Portugal has its fair share of package holidays, tourist blocks and concreted coastal towns. Nevertheless, if you're prepared to explore the less-travelled parts of the interior, you'll find idyllic country house lodgings that are perfect places to relax. Head to the village of **Brejão** in the south-west, for example, and stay at the friendly Cerro da Fontinha (tel: 282 949 083; www.cerroda fontinha.com) – an impressive country retreat with rustic little houses and its own private lake.

FEELING

Portugal's markets are a real treat for all the senses

That Portugal Feeling

JOURNEY TO THE CENTRE OF THE EARTH

Come and marvel at Portugal's beautiful caves and their fantastic rock formations. Make the short trip from Fátima, the nation's best-known pilgrimage site, to delve into the **Grutas da Moeda** (tours daily, April–June 9–6; July–March 9–5; admission €6; www.grutasmoeda.com). Visitors to these caves, discovered in the 70s, can explore down to a depth of 45m (150ft). Alternatively, head 15km (9.5mi) southwest of Fátima to the **Grutas de Mira de Aire**, an even more impressive natural phenomenon (daily, July, Aug 9:30–8; June, Sep 9:30–7; April, May 9:30–6; Oct–March 9:30–5:30; admission €6.60; www.grutasmiradaire.com). Both caves make great family destinations.

Time for a break? It's best with a _bica_

PORTUGAL: KING OF THE CASTLES

Portugal boasts a large number of imposing castles, whose storied walls, halls and dungeons are steeped in dramatic tales and fascinating history. The nation is also home to such impressive fortified settlements as **Óbidos** and **Marvão**. You'll find one of the best preserved – and most mysterious – castles on the Iberian Peninsula in **Tomar**. Once the medieval seat of the Knights Templar, it's a World Heritage Site today.

RELAX AND SMELL THE COFFEE

The Portuguese have mastered the art of living – they relax, take their time, and enjoy life at their own pace. Their favourite method of chilling out is to meet some friends and drink a _bica_ – a short, black coffee – while having a chat and watching the world go by.

TAKE A HIKE

You don't have to do anything as daring as parachuting to truly experience Portugal – setting out on foot is just as good. Such mountainous regions as the **Serra da Estrela** and the **Serra de Monchique** are great places to walk, as are coastal sections of the **Algarve**. Try the **Rota Vicentina**, a long-distance hiking route in the southwest, where you'll catch the scent of lavender, sea salt and samphire, see carpets of icicle plants and watch storks and sea-gulls soaring through the skies.

The Magazine

21st-century PORTUGAL

Visit Portugal today and you are just as likely to hang out in a trendy lounge bar, play on some of Europe's best golf courses or shop in the chic Chiado quarter of Lisbon as you are to sit on a beach or watch a religious procession.

21st-century Portugal is changing fast. This dynamism is partly due to entering the European Economic Community (EEC, now the European Union (EU)) in 1986, when Portugal broke with its more traditional past. The nation's fortunes have been mixed ever since. At the turn of the century, Portugal enjoyed several years as one of Europe's fastest-growing economies – despite having the longest working hours in the EU and some of its lowest salaries. The financial crisis then tore through the country, however, putting an end to the party.

Economic Woes

In the latter half of the decade, with crippling public debt, low productivity and disappointing growth in the wake of the global recession, the country began to suffer. In 2011, there was widespread opposition to the proposed austerity measures to tackle the budget deficit, which included tax increases and cuts to pensions, salaries and unemployment benefits. Faced with a struggling economy, Portugal followed Greece and Ireland, becoming the third country to receive a bail-out from the EU and the International Monetary Fund. The nation's austerity measures, which were further increased by politicians in 2014, hit lower and middle class citizens extremely hard. More and more people began to demonstrate in the streets. In 2015, the Portuguese rejected the EU's help and formed a new government with the aim of loosening their economic shackles. Tourism is one of the things they're hoping will help them recover.

Bright Future

Despite all all its woes, Portugal has progressed rapidly over the past few decades. Airports, stations and harbours have been modernized, mainly with a view to tourism, which now brings over 8 million visitors to the country every year. For much of the 20th century, Portugal was inaccessible for the average traveller – as late as 1985, there was just one motorway running between Porto and Lisbon, and very few ways of exploring further afield. Today, there are dozens of new roads opening up the interior and linking previously unreachable regions with Lisbon and Spain.

The staging of Expo'98 in Lisbon (➤ 69) on the 500th anniversary of Vasco da Gama's journey to India unleashed a building boom in the capital, bringing new bridges, Metro lines, skyscrapers and malls; Euro 2004 also meant vast sums were spent on new stadia and upgrading hotels.

The most recent example of the nation's wide-scale urban

The Ponte Vasco da Gama in Lisbon

The Magazine

regeneration is the northern Portuguese city of Guimarães (➤ 101), Europe's Capital of Culture in 2012. Once famous as a textile-manufacturing hub, Guimarães is getting a new lease of life today, with design-oriented restaurants, artists' studios and cultural centres giving the UNESCO-listed town a new buzz and energy.

Breaking with the Past

The first seeds for this intense period of change came with the Carnation Revolution of 1974, when the people of Lisbon ended over 40 years of dictatorship under António Salazar by stuffing carnations down the barrels of soldiers' guns. At the same time, the end of the colonial wars and giving independence to their former African colonies brought thousands of Angolans, Cape Verdeans and Mozambicans to Lisbon, creating a vibrant, racially diverse, tolerant city.

> "Catholic priests are no longer seen as the guardians of public morality in Portugal"

During the 1980s, Portugal moved into the European mainstream, and some of its more entrenched traditions began to wane; the influence of the Catholic church, for example, is declining and, although over 79,5 per cent of the population declared themselves Catholic and religious festivals are as popular as ever, attendance at church is low. Catholic priests are no longer seen as the guardians of public morality, and contraception is widely available. Unmarried sex is not taboo and homosexuality is more widely accepted.

Portuguese Heroes

Portugal is also making more of an impact outside its borders. Novelist José Saramago (1922–2010) won the Nobel Prize for Literature in 1998; Paula Rego (b. 1935) is an internationally fêted artist; and Álvaro Siza Vieira (b. 1933) is a Pritzker Prize-winning architect. Cristiano Ronaldo has been crowned FIFA World Player of the Year no fewer than three times, and football manager José Mourinho has won the Champions League and been in charge of Portugal's FC Porto, Spain's Real Madrid, England's Chelsea and Manchester United, and Italy's Inter Milan.

SPEAKING PORTUGUESE

Today, the population of Portugal stands at around 10.6 million, with a further three million citizens living abroad. Portuguese is spoken by more than 215 million people worldwide and is the official language of Brazil and five African nations, including Angola and Mozambique. Other Portuguese-speaking countries include Macau and East Timor. This makes Portuguese the world's seventh most spoken language – it's even more common than French.

Portugal in a Glass
PORT AND WINE

It is many years since Portugal's wine industry has been just about port and Mateus Rosé. Inspired by indigenous grape varieties and helped by a warm sunny climate, winemakers are now making rich, smooth red wines and crisp, fresh whites that compete with other quality wine regions.

It takes grit to make wine in much of the country. Many of the vines grow on sharp, heat-baked schist rocks that can only be cared for by hand because of steep slopes that sit at around 700m (2,297ft) above sea level. Nowhere is this more evident than the beautiful Douro Valley (▶ 188) in the north of Portugal, which has long been famous for its production of grapes destined for port and is the oldest demarcated wine region in the world. Today, it is also producing well-structured, powerful red wines that have deservedly been getting more and more international attention – perfect for pairing with a rich steak sauce.

The mild and sunny Portuguese climate creates the perfect conditions for winegrowers

The Magazine

Fruity Reds and Crisp Whites

Heading further south, the pretty Beiras region halfway between Porto and Lisbon produces the full-bodied reds of the Dão and the fruity reds of Bairrada. Further south still, the Alentejo (between Lisbon and the Algarve) is one of Portugal's most prestigious wine regions, with new producers bringing in fresh ideas and outside investment.

> ## "Alentejo is probably the fastest-growing wine region in the country"

White-wine lovers shouldn't dismiss the vibrant, slightly sparkling Vinho Verde that comes from northwest Portugal. It has managed to shake off much of its old-fashioned image in recent years, and is the perfect aperitif; order it on a shaded terrace in the hot sunshine, or pair it with an appetizer of grilled sardines.

Port – Perfect Anytime

While the vineyards of Portugal develop, port still remains the symbol of the local drinks industry and is a drink to be enjoyed at any time – a white port and tonic as an aperitif or an aged tawny with chocolate cake.

Wine has been made in the 100km (62-mile) stretch of the Douro Valley since Roman times, but the origins of port lie in the 17th century, when British traders, cut off from their supplies of claret by wars with France, developed a taste for strong Portuguese wines. The Methuen Treaty of 1703 lowered the duty on Portuguese wine coming into Britain in return for concessions for British textile merchants in Portugal. Unfortunately, the wines did not travel well, so the port shippers began adding brandy to fortify them during their voyage. Port was born, along with the names (Croft, Dow's and Taylor's) that still control much of the trade.

Insider Tip

VISITING THE PORT HOUSES

Both the Douro vineyards and Vila Nova de Gaia are UNESCO World Heritage Sites. Wine tourism in these areas has meant that many port houses have opened up to visitors, and a variety of car, boat and train trips have emerged to up to help you explore the terraced vines. The town of Porto (►90) is a perfect weekend destination with its narrow winding streets and large, handsome squares. Climb to the highest point in the city to enjoy some beautiful views out over the river to Vila Nova de Gaia (►88), where you'll see neon signs for famous brands of port that make it look like a tiny Hollywood Hills. Over in Vila Nova de Gaia itself are some attractive wine bars and restaurants, and extensive restoration work has been done on the waterfront. Some of the best port houses to visit include Ramos Pinto and Taylor's (►89; although lots of other houses also open their doors). It goes without saying that you'll get to taste and buy their wares during your tour.

STYLES OF PORT

White: Dry or sweet, and served chilled as an aperitif.

Pink: Light and fruity style of port designed to appeal to younger drinkers.

Ruby: Dark, full-bodied and fruity.

Tawny: Amber-coloured, aged in wood for ten years or more.

Colheita: Complex, spicy, single-harvest tawny aged for at least seven years.

Late Bottled Vintage (LBV): Smooth and light-bodied port from a single-harvest wine aged in wood for four to six years.

Vintage: In exceptional years, a vintage may be declared and the very best wine will be transferred into bottles after two years in the cask. It will age in the bottle for at least ten years, developing a dark colour, a heady aroma and a crusty sediment. Vintage port should be decanted before being served, and it needs to be consumed within a day of being opened.

Insider Tip

The grapes – usually Tinta Roriz and Touriga Nacional – are harvested by hand in autumn, and crushed in stone vats or (more usually) fermented in steel tanks. After two days, the fermentation process is stopped by the addition of grape spirit and the wine is transferred into wooden casks (known as pipes). The following spring, the casks are taken to mature in the port lodges at Vila Nova de Gaia (➤ 88). Since the construction of several dams, traditional *barcos rabelos* (➤ 88) can no longer travel along the Douro. Today, trucks are often used to transport the casks from the *quintas* (farms) to the lodges in Vila Nova de Gaia, which has led to the emergence of smaller houses that sell direct from the Douro.

The port houses in Vila Nova de Gaia open their doors to visitors

Nautical NATION

On the edge of the Atlantic and at odds for much of its history with Spain, its only land neighbour, the coastline defines Portugal's identity as a seafaring nation, and its influence is seen in everything from architecture to food.

The Age of Discovery

The Portuguese like to look back to the golden age when their explorers sailed uncharted waters in search of new lands. The greatest of all these heroes is Henry the Navigator (1394–1460, ➤ 90, 167), Grand Master of the Order of Christ and architect of the *descobrimentos* (discoveries).

Henry took part in the capture of Ceuta in Morocco in 1415, but never sailed again, retiring instead to Sagres (➤ 156–157) where – according to one controversial theory – he established a school of navigation to train the nation's best minds. Here, new forms of navigational instruments were developed and a design was created for the *caravel*, a novel type of ship that was a cross between a traditional Douro cargo boat and an Arab *dhow*. The *caravel* revolutionized sea travel. Its triangular sails allowed sailors to take advantage of side winds and travel much faster. Columbus (1451–1506) even used them during his voyages to the New World.

Great Explorers

During Henry's lifetime, Madeira and the Azores were "discovered" and the explorer Gil Eanes rounded the Cape Bojador in West Africa – believed

at the time to be the end of the known world, beyond which were thought to lurk sea monsters and unknown perils.

The holy grail was the discovery of a sea route to India by Vasco da Gama in 1498, which allowed Portugal to control the trade of oriental spices, silks and carpets that crossed Asia, and establish colonies in Angola and Mozambique as well as trading posts in Goa,

A statue of Henry the Navigator in Lagos

According to one theory, Henry the Navigator set up a Nautical School on the Cabo de São Vicente

Timor and Macau. The Ponte Vasco da Gama in Lisbon is a fitting tribute to the great man; the bridge crosses the Rio Tejo at 17.2km (10.7mi).

In the meantime, Pedro Álvares Cabral had found Brazil somewhat accidentally. It was awarded to Portugal under the 1494 Treaty of Tordesillas, which divided the known world into Spanish and Portuguese spheres of influence. The country's naval power declined during the 17th century as the Dutch and English fleets grew in strength, particularly in the East Indies and Asia. Nevertheless, Macau, Portugal's last overseas colony, was only handed back to China as late as 1999.

PORTUGAL'S GREAT VOYAGES OF DISCOVERY

1419 Madeira

1427 The Azores

1434 Gil Eanes manages to sail round West Africa's legendary Cape Bojador

1460 Cape Verde

1482 Diego Cão reaches the mouth of the Congo, leading to the Portuguese conquest of Angola.

1488 Bartolomeu Dias rounds the Cape of Good Hope, South Africa.

1498 Vasco da Gama discovers a sea route to India.

1500 Pedro Álvares Cabral discovers Brazil.

1519 –1522 Fernão de Magalhães (Ferdinand Magellan) leads the first circumnavigation of the world. He dies en route and the journey is completed under the leadership of Juan Sebastián Elcano.

To learn more about Portugal's relationship with the sea, visit the Museu de Marinha in Belém (► 52), which is devoted to Portugal's maritime history.

Padrão das Descobrimentos, Lisbon, built to commemorate Portugal's great explorers

Portuguese Fishing Industry

In the 20th century, Portugal still had one of the world's largest fishing fleets. Cod fishing off the coast of North America and Canada became the driving force of the Portuguese economy, with elaborate ceremonies held to wave the men off on fishing voyages. In recent years, however, the Portuguese fishing fleet has declined due to overfishing and stringent rules aimed at conserving the world's deep-sea fish stocks. Nevertheless, fishing is still an important source of income for some, and brightly coloured wooden boats remain a familiar sight in ports like Peniche and Nazaré (➤ 6) on the west coast, and Lagos (➤ 177) and Olhão in the Algarve.

These days, the sea is yielding a different but nonetheless lucrative harvest: tourists are attracted to the superb beaches of the Algarve, Costa de Lisboa, Costa de Prata and Costa Verde. As well as swimming and sunbathing, these visitors love boat trips, and set sail from the nation's traditional harbours like the early explorers before them.

MANUELINE ART

King Dom Manuel I is known as Manuel the Fortunate as it was during his reign (1495–1521) that the sea route to India was discovered, bringing riches to Portugal in the form of spices, ivory and gold. The king has lent his name to a uniquely Portuguese version of late Gothic architecture, inspired both by the florid forms of Indian art and by the discoveries themselves. The most typical symbols of Manueline art are the armillary sphere (a navigational device consisting of a celestial globe with the earth at the centre, which became the emblem of Manuel I), the cross of the Order of Christ, seafaring imagery such as anchors and knotted ropes, and exotic fauna and flora from the newly discovered lands. The finest examples of Manueline art are the monastery and tower at Belém (➤ 51), the cloisters and unfinished chapels of the abbey at Batalha (➤ 114) and the windows of the Convento de Cristo at Tomar (➤ 128).

POUSADAS
and *Solares*

A Portuguese guest house is a great way to experience local traditions. Choose between *pousadas* (historic buildings converted into atmospheric hotels) and *solares,* usually former manor houses now upmarket family-run B&Bs.

Convento dos Lóios in Évora is a 15th-century monastery converted into a *pousada*

On 19 April 1942, the first *pousada* opened in the border town of Elvas to cater for travellers from Spain. The price of a double room was 80 escudos (€0.40). The *pousadas* were state-run inns along the lines of the Spanish *paradores*, offering simple hospitality and regional cuisine, and were the brainchild of the minister for popular culture and tourism, António Ferro. "At the current time, nearly all construction in Europe is intended for war," he said at the opening ceremony. "Our *pousadas* will be fortresses of peace, refuges of grace and quiet."

Pousadas Today

Today, more than 70 years later, there are around 35 *pousadas* in Portugal, but they are no longer state-owned and are anything but modest. All of them are housed in historic buildings, such as restored castles in Óbidos (➤ 134) and Estremoz (➤ 152), or situated in places of natural beauty –

a village house in Marvão (► 155), for example, or a convent in Évora ► 155 and Beja ► 156.

Insider Tip Perhaps the finest of all the *pousadas* is the Pousada Mosteiro de Guimarães (► 105), a converted 12th-century Augustinian monastery overlooking the historic city of Guimarães. Its bedrooms are located in former monks' cells around the cloisters, with gorgeous tile-lined stairways and corridors filled with antiques. In contrast, the *pousada* at Bragança in the far northeast of the country is much more modern, but still manages to impress thanks to its magnificent city views.

António Ferro wanted the *pousadas* to be "small hotels where people could feel at home". For Ferro, rustic furniture and local crafts were part of the experience, which was summed up as unostentatious comfort.

Ironically, as levels of service rise ever higher in response to customer demands, the *pousadas* are in danger of moving away from their roots and Ferro's ambition to make guests feel truly at home: "If a guest walks into one of our *pousadas* and feels as if he has returned to his own house, then we will have achieved what we were striving for."

Solares de Portugal

For a home-from-home experience, you could stay in a Portuguese family *solar*. This is hardly a low-key option, as many *solares* are manor houses converted into guest houses where you will be warmly welcomed, have the chance to brush up your Portuguese and sample home cooking at its best

All of the accommodation is arranged by an umbrella organisation, Solares de Portugal (► 39). A typical example of the classy lodgings they offer is the Paço de Calheiros (tel: 258 947 164; www.pacodecalheiros.com), a noble family's home that sits above the Rio Lima valley. The beautiful house, built in the 17th century, stands at the end of an avenue of magnolia trees with a stone fountain in the yard. Chestnut ceilings are weighed down with chandeliers, and family portraits hang on the walls. The chapel has a carved 17th-century altarpiece and a vault where the last Count is buried. The old stables have been turned into apartments and there is a swimming

The elegant and comfortable interior of the Pousada Mosteiro do Crato

Many *pousadas* are converted historic buildings, such as this castle in Palmela

pool and tennis court in the grounds. The terrace boasts views out over the vineyards to Ponte de Lima – the headquarters of Solares de Portugal and the town with the largest concentration of manor houses in the scheme.

A few hours east at Trás-os-Montes (▶ 85) in the municipality of Macedo de Cavaleiros, you'll find the Solar das Arcas (tel: 278 400 010; www.solaresdeportugal.pt). This 17th-century mansion belongs to the Pessanha family and was built for the descendants of a Genoese navigator who came to Portugal in the 14th century at the invitation of Dom Dinis. The thoroughly rustic apartments are filled with wooden furniture, interspersed with touches of modernity and little works of art. The only sounds you can hear in the rooms are

> "From your room, the only sounds you can hear are church bells and horses' hooves"

church bells and horses' hoofs clip-clopping on the village street outside. The Pessanhas offer guests their own wine, home-cured sausages and advice on walking, cycling and horse-riding in the area.

Solares de Portugal offers around 100 properties, from manor houses and country estates to rustic farmhouses and cottages. Most are in the Minho, but others are scattered across Portugal, right down to the Alentejo and the Algarve. Most are in quiet rural locations and many have swimming pools. However, what makes this experience really special is that guests enjoy a real insight into Portuguese family life.

USEFUL ADDRESSES
- Pousadas de Portugal, Rua Soares de Passos 3, Alto de Santo Amaro, 1300-314 Lisbon; tel: 218 442 001; www.pousadas.pt (▶ 39).
- Solares de Portugal, Praça da República 4990, Ponte de Lima, Lisbon; tel: 258 931 750; www.solaresdeportugal.pt (▶ 39).

FADO
Lisbon's Urban Blues

You may not have heard of *fado*, but this bittersweet music will plunge you headfirst into the nation's folk and blues traditions with its tales of destiny, love, death and despair.

A traditional *fado* evening can be dramatic – all eyes are on the musicians, one with a *guitarra* (a Portuguese guitar that looks like a mandolin), the other with a *viola* (an acoustic Spanish guitar). There is silence as a woman dressed in black rises to sing. She sings of love and death, of triumph and tragedy, of destiny and *fado* (fate). Above all she sings of *saudade,* that Portuguese sentiment best translated as a longing for that which has been lost – perhaps a broken love affair or the days when Portugal was a great seafaring nation. UNESCO placed *fado* on their Intangible Cultural Heritage list in 2011.

Fado Clubs

There are singers today who are renewing *fado* and finding fresh audiences both in Portugal and abroad. Nevertheless, you'll still find lots of musicians who enjoy playing it in its old, luxurious form. *Fado* makes for a great night out. Some venues will try and overcharge for meals, but in general the music is taken very seriously, and the *fado* clubs in Lisbon are wonderful places to go. For the most authentic experience, try the backstreet cellar clubs of Alfama. If you're in Bairro Alto, check out the reliable Café Luso. A few streets away, guitarist Mário Pacheco

---

THE ORIGIN OF *FADO*

Fado has its origins in the working-class *bairros*, or neighbourhoods, of Lisbon in the early 19th century where it was played in taverns and brothels. In the 1920s, the first *casas de fado* opened, with professional singers making records and putting on shows for tourists. It is only now that *fado* is making a comeback among young Portuguese as a genuine art form. It is melancholy, dramatic and heart-wrenching – think of the blues. All female *fadistas* wear a black shawl in memory of Maria Severa (1820–46), the first great *fado* singer, whose scandalous affair with a bullfighter and tragically early death are the subject of many songs.

A traditional *fado* singer in a restaurant in Lisbon

plays every night in the intimate, vaulted surrounds of his Clube de Fado, one of Lisbon's top-drawer *fado* clubs. Apart from levying a minimum charge, these venues are largely untouched by commercialism, and most of the customers are Portuguese. Outside Lisbon, the other *fado* centre is Coimbra, where it's usually sung in the city's streets and squares by men in academic robes.

For a more spontaneous experience, head for bars and clubs where house musicians play *fado vadio*. Anyone can turn up to sing there: *fado vadio* (literally "vagabond *fado*") is the amateur music of the people.

Visit Lisbon's Fado Museum if you want to explore this art form in even greater depth.

Modern *Fado*

The *fado* scene nourishes generation after generation of talented new voices. The selection of up-and-coming singers who have emerged at the top of the pile include Ana Moura and Cuca Roseta. Carminho, born in Lisbon, has also already made a number of international appearances.

LISBON'S *FADO* CLUBS

- **Café Luso**, Travessa da Queimada 10, Bairro Alto, tel: 213 422 281; www.cafeluso.pt
- **Adega Machado**, Rua do Norte 91, Bairro Alto; tel: 213 422 282; www.adegamachado.web.pt
- **Maria da Mouraria**, Rua do Capelão/Largo da Severa 2/2B, Alfama, Tel. 218 860 165, http://mariadamouraria.pt
- **Clube de Fado**, Rua São João da Praça 94; tel: 218 852 704; www.clube-de-fado.com

BEYOND THE BEACHES

Portugal has 960km (600mi) of beaches, but a few days exploring the interior will reveal traditional villages, vast acres of cork trees and breathtaking mountain ranges that offer excellent walking, hiking and adventure sports.

The highest mountains in Portugal – known as *Terra Fria* (Cold Lands) – are concentrated in the north and east and have a climate often described as "nine months of winter and three months of hell". Until fairly recently, these regions were very difficult to reach, but a new highway from Porto to Bragança has opened up the route to northern Spain, which passes through many of them. Today, you can easily reach the spectacular Douro Valley (▶ 188), with its terraced vineyards and craggy peaks that cover 250,000ha (617,763 acres), the bleakly beautiful Trás-os-Montes (▶ 85)

and Serra da Estrela (▶ 124), the highest range in mainland Portugal. For a gentler experience, explore the Peneda-Gerês ranges (▶ 99), a stunning national park that has several camping sites, beautiful waterfalls and plenty of activities, including walking trails.

Behind the Mountains

In Trás-os-Montes (which translates literally as Behind the Mountains, giving you some idea of how cut off the region has been), cars and tractors are replacing horse-carts and bullock-ploughs, and the emigrants who abandoned the area for lack of work opportunities are returning to build chic new houses (*casas de emigrante*) with the money they have made in France, Germany, Luxembourg and the USA, bringing with them cosmopolitan values and a taste for fast food.

However, the sense of other-worldliness has not entirely left Trás-os-Montes, making it fascinating to explore. Until recently, when people were ill, they used folk remedies or consulted the local witch. The winter solstice is still marked by masked dancers running through the village with cowbells round their waists in a ritual that dates to pagan times.

Vines growing on the terraced slopes in the Douro Valley

The Magazine

Tranquil scenery in Parque Nacional da Peneda-Gerês

As you move further down the country, the mountains may lose a little height, but that doesn't mean you can't find excellent opportunities to walk and explore. Head around 10km (6mi) south of Fátima, the famous pilgrimage site, to check out the 👬 dinosaur footprints near the village of Bairro in the Serras de Aire natural park – they're some truly impressive fossils! Kids will also love the many donkeys that live in the area. Limestone is the dominant rock in both the Serras de Aire and the Candeeiros natural park, and the region's dramatic caves and gullies are worth a visit.

For beach lovers who want a day off from the Algarve coast, there are a couple of very good walking opportunities in Serra de Monchique (➤ 172). This low-lying mountain range is within an hour's drive of the coast and is blanketed with cork, chestnut and eucalyptus trees.

INTO THE WILD

Some of the wildest parts of Trás-os-Montes are in the Parque Natural de Montesinho, between Bragança and the Spanish border. The heather-clad uplands rise to 1,480m (4,855ft), while the lower slopes support chestnut and holm oak. Golden eagles hover above the hills, wolves hide in the forests, and at weekends the local farmers go hunting for partridge, deer and wild boar (depending on the season). At least 90 villages are scattered about the park, with horseshoe-shaped dovecotes and slate-roofed houses where the oxen sleep downstairs and granite staircases lead to the living quarters above.

The village of Rio de Onor, right on the border, is half-Spanish, half-Portuguese. The only sign that you are crossing from one country to another is a stone block marked with the letters "E" (España) and "P" (Portugal). A study by the Portuguese anthropologist António Jorge Dias in 1953 found that the people of Rio de Onor lived a communal existence, sharing land and cattle with their Spanish neighbours quite independently of the State and speaking a dialect common to them both, Rionorês. Although the village has become depopulated in recent years, some traditions still survive.

TRÁS-OS-MONTES FOLK TRADITIONS

To find out more about Trás-os-Montes folk traditions, visit the local museums in Bragança (➤ 102) and Miranda do Douro (➤ 103).

Portuguese
PASSIONS

There is probably a festival going on somewhere in Portugal every day of the year. Outside these celebrations, Portuguese culture is full of drama, from the national obsession of football to the traditional spectacle of running with the bulls.

Festa!

Nothing quite matches the colour and spectacle of a Portuguese *festa*. Every town and village has its own saint's day, marked by religious processions, music, dancing and parades. Many of these festivals combine Christian and pagan elements, and all provide an excuse for partying, drinking, flirting and fireworks.

The biggest celebrations of the year centre around Holy Week in March or April, when candlelit processions are held. Another excellent event is the Festa de São João, which takes place in Porto (➤ 90) and Vila Nova de Gaia (➤ 88) at the summer solstice in June. Food plays an important part in almost all Portuguese festivals, and tiny roadside stalls sell sweet treats and grilled sardines. The Portuguese often spend all the money they have on festivities to put their everyday cares behind them.

Traditional costume of the Costa Verde

Festival of Tabuleiros, Tomar

The Magazine

Football...the Beautiful Game

There are plenty of secular pleasures to enjoy in Portugal as well, and football is the true modern-day obsession. Football has been played in the country since the 19th century, and the main competition is the Portuguese Liga. This highly popular league usually comes down to a play-off between FC Porto and two Lisbon teams – Benfica (in red) and Sporting (in green) (► 82). Until very recently, Portugal's national team had never managed to bring home any significant silverware from major competitions. That all changed at the Euros in 2016, however, when the squad managed to fend off host nation France to get their hands on the cup. Their captain, record goal-scorer Cristiano Ronaldo, has won far more awards than his country – he's been crowned FIFA World Player of the Year on no fewer than three occasions (2008, 2013 and 2014).

Best Annual Festivals

Carnival (Feb/March): Masked dances, fancy-dress and processions mark the arrival of Lent. The Loulé (► 175) and Elvas (► 152) parades are especially colourful.

Holy Week (March/April): Torchlit processions of hooded and barefoot penitents on the Thursday and Friday before Easter in Braga (► 96).

Festa das Cruzes (first weekend in May): A country fair in Barcelos, with processions of crosses along flower-strewn streets.

Queima das Fitas (May): A vibrant student festival with a big parade through the streets of Coimbra, a university town.

Festas dos Santos Populares (12–29 June): Three weeks of merrymaking takes place in Lisbon to mark the feasts of the "popular saints". On 12 June, the *bairros* of Lisbon are decorated and people pour into Alfama to eat grilled sardines at tables set up on the street.

Festa de São João (23–24 June): Bonfires and fireworks mark the summer solstice in Porto (► 90) with a regatta on the River Douro.

Germany and Portugal soccer fans

Festival celebrations

A LOAD OF BULL(S)

Especially over the summer months, you are likely to see a bullfight taking place somewhere in Portugal. The biggest difference with Spanish bullfights is that in Portugal bulls are not killed in the ring (though don't be fooled by the large declarations on posters, as they are invariably mortally wounded and dispatched out of sight after the fight).

The spectacle during a fight is dramatic, with bullfighters in 18th-century costumes and scarlet cummerbunds leaping onto the bull and wrestling it to the ground. If you'd prefer to witness a slightly less controversial tradition, however, check out bull-running. This takes place in the streets of Vila Franca de Xira, c. 35km (22mi) northeast of Lisbon, during the Festa do Colete Encarnado (Festival of the Red Waistcoat) in early July and the Feira de Outubro in early October. As in Pamplona in Spain, this event involves members of the public running through the streets with rampaging bulls. Don't decide to join in on a whim – people have been seriously injured in the past!

Romaria de Nossa Senhora da Agonía (weekend nearest 20 Aug): A huge, traditional *romaria* (religious festival) in Viana do Castelo (➤ 102) with concerts, parades, fireworks, folk dancing and the blessing of fishing boats.

Feiras Novas (Sep): A market, fairground, brass bands, parades and fireworks in Ponte de Lima, a centre of Minho culture. Usually held early in the month.

Festa dos Rapazes (25 Dec–6 Jan): Christmas in Portugal is a family affair, a time for eating *bacalhau* (salt cod) and *bolo rei* (fruit cake) – except in the villages around Bragança (➤ 102), where young men put on masks, cowbells and suits of ribbons and run through their villages in an ancient rite of passage that dates back to pre-Christian times.

Dignitaries assemble in front of a large crucifix during the Festa das Cruzes, Barcelos

FOOD Traditions

The Portuguese like to eat, and not only is there an enormous variety of traditional ingredients and cooking styles, but these are being interpreted and highlighted by young, world-class Portuguese chefs.

Grilling fresh sardines in Portimão

Seafood Delights

Portugal is an old seafaring nation, so there are no prizes for guessing that many of its restaurants feature plenty of fresh fish. Depending on the region and season, you can find pretty much every kind of fish you can imagine. The most sought after include sardines, red mullet (*salmonete*) and swordfish. If you can't decide on your favourite fish, try a *cataplana* – a mixed seafood dish of shellfish cooked with onions and potatoes – or a fish stew known as *caldeirada* – a delicious blend of fish, onions, garlic, potatoes and peppers. Wash it all down with a good glass of wine.

Regional Dishes

There are also many regional dishes that give clues to the history of the individual areas. In the Trás-os-Montes, for example, you often find a chicken sausage on the menu known as an *alheira*. This dates back to the 15th century, when Jews fled to the remote mountainous region from the Spanish Inquisition. The chicken sausage was first made as a way of fooling the Inquisitors that they had renounced their Jewish ways and had started to eat pork. They are still eaten today.

The Portuguese love to eat meat, and vegetarians may find a rather limited selection on offer. Meat eaters, however, will discover a succulent array of hams, sausages, salamis (in fact 40 per cent of meat eaten in

Portugal is pork). One of the best of these cured hams comes from Alentejo's acorn-fed black pigs and is known as *presunto de porco preto bolata*. These pigs have grazed in the gentle Montados countryside and are said to offer the same benefits to your heart as olive oil.

Cheese, Wines and Olive Oils

The region's cheeses are also found in a seemingly endless array of varieties. Most cheeses come either from ewes or goats, or a combination of both. The best known is probably Queijo da Serra da Estrela (► 125) from continental Portugal's highest mountain range. This is a delicious mountain sheep's cheese that is rich and creamy, and usually eaten straight out of the pot after six weeks of ripening.

In addition, regional wines and olive oils are also increasingly available with more and more regional single-*quinta* (from one estate) wines from quality-conscious producers, and new single-*quinta* olive oils from the Douro, Trás-os-Montes, Alentejo and Ribatejo.

> "the locals can't resist a sweet start to the day, or end to a meal"

Order of Play

All meals in Portugal are likely to start with soup (and again, vegetarians beware, as even vegetable soups usually have bits of meat lurking within them). Typical soup of the north is the *caldo verde,* with cabbage, onions and potatoes, while a chilled Alentejo soup is made of bread, egg and garlic. Many dishes have spicy touches that contain flavours of cumin, cinnamon, paprika and sweet peppers brought back from former Portuguese outposts in Brazil, Goa, the Azores and further afield.

The Portuguese really come into their own with their sweet specialities. All over the country, you'll find that the locals can't resist a sweet start to the day, or end to a meal. Among the stickiest treats on offer are the *doces conventuais,* little egg-yolk sweets. Look out also for *marmelada* – not marmalade as the name suggests, but a quince paste – and jams made from the delicious Elvas (► 145) plums. Towns large and small can be counted on to contain at least one or two bakeries, where you should ensure you stock up on egg custard *natas.*

BACALHAU

The Portuguese passion for *bacalhau* (dried salted cod, ► 41) has its origins in the fishing fleets that sailed the waters off Newfoundland in the early 16th century. At that time, there was an abundance of cod, but it had to be preserved for the journey back to Portugal. Despite the presence of numerous fresh fish off the coast, *bacalhau* remains a Portuguese favourite and there are said to be 365 different ways of cooking it.

ON THE TILES
The Art of *Azulejos*

If a single item could define Portuguese style, it'd be the *azulejo* tile. You'll see them everywhere you look, adorning stations, churches, shops, palaces, backstreet bars and entire façades of Lisbon buildings.

Azulejos are not unique to Portugal, but it is perhaps here that they have achieved their finest expression. Similar glazed and painted tiles are found across the Arab world and in the Spanish region of Andalucía, from where *azulejos* originally came.

The name probably derives from an Arabic phrase meaning "azure polished stone" and they were first introduced to Portugal in the late 15th century when Manuel I imported Hispano-Arabic tiles from Seville for his royal palace at Sintra (► 56).

Early Tiles
These early tiles were called *alicatados* and were made of monochrome pieces of glazed earthenware that were cut into shapes or separated by strips to form mosaic-like geometric patterns.

The Majolica technique was introduced from Italy during the 16th century. This involved coating the clay in a layer of white enamel onto which the artist could paint directly. In the 17th century, the fashion was for *tapetes* (carpet tiles), painted blue and yellow and resembling Moorish tapestries and rugs.

Mass Production

The first mass-production tile factory was set up after the 1755 earthquake in Lisbon, which also saw the development of the familiar blue-and-white tiles, heavily influenced by Chinese porcelain. The custom of covering entire house- and shop fronts with *azulejos* began in Lisbon during the mid-19th century and came from Brazil, where Portuguese settlers used it as a way of keeping out the tropical rain.

Visible throughout the whole of the country, *azulejos* tiles are a popular decorative addition to a wide variety of settings. They're used to create

Left: Cloisters of the Sé (Cathedral), Porto. Right: Jardim Zoológico de Lisboa, Lisbon

WHERE TO SEE *AZULEJOS*

- Museu Nacional do Azulejo, Lisbon (➤ 72)
- Palácio Nacional de Sintra (➤ 56)
- Sé Velha, Coimbra (➤ 120)
- Igreja dos Lóios, Évora (➤ 145)
- Igreja de Nossa Senhora da Consolação, Elvas (➤ 1453)
- Museu Regional, Beja (➤ 154)

The Magazine

gigantic mosaics of historic and religious scenes in monasteries and churches, add ornamental folk and rustic motifs to gardens and interior courtyards, and produce flowing geometric patterns around the doors and windows of private houses.

These colourful Portuguese ceramics help keep places cool in hot weather and add a ray of sunshine to otherwise polluted, asphalt grey streets. Monumental *azulejos* images make Porto's central Estação São Bento seem less severe and change the mundane space surrounding the station into a treasure trove of art. The same is true of Lisbon's underground rail network, where tiles have been used to transform the walls and staircases into unique *azulejos* galleries.

Azulejos add a touch of authentic Portuguese flair to Porto's São Bento station

Versatile Tiles

Azulejos are so wonderfully versatile: you'll spot their light blue, glowing red, subtle green and sharp orange tones adorning the interiors of bars and restaurants, covering public benches and fountains, and decorating terraces, stairs, street signs and advertising hoardings throughout Portugal.

It doesn't really matter that the tiles and the buildings they decorate are sometimes in a state of disrepair – they provide a constant whirl of colours and motifs that enriches everyday life and transforms the country into a unique open-air museum!

Finding Your Feet

First Two Hours

Lisbon, Porto and Faro all have international airports with tourist offices and car hire outlets. Airlines with frequent flights there include British Airways, TAP, Monarch, and such low-cost operators as Ryanair and easyJet.

Lisbon

■ **Portela Airport** (www.ana.pt) is 7km (4.3mi) north of the centre (tel: 218 413 500 for enquiries; tel: 218 413 700 for arrivals/departures) and 218 450 660 (tourist information).

■ The **Aerobus** to the city centre (final destination: Cais do Sodré) costs €3.50 (return: €5.50). Thebus leaves from Terminals 1 and 2 (daily 7am–11pm, every 20 mins). A further line (daily 7:30am–11pm, every 40 mins; every 60 mins after 8pm) serves the financial district (Av. José Malhoa Sul).

■ The **Metro** (www.metrolisboa.pt) starts at the station named Aeroporto ("airport") at the end of the Red Line. Change at S. Sebastião for the city centre (single: €1.40; 24-hrs: €6).

■ **Taxi** to central Lisbon cost about €26 (more for extra luggage or at night).

Porto

■ **Francisco Sá Carneiro Airport** is 11km (6.8mi) north of the city centre (tel: 229 432 400; www.ana.pt).

■ Take **Metro** Line E (the "violet" line; 6am–1am every 20 mins). It's 20–35 mins to the centre. Tickets €1.85–€2.70, depending on the zone.

■ A **taxi** to central Porto should cost around €25–30, with supplements for extra luggage or night travel.

Faro

■ **Faro Airport** is 6km (3.7mi) west of the city centre (tel: 289 800 800; www.ana.pt).

■ From the airport, take **buses** (www.proximo.pt) No. 16 and No. 14 into Faro. A ticket costs €2.22 (day ticket €5.29).

■ **Taxi** fares to Faro shouldn't cost more than €20–25. Book in advance at www.faroairporttransfersto.com

Tourist Information Offices

■ **Lisbon**: **Lisboa Welcome Center** (the main office), Praça do Comércio (tel: 210 312 810; www.askmelisboa.com; daily 9–8). You'll also find tourist offices at Santa Apolónia railway station and on Praça dos Restauradores (Palácio Foz, daily 9–8). There's an info kiosk at the Mosteiro dos Jerónimos in Belém (Mon–Sat 10–1 and 2–6).

■ **Porto:** The main tourist office is at Rua Clube dos Fenianos 25, near the top of Avenida dos Aliados (tel: 223 393 472; www.portoturismo.pt; June–Oct daily 9–8, Sep–May 9–7). You'll also find another at the central Terreiro da Sé; www.visitporto.travel

■ **Faro:** The tourist office is at Rua da Misericórdia 8 near the entrance to the Old Town (tel: 289 803 604). There is also an office at the airport (late June to late Sep daily 9–7, late Sep to late June 9–5:30); www.turismodoalgarve.pt, www.cm-faro.pt.

■ **The Algarve:** There are also tourist offices at Albufeira, Alcoutim, Castro Marim, Lagos, Loulé, Monchique, Portimão, Silves, Tavira and Vila Real de Santo António.

Getting Around

Portugal's compact size makes it easy to get around. There are excellent bus and train connections between the major cities in Portugal, but to get to the more out-of-the-way places you will need a car.

Driving

- Drivers **bringing their own cars** into Portugal need to carry their driving licence, registration document, insurance certificate and display a nationality sticker on their car.
- **Car rental** is available at all airports and in major towns and resorts. To rent a car you must be aged over 21 (sometimes over 25!), and have a passport, a driving licence and a credit card. You can book in advance through one of the reliable major international car rental agencies – this tends to be the cheaper option. Local firms also offer competitive rates, but you should check the level of insurance cover and excess they provide carefully before handing over your money. Keep the car-rental documents and your driving licence with you at all times.
- Theft from rental cars is common. Never leave items on display in the car, and take all valuables with you or lock them out of sight.

Driving Essentials

- Drive on the **right**.
- **Seat belts** are compulsory for the driver and all passengers.
- The legal **alcohol** limit is 0.05 per cent.
- **Speed limits**: 120kph (74mph) on motorways, 90kph (56mph) on main roads, and 50kph (31mph) in urban areas. (Beware speed cameras!).
- **Driving standards** are generally poor and Portugal has one of the highest accident rates in Europe. If you are involved in an accident, use an orange SOS phone on the motorway to call the police.
- A network of **motorways** and **main roads** connects Lisbon, Porto and the major cities. Motorways are prefaced with A and incur tolls. Other main roads are prefaced with IP or IC, or N (for *nacional*).
- Some stretches of the motorway charge an electronic **toll** (and don't have ticket booths anymore). Whatever you do, find out more before your trip, e.g. at www.visitportugal.com ("Electronic tolls").

Buses and Trains

- Bus and train services connect the main towns and cities. Under-4s travel free (as long as they don't take up their own seat), 4–13 year-olds travel half fare, and over-65s receive a **discount**.
- The bus company with the largest national coverage is **Rede Expressos**. Visit their homepage (www.rede-expressos.pt) to check prices and connections and book tickets in advance.
- **Train** services are operated by **Caminhos de Ferros Portugueses** (**CP**; tel: 707 210 220, call charges apply; +351 707 210 220 from abroad; www.cp.pt). Tickets can be purchased directly from their homepage. Keep your eyes peeled for current discounts, e.g. for families, younger travellers (aged 25 and under), and return tickets.
- The Alfa Pendular is a **fast train service** that connects the cities of Braga, Porto, Coimbra, Lisbon, Albufeira and Faro.
- There are several **railway stations** in **Lisbon**. Trains depart from Sete Rios for Sintra, from Cais do Sodré for Estoril and Cascais and the west coast

from Santa Apolónia or Oriente for Porto and Madrid and from Entrecampos for Faro and Évora.

City Transport

■ **Lisbon** has an excellent network of buses, trams, Metro trains and *elevadores* (funiculars). **Single tickets** can be bought on buses or at Metro stations and validated at the machines behind the driver or at the station barriers. It's cheaper to buy a **Carris ticket** instead of paying for lots of single journeys, however – it lasts **24 hours**, costs €6 and lets you use the Metro, too (www.carris.pt, www.metrolisboa.pt). Tourist offices sell the **Lisboa Card**, which is valid for up to three days and gives you unlimited travel on public transport and free or discounted admission to more than 80 museums, tours and places of interest. The Lisboa Card costs €18.50 for 24 hours (kids aged 5–11: €11.50), €31.50 for 48 hours (kids aged 5–11: €17.50), and €39 for 72 hours (kids aged 5–11: €20.50).

■ **Porto** has a good metro system with six different lines (named A–F). It covers most of the city, including the main part of Porto, over the bridge to Gaia and out to the airport (www.metrodoporto.pt). There is also a good network of local **buses**. Single-journey tickets and one-day passes can be bought on the bus. Tourist offices sell the **Porto Card**, which gives you discounts at museums and other sights, and free travel on buses, trams and the Metro. It also lets you take advantage of some extra offers (at restaurants, for example). The Porto Card costs €13 for one day, €20 for two days, and €25 for three days.

Accommodation

Accommodation in Portugal is very good value, especially outside Lisbon and the Algarve. Independent travellers can choose from a wide range of lodgings and the luxury end of the market is refreshingly informal.

Booking

■ Advance booking is vital in the **high season** (July and August) or if your stay coincides with such events as local festivals and pilgrimages. In quiet periods, rates can drop to 60 per cent of the high-season price, and even more in some areas.

■ **Tourist offices** have comprehensive lists of official accommodation and the addresses of *dormidas* or *quartos* (rooms for rent).

■ Many hotels and tourist complexes in the Algarve are **block booked** throughout the summer; either reserve months ahead or choose a guesthouse, *pousada* (➤ 39) or *estalagem* (country inn) instead.

Hotels

■ Hotels are invariably **clean and safe**, but you might find alternative types of accommodation (➤ 39) more attractive and welcoming than budget hotels, especially in cities.

■ An **official price list** must be displayed inside the door of every room.

■ **IVA** (VAT) or sales tax must be included in the advertised room rate; breakfast tends to be included and varies from continental to a buffet.

■ You may be **charged extra** for using a garage or gym.

- **Extra beds** are often supplied for a small fee.
- **Children** (usually under four years) can stay free or at a discount.

Pousadas and Accommodation with Character

- *Pousadas* (which means "a place to rest", ➤ 19) are hotels located throughout the country (many in the Alentejo, ➤ 127–146), aimed at tourists looking for somewhere special to stay, usually near centres of interest. They are set in **fabulous surroundings** and have elements of traditional architecture and furnishing, as well as good to excellent restaurants – open to non-residents – where you can sample Portuguese specialities and wine, often in highly atmospheric dining rooms. **Standards of comfort** are reliably high.
- With around 40, there are **four categories**: historical *pousadas*, converted castles and monasteries; historic design *pousadas*, as above but with modern boutique-style elements; nature *pousadas,* in spectacular natural settings; and charm *pousadas,* often in converted village houses. All *pousadas* are good value for money and even the most expensive, such as those at Estremoz (➤ 156) and Guimarães (➤ 105), cost less than the equivalent luxury establishments in most other countries.
- To stay competitive, *pousadas* offer a whole range of different **special deals**, including romantic getaways for two, early booking discounts (via the homepage) and offers for over-55s.
- The *pousadas* described in this guide are not necessarily the best, but form part of a balanced selection of accommodation for each region. For a complete listing and detailed information, including promotions and booking facilities, contact www.pousadas.pt. The *pousadas* have been taken over by Pestana hotels: Intervisa Viagens e Turismo, Lda., Rua Ivone Silva, Ed. Arcis, 6 – 5º andar, 1050-124 Lisboa; tel: +351 218 442 001 (call charges apply, but they can ring you back on Skype); reservations and enquiries: guest@pousadas.pt.
- The **Solares de Portugal** and other similar schemes are on a more intimate scale. They offer a huge choice of alternative accommodation in the mid-budget range across the whole country. Government-approved but privately owned, these tend to be farmhouses and country houses with around 12 rooms. They sometimes have such facilities as swimming pools, but seldom offer meals other than breakfast. **Solares de Portugal**, Praça da República, 4990 Ponte de Lima; tel: 258 931 750, www.solares deportugal.pt. Additional organisations and websites for Portuguese country tourism include: **Privetur** (Associação Portuguesa de Turismo Rural), tel: 258 743 923 www.privetur.pt and **CENTER** (Central Nacional do Turismo na Espaça Rural), tel: 258 931 750; www.center.pt.
- Another thing to look out for is the official green tree symbol awarded to government-approved country guesthouses often advertised as a *turismo rural*. These also offer charming accommodation in manors and farms, usually on a bed-and-breakfast basis, plus facilities such as horse-riding.
- Traditional farmhouses on the Costa Alentejana and Costa Vicentina in the southwest have grouped together to form **Casas Brancas** (http://casasbrancas.pt).

Residenciais, *Pensões* and *Hospedarias*

- In addition to rooms for rent, at the lower end of the budget range is the *residenciais*. These are nearly always clean and comfortable, if basic, but do not provide any meals, except possibly breakfast.

Finding Your Feet

■ The **pensão** sometimes offering no meals at all, or sometimes breakfast and an evening meal. Often family-run, *pensões* tend to have a more local flavour than hotels and can be a charming place to brush up on your Portuguese

■ Alternatively, there is the **hospedaria,** the lowliest of all. Some rooms have their own bathroom, sometimes at a far higher rate than if you share facilities. These are often better value than a low- to mid-budget hotel, and some of these places have wonderful character.

Youth Hostels

■ *Pousadas de Juventude* (youth hostels) are good on the whole and some are excellent – clean, safe and friendly. Bed linen and a breakfast are generally included in the price, and facilities often include shared kitchens, snack bars and wireless internet access.

■ Make sure to book ahead during the **high season**, either direct at individual youth hostels or via the **Portuguese Youth Hostel Association** (Rua Rodrigo da Fonseca, 55, 1250-190 Lisboa; tel: 707 203 030 for reservations (call charges apply); www.juventude.gov.pt).

■ The **prices** of bunk beds in youth hostel dorms don't change much at different times of the year. Expect to pay around €10/11 in the low season and €16/17 in the high season. If you're prepared to fork out quite a bit more, you can also rent double rooms (with and without private bathrooms), family rooms and apartments for several people.

Camping

■ *Parques de Campismo* (campsites) are usually well run, with facilities ranging from basic to quite luxurious, again at relatively low prices. The best ones in **prime seaside locations**, especially in the Algarve where there are several, are crowded in high season – and be warned that theft can be a problem.

■ Sites belonging to **ORBITUR** (Avenida da Boavista 1681, 3º, Salas 5 a 8, 4100-132 Porto; tel: 226 061 360; www.orbitur.pt) are more expensive but slightly better.

■ For more information, check out the **Federação Portuguesa de Campismo e Caravanismo** (Avenida Coronel Eduardo Galhardo 24 D, 1199-007 Lisbon; tel: 218 126 890; www.fcmportugal.com) and **Roteiro Campista** (Rua do Giestal, 5, 1 F, 1300-274 Lisbon; www.roteiro-campista.pt).

Self-catering

■ Self-catering apartments and villas are located mostly along the **south coast**, though they can be found throughout Portugal. **Facilities** range from a basic refrigerator and cooker to fully equipped kitchens, swimming pools, large gardens and a regular maid service.

■ It's worth **booking privately** rather than through a tour operator to get better value for money.

■ Local and national **tourist offices** should be able to supply contact names and addresses.

■ Also try www.ownersdirect.co.uk or www.holidaylettings.co.uk.

Accommodation Prices

Expect to pay for a double room per night in high season

€ under €80	€€ €80–€110	€€€ €110–€150	€€€€ over €150

Food and Drink

There are said to be 365 ways of preparing the national favourite, *bacalhau*, so you are sure to find it on the menu. Given the subtle regional variations, the advent of several imaginative chefs, plus some remarkably low prices, you can enjoy some memorable meals.

Eating Out – A Practical Guide

- Strict **dress codes** are almost non-existent, though Sunday best is still customary in the provinces. Jacket and tie is *de rigueur* in only a handful of restaurants in Lisbon and Porto.
- Often as smart as restaurants and mostly found in cities, *cervejarias* (beer houses) also serve high-quality Portuguese food. *Marisquerias* specialize in *marisco* (seafood), where *gambas* (prawns), lobster and luxury fish, served by weight, are expensive.
- **Restaurant terraces** (as opposed to café *esplanadas*) are a rarity, so the coolness of deep cellars where some dining rooms are located may prove welcome in the height of summer.
- All but the most modest places now accept **credit cards**, but check first in case you don't have enough cash on you.
- **Lunch** is over by 2, maybe 3 in the south. **Dinner** is served around 8 and you may find it hard to find a kitchen open after 10 or 11, especially in rural areas. In **Lisbon**, fashionable places serve until very late into the night, while *cervejarias* (beer houses) may stay open all afternoon, too. Some establishments may close Sunday evening; many more are closed all day Monday.
- Standard servings are **enormous**, except in chic restaurants: you can often ask for a *meia dose* (half portion) for one person. *Insider Tip*
- **Service** is rarely included and never compulsory, but a 5–10 per cent tip will always be welcome even in cafés and tea-rooms.
- The *ementa turística* (daily set menu) can be very good value (usually from €8–€10 in the countryside). It's normally only available at lunch-time.
- Many restaurant owners have been forced to raise their prices in recent times as politicians have increased their sales tax dramatically.

Portuguese Cuisine

- **Seafood**, usually top quality and priced accordingly, is served along Portugal's long coasts. Lamb, pork and game (in season) feature inland.
- *Carne de porco à alentejana* (pork simmered with clams and fresh coriander) is Portugal's answer to "surf and turf", the North American dish combining meat and seafood. The pork is marinated for four hours in white wine and spices and is then fried. The clams are added at the end. It is often served with diced potatoes or French fries.
- *Bacalhau* (salt cod, soaked to remove most of the salt, ►31) is a favourite. There are several different recipes, such as *à Gomes de Sá* (with hard-boiled egg, boiled potatoes and black olives), *à brás* (stir-fried with eggs, onions and potatoes), *à Minhota* (with fried potatoes) and *com natas* (baked in a rich cream sauce).
- *Churrasco* (barbecued chicken, beef or pork), sometimes served Brazilian-style (*rodízio*), is the house speciality of many roadside grills.
- *Leitão* (suckling pig), cooked until crisp and succulent and infused with local herbs, is the speciality of the region between Lisbon and Coimbra.

Finding Your Feet

- **Vegetarians** have a fairly hard time in Portugal – ask for salads or side orders, such as spinach. Although rice and potatoes are frequently on the menu, the only true concession to vegetarians will be omelettes.

Snacks and Sweets
- The Portuguese are great on **snacks** (*petiscos* are the local answer to *tapas*). Choose a slightly sparkling Vinho Verde white wine to go with *petiscos* like *bolinhos de bacalhau* (codfish cakes), *presunto* (cured ham), *polvo* (octopus) and *caracóis* (snails) cooked in garlic and herbs. *Lanche* (afternoon tea) is faithfully observed.
- With a good breakfast (coffee or tea, bread and jam or cheese, cold meats and eggs), you can probably survive until the evening by eating in cafés, *confeitarias* and *pastelerias* (cake shops), and *casas de chá* (tea rooms).
- **Coffee** is good and popular. *Bica* (*um café* in Porto) is a strong espresso, while *galão* is a milky coffee served in a glass, perfect with a *torradas* (thick slices of toasted bread dripping with butter).
- In addition to *sandes* (sandwiches), *pregos* (bread rolls with hot slices of beef) and *bifanas* (like *pregos* but with pork), try *rissóis* (deep-fried meat or prawn patties) and *pastéis de bacalhau* (mini cod fishcakes).
- Portuguese **cakes** (*pastéis* or *bolos*) are very sweet. The best are the cheese-based *queijadas* from Sintra and custard-filled, cinnamon-dusted *pastéis de nata* (especially the fabulous ones at Belém, ➤ 77).
- **Dessert** fans will appreciate *arroz doce* (rice pudding with cinnamon), *pudim flan* (crème caramel) and a whole range of nut and chocolate concoctions. Baked apple (*maçã*) and quince (*marmelo*) are delicious.

Cover Charges and Starters
- In nearly every restaurant there's a *couvert* or **cover charge** – ostensibly for the bread – and in more expensive places this can be quite high.
- ***Acepipes*** – an array of olives, ham, cheese (traditionally served before rather than after meals), fish pâté and pickles. Note that even if un-solicited, they will be itemized on your bill if you so much as touch them. Politely but pointedly refuse them if you don't want to be charged.
- ***Entradas*** (starters) come in the form of vegetable soups (such as *caldo verde*, containing strips of kale cabbage) or seafood, or maybe a salad.

Drinks
- **Mineral water** is inexpensive – ask for *agua sem gas* (still) or *agua com gas* (sparkling) served *fresca* (chilled) or *natural* (room temperature).
- Apart from **vinho do Porto** (port, ➤ 14) and **Mateus Rosé**, there are other excellent **wines**, the best coming from the Dão and Douro valleys, plus full-bodied reds from Bairrada and the Alentejo. Or there's Vinho Verde – slightly sparkling young wine from the Minho (mostly whites).
- **Beer** is popular in big cities and on tap should be ordered by the *imperial* (in the south) or *fino* (in the north).
- There are some good **brandies** (*conhaque*) as well as *aguardente*, *bagaço* and *medronho*, made in the Algarve from arbutus berries. Cherry-based *ginginha* is a popular tipple.

Restaurant Prices
Expect to pay per person for a three-course meal, excluding drinks and tips.
€ under €20 €€ €21–€30 €€€ €31–€40 €€€€ over €40

Shopping

Traditional markets across Portugal can be colourful spectacles as well as great places to shop. Ceramics are often on sale along with foods, but the finest items are only sold during local fairs *(feiras)*. With its juxtaposition of extravagant boutiques and dusty groceries alongside state-of-the-art shopping malls and beguiling bookstores, Lisbon is Portugal's undisputed shopping capital, though Porto does its best. Every town and city has a busy commercial street or two where you can pick up bargains. Perhaps the best gifts are food or wine related, though sometimes you can come across interesting arts and crafts. Footwear and other leather goods are also good value.

Opening Hours

■ Shops usually open daily 9–7, except Sunday, with a two-hour lunch break – *sestas* (siestas) are rare outside the rural interior.

■ Modern shopping centres open 10am–midnight, seven days a week.

Clothes and Footwear

■ **Leather goods** are relatively cheap. They're often still sold at old-fashioned, booth-like shops.

■ **Home-grown designers** are worth investigating, though few have branches outside Lisbon.

Food and Wine

■ In addition to **wine** and port, **brandy**, *aguardente* (firewater) and, in the Algarve, *medronho* (➤ 42, 181) make good gifts. Decanters and other wine-connoisseur paraphernalia can be interesting – some are designed by fashionable artists.

■ The easiest foodstuffs to transport include **olive oil** (try and get "luxury" oil – 0.1 or 0.2 per cent acidity, packaged in smart, corked bottles), cheese (some of it at astronomical prices, so beware), *bacalhau* (➤ 31, 41), and non-perishable **cakes** and **biscuits**.

Art & Crafts

■ **Ceramics, basket- and wicker-ware**, and **copper pans** tend to be the traditional items appealing to all tastes. Pottery and porcelain can be more of an acquired taste.

■ The yellow-dotted brown **earthenware dishes from Barcelos** are universally popular with tourists – as is the *Galo* (rooster) commemorating a folk legend originating in the eponymous northern town, and now a national symbol (➤ 102).

■ **Cork** isn't just for coasters – it's also used to make cork leather, which is turned into a variety of creative bags, hats and purses, etc.

Souvenirs

■ *Azulejos* (traditional glazed tiles) range from mass-produced souvenirs to whole sets of antique tiles. You can have a set tailor-made, to your own design.

■ *Cataplanas* are metal cooking pans used to make seafood dishes.

■ *Arraiolos carpets* are exquisite (and expensive) rugs made in the picturesque town of the same name, to ancient designs.

■ *Fado* (➤ 22) – a CD of Portuguese "blues".

Entertainment

Portugal is noted for its traditional festivals – the calendar is packed with them – *fado* and, of course, football so there's usually something to suit every taste.

Information

Many regions and towns produce their own weekly and monthly **English-language info publications**. All are available from tourist offices and hotels. Alternatively, check out the relevant websites (➤ 200).

Nightlife

■ Lively student populations keep the nightlife upbeat and the arts scene buoyant in **Lisbon** (➤ 72), **Porto** (➤ 108) and **Coimbra** (➤ 138), where there's a good mix of **nightclubs**, **wine bars**, **concert halls**, *fado* **venues** and **cultural centres**. Most *fado* venues (➤ 222) double up as restaurants and have entry fees and minimum spends.

■ Nightlife in the **Algarve** is **seasonal** from about Easter to September, though a few clubs, bars and pubs are open all year. **Albufeira** (➤ 182) is party central, but **Faro** (➤ 182) offers a more stylish, Portuguese scene.

■ **Opening hours** vary widely. **Bars** open around midday and close at midnight; lounge bars with DJs or live music may stay open until 2am or 3am. **Nightclubs** open around 10pm or 11pm and close between 4am and 6am. Most have relaxed dress codes, though more exclusive clubs may rule out denim, trainers and T-shirts. Nightclub entrance charges tend from €5 –€10, though small venues are often free.

Festivals

The most important festivals are covered in the regional listings, but look for others – it's important to know if only because accommodation can be scarce. Check at local tourist offices.

Spectator Sports

■ Cristiano Ronaldo is the most prominent Portuguese footballer since Eusébio and Luís Figo. Porto's Boavista and FC Porto and Lisbon's rival teams, Benfica and Sporting, have the national championship stitched up between them and fans might like to see them play at home (➤ 74).

■ **Roller-hockey** is the only international sport at which Portugal regularly excels, while **bullfighting** (*touradas*, ➤ 29) is primarily popular in the south.

Sport and Outdoor Pursuits

■ Some of Europe's best **golfing** fairways (➤ 182), **tennis courts, watersports** and **diving clubs** are found on the warm southern Algarve coast.

■ The western seaboard – where wind and rollers are perennially reliable – is better for **surfing**, **windsurfing** or just a refreshing dip.

■ Inland, unspoiled mountain scenery lends itself to **hiking**, **mountainbiking**, **hang-gliding** and **horse-riding** – ask at local tourist offices for outfits.

■ **Boating**, **fishing** and other **watersports** can be practised at sea or on inland waterways; many places hire equipment.

■ Algarve boat trips take you **dolphin watching**, riding centres throughout the country provide horseback lessons and outings, and you can explore Portugal's rivers and Atlantic coast in **kayaks** and **canoes**.

Lisbon & Around

Scintillating Stonework

Admire the artistry in the cloister of the **Mosteiro dos Jerónimos** (➤ 52), the ultimate expression of the Manueline style.

A Musical Mélange

Pick up an audio guide in Lisbon's **Fado Museum** (➤ 67) and listen to the musical samples at its numbered stations.

Moorish Masonry

The strenuous climb up to Sintra's historic castle complex (**Castelo dos Mouros**, ➤ 56) is definitely worth the effort.

Getting Your Bearings

The capital of Portugal since around 1255, Lisbon (Lisboa) is one of Europe's smallest and most atmospheric metropolises. Tumbling down seven hills on the north bank of the Tagus (Tejo) estuary, it has a vibrant, multicultural appeal thanks to its large number of immigrants from the former African and Asian colonies. A tenth of Portugal's population live here, creating a lively, Latin atmosphere.

Most visitors arrive in Lisbon by plane, but there's nothing like arriving on one of the ferries that breeze across the River Tagus to get a true sense of the city's layout. In front of you is Praça do Comércio, the former parade ground and symbolic entrance to the city. Ahead, beyond a triumphal arch, Rua Augusta leads through the Baixa (lower town), the downtown business and shopping district. To the west rises the Bairro Alto (upper town) and boutique-dotted Chiado; to the east, the labyrinthine Alfama, crowned by a splendid Moorish castle. Across the water, beyond the Ponte 25 de Abril, a giant statue of Christ gazes down from the south bank.

The shape of Lisbon today is largely the result of the earthquake of 1755. It struck on All Saints' Day, when most people were at church, causing a tidal wave and hundreds of fires. At least 40,000 people died. The rebuilding of the Baixa on a grid plan was largely the architectural vision of the chief minister, Marquês de Pombal.

Two buildings that mostly survived the destruction were the Manueline tower and monastery at Belém (►51), inspired by the discoveries and built on the riches that made Lisbon great – Indian spices and Brazilian gold.

In the last few years, Lisbon has seen another transformation, with new dockside leisure facilities, one of Europe's longest bridges and glittering new façades. As Lisbon sails into the 21st century, its cityscape is a striking blend of old and new, its people at once nostalgic and innovative.

The Parque Eduardo VII, Lisbon's green oasis, is a perfect place to stroll and relax on a bench in the heat

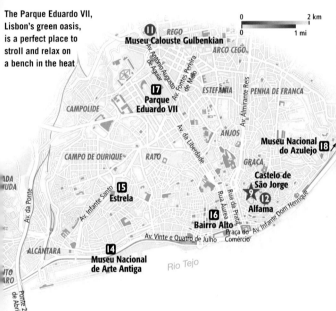

TOP 10

⭐ Belém ➤ 50
⭐ Sintra ➤ 56
⭐ Castelo de São Jorge ➤ 61

Don't Miss

⓫ Museu Calouste Gulbenkian ➤ 63
⓬ Alfama ➤ 65
⓭ Parque das Nações ➤ 69

At Your Leisure

⓮ Museu Nacional de Arte Antiga ➤ 71
⓯ Estrela ➤ 71
⓰ Bairro Alto ➤ 71
⓱ Parque Eduardo VII ➤ 72
⓲ Museu Nacional do Azulejo ➤ 72
⓳ Estoril & Cascais ➤ 73
⓴ Palácio de Mafra ➤ 74

Perfect Days in...

Four Perfect Days

If you're not quite sure where to begin your travels, this itinerary recommends a practical and enjoyable four days exploring Lisbon and the surrounding area, taking in some of the best places to see. For more information see the main entries (➤ 50–74).

Day 1

Morning

From Praça do Comércio, take tram No 15E to ⭐ **Belém** (➤ 50) to immerse yourself in Portugal's maritime past. Walk along the waterfront to the Torre de Belém, and allow plenty of time for the Museu de Marinha. Explore the Manueline **Mosteiro dos Jerónimos** (➤ 52), its intricate stonework celebrating the Portuguese explorer Vasco da Gama. Have a custard tart at the *azulejo*-tiled **Antiga Confeitaria de Belém** (➤ 77).

Afternoon and Evening

Return by tram as far as the Alcântara docks and explore the **14 Museu Nacional de Arte Antiga** (➤ 71). If you want to party, head to the revitalized docks area and choose one of the sleek lounge bars or warehouse clubs (➤ 82). Otherwise return to Belém for a concert at the **Centro Cultural de Belém** (➤ 82) – the arts centre has an exciting programme of classical music, opera, jazz and dance.

Day 2

Morning

Take the Metro to São Sebastião for the wonderful **11 Museu Calouste Gulbenkian** (➤ 63). Plan to spend a great deal of time exploring this outstanding cultural institution.

Afternoon and Evening

Walk downhill to the centre through **17 Parque Eduardo VII** (➤ 72) and along the tree-lined Avenida da Liberdade. Take Tram 28 through the narrow streets of Castelo to the maze-like Moorish district of **12 Alfama**. (➤ 65). Climb up to the ⭐ **Castelo de São Jorge** (➤ 61) to watch the sun set over the River Tagus. Wander back down to Alfama for a delicious fish supper and authentic *fado* in an intimate club (➤ 22).

Day 3

Morning

Take the Metro to Oriente for the cutting-edge ⑬**Parque das Nações** (▶69). Visit the huge oceanarium (left) and a stroll along the water-front. Have lunch at one of the riverside restaurants.

Afternoon and Evening

Shop for the latest Portuguese styles in the Centro Comercial Vasco da Gama, then take the Metro to Rossio for a drink at a pavement café. Ride the Elevador da Glória up to the Bairro Alto and have an apéritif at the **Solar do Vinho do Porto** (▶80). Head out to find something more to eat and drink afterwards – there are lots of good places nearby. Finish up at at one of the lively hole-in-the-wall bars around ⑯**Bairro Alto** (▶71).

Day 4

Morning and Afternoon

It's time for a day trip! Take the train from Cais do Sodré to ⑲**Estoril** (below, ▶73) and stroll along the seafront to ⑲**Cascais** (▶73). Explore this fishing port, then get a bus to ★**Sintra** (▶56) with its easily navigable town centre that's full of places to eat. Hike up through the trees to visit the fantastical Castelo dos Mouros and the Palácio da Pena before hopping on the bus or the train back to Lisbon.

⭐③ Belém

More than anywhere else in Portugal, it is at Belém that you feel the pull of the Atlantic and the magic of the great Age of Discovery. For more than a century, Portuguese ships left from Belém in search of new worlds, bringing back untold riches. Add to that its status as Lisbon's museum district, along with the crowning glories of Manueline architecture, and there is plenty to keep you occupied here.

The best way to reach Belém is on the No 15E tram that clatters along the waterfront from central Lisbon. On arrival, head for the imposing **Padrão dos Descobrimentos** (Monument to the Discoveries), built in 1960 to mark the 500th anniversary of Prince Henry the Navigator's (➤ 12) death. A *padrão* was a stone cairn surmounted by a cross, built by

The Torre de Belém is Lisbon's most emblematic building

Portuguese explorers to mark their presence on new territory; this modern version neatly combines the form of a *caravel*, a cross and a sword. The prow of a ship faces out to sea with an image of Prince Henry at the helm. Behind him are other heroes of the discoveries (➤ 16), including Gil Eanes, Vasco da Gama, Pedro Álvares Cabral and poet Luís de Camões, who celebrated the Age of Discovery in his epic work *Os Lusíadas* (*The Lusiads,* ➤ 95). Take the lift to the top of the tower, which is 52m (171ft) high, for harbour views, then wander around the marble world map at its base, with dates showing Portuguese conquests in Africa, Asia and America.

Portuguese heroes are carved in stone on the Padrão dos Descobrimentos

Manueline Masterpiece

Just along the waterfront is the **Torre de Belém**, built by Dom Manuel I between 1515 and 1520 to guard the entrance to Lisbon harbour. This elegant fortress is a good example of what has come to be called the Manueline style (➤ 18), a Portuguese version of late Gothic architecture inspired by the discoveries. It's particularly associated with Dom Manuel.

The hallmark of the Manueline style is the extravagant use of seafaring imagery, with windows and doorways decorated with stone carvings of knotted ropes, anchors, globes, exotic fauna and flora and other maritime motifs. Two symbols that are ever present are the armillary sphere (emblem of Dom Manuel, ➤ 18) and the Cross of the Order of Christ. You can go right inside the tower and up onto the terrace for closer views.

Insider Tip

Art & Culture

The other main sights of Belém are across the railway line, around the Praça do Império gardens.

On one side is the **Centro Cultural de Belém**, built out of the same limestone as the Mosteiro dos Jerónimos (➤ 52), which has become one of Lisbon's most vibrant cultural centres.

The star attraction for art buffs is the free **Museu Colecção Berardo**, harbouring the magnificent art collection of billionaire José Berardo, which includes masterpieces by Picasso, Warhol, Yves Klein and Portuguese artist Paula Rego. The works are shown in rotating exhibitions.

Lisbon & Around

A Long History

However, the sight that really takes your breath away is the UNESCO World Heritage site **Mosteiro dos Jerónimos** (➤ 54) begun in 1502 on the site of a hermitage founded by Prince Henry the Navigator. In 1497, Vasco da Gama spent his last night here before sailing to find a sea route to India. Dom Manuel vowed he would build a church to the Virgin if he was successful. Begun by French architect Diogo de Boytac and continued by Spaniard Juan de Castillo, the monastery is full of Manueline flourishes. Just inside the web-vaulted church are the tombs of Vasco da Gama and Luís de Camões. Go through a separate entrance to the two-storey cloister, a Manueline masterpiece. Portugal's treaty of accession for entry to the EEC (now EU) was signed here in 1986.

Maritime History

A 19th-century wing of the monastery houses the **Museu de Marinha**. Highlights include graffiti carved onto the African rocks by Portuguese explorer Diogo Cão in 1483, a model of Vasco da Gama's flagship, maps of the known world and a reconstruction of the state rooms from the royal yacht *Amélia*, right down to the king's private piano and roulette table.

A separate building contains the **royal barges**, including the sumptuous gilded barge built for the wedding of João VI in 1780.

Fairy-tale Coaches

Only part of the popular **Museu Nacional dos Coches** is still housed in the former Royal equestrian arena from the 18th century. Most of the extraordinary collection of 17th to 19th-century coaches can now be seen in the modern white building opposite. Highlights include Pope Clement XI's lavishly gilded Coach of the Oceans (1716) that's covered with red silk velvet and lined with gold brocade.

TAKING A BREAK

Treat yourself to a coffee and a custard tart at the **Antiga Confeitaria de Belém** (➤ 77).

✚ 208 off A1
🚊 Tram 15E 🚆 Belém (Lisbon to Cascais line)

Padrão dos Descobrimentos
✉ Avenida de Brasília ☎ 213 031 950; www.padraodosdescobrimentos.pt
🕐 Daily March–Sep 10–7; Oct–Feb 10–6 ✋ €4

Torre de Belém
✉ Avenida de Brasília ☎ 213 620 034; www.torrebelem.pt
🕐 May–Sep 10–6:30; Oct–April Tue–Sun 10–5:30
(last entry 30 mins before closing)
✋ €5; combined ticket with Mosteiro dos Jerónimos €10; free Sun 10–2

Museu Colecção Berardo

Praça do Império ☎ 213 612 878; www.museuberardo.pt

🕐 Mon–Sun 10–7 (last entry 30 mins before closing) 💷 Free

Centro Cultural de Belém

✉ Praça do Império ☎ 213 612 400; www.ccb.pt

🕐 Mon–Fri 8–8, Sat, Sun 10–6

💷 Free. Prices vary for workshops, concerts, etc.

Mosteiro dos Jerónimos

✉ Praça do Império ☎ 213 620 034; www.mosteirojeronimos.pt

🕐 May–Sep Tue–Sun 10–6:30; Oct–April Tue–Sun 10–5:30

💷 €10; combined ticket with Torre de Belém €12 (free 1st Sun of the month)

Museu de Marinha

✉ Praça do Império ☎ 213 620 010; http://museu.marinha.pt

🕐 May–Sep Tue–Sun 10–6; Oct–April Tue–Sun 10–5

💷 €5; free Sun until 2pm

Museu Nacional dos Coches

The ornate façade of the Museu de Marinha in the Belém area

✉ Picadeiro Real, Praça Afonso de Albuquerque; new site: Avenida da Índia 136

☎ 213 610 850; Museu 210 732 319, www.museudoscoches.pt

🕐 Tue–Sun 10–6 (last entry 30 mins before closing)

💷 €8 for both, €4/€6 each

INSIDER INFO

Insider Tip

■ Many of the museums and sights are **free on the first Sunday of the month**. Avoid Mondays when almost everything is closed (apart from the Museu Colecção Berardo).

■ Don't miss the chance to **take a walk along the banks of the river** – the best spot for a stroll is near the Padrão dos Descobrimentos.

Mosteiro dos Jerónimos

The Mosteiro dos Jerónimos ("Monastery of the Hieronymites") is a symbol of Portugal's Golden Age, the economic and cultural blossoming that followed its discovery and colonization of lands overseas.

❶**South Portal:** Dedicated to Saint Jerome. Depicts scenes from his life and two lions, the saint's heraldic animals.

❷**Entrance and West Portal:** Decorated in the Manueline style, its ornamentation includes the figures of Manuel I and Jerome, his patron saint.

❸**High Choir:** Boasts the royal graves of Manuel I and João III that are held up by elephants.

❹**Southern Transept:** Houses the grave of King Sebastião. His demise in Morocco led to the advent of Spanish rule in Portugal.

❺**Cloister:** Often called the world's most magnificent cloister. Its Renaissance architecture with Manueline decoration tells the story of the Portuguese discovery of foreign lands. There's also a monument to Fernando Pessoa.

❻**Sacristy:** The monastery's sacristy is found between the church and the chapter house.

❼**Chapter House:** Graced with a beautiful Gothic vaulted ceiling. The chapter house is home to the grave of Alexandre Herculano, a famous poet and historian.

❽**Refectory:** The monks' former eating hall. It has a net-vaulted ceiling, and part of the walls are surrounded with decorative tiles.

❾**Museu Nacional de Arqueologia:** The dormitory was once located in the monastery's elongated western wing. It plays host to the Portuguese National Museum of Archaeology today.

Belém

The monastery's 32m (105ft)-high south portal is regarded as one of the finest examples of the Manueline style

The monastery's magnificent cloister with its wonderfully delicate decorations

Sintra

If you only have time for one excursion, you should make it Sintra. Once the summer residence of the kings of Portugal, this UNESCO World Heritage site is pure fairy-tale stuff with its whitewashed *quintas* set on green hillsides among palaces, pinewoods and granite crags.

Palácio Nacional de Sintra

The centre of the town is dominated by the fairy-tale **Palácio Nacional**, with its two enormous conical chimneys. This royal palace was begun by João I in the late 14th century and completed by Manuel I (1469–1521) in the Manueline style.

Look out for the Renaissance-inspired **Sala dos Cisnes** (Swan Room) and **Sala das Pegas** (Magpie Room), named after the 136 magpies in the ceiling frescoes.

The **Sala dos Brasões** (Arms Room) has *azulejo* (➤ 32) walls depicting hunting scenes and a coffered gilded ceiling with the coats of arms of 72 noble families.

Also in the palace is the **bedchamber of Afonso VI**, the deranged king held prisoner here by his brother Pedro II, who added insult to injury by marrying his queen.

The Castle

Sintra's other main sights speckle the hills above it. The **Castelo dos Mouros** (Moors' Castle) was built in the ninth century and captured by Afonso Henriques in 1147. You can walk around the snaking ramparts, with views stretching beyond Lisbon and out to sea, to reach the royal tower, where there is a fine view of the Palácio da Pena, on a granite peak.

The mighty complex of the Palácio Nacional de Sintra

The fantastic façade of the Palácio da Pena

Palácio Nacional da Pena

The climb to the **Palácio Nacional da Pena** (▶ 58) winds through the woodlands of Parque da Pena, dotted with lakes and follies. With its minarets, towers and golden domes, the palace is famous throughout Portugal. It was built in the 1840s by Prince Ferdinand of Saxe-Coburg-Gotha-Koháry, husband of Dona Maria II and honorary king of Portugal, on the site of a monastery established by Manuel I to give thanks for the sighting of Vasco da Gama's fleet returning from India.

This was the last royal palace built in Portugal and Baron Eschwege, the German architect, let his imagination run wild. Gargoyles gaze down from doorways and life-size statues hold up chandeliers. Meissen porcelain dominates the queen's antechamber and the Arabic Room features playful *trompe-l'œil* walls. Everything is preserved as it was when Dom Manuel II went into exile in 1910. From the belvedere you can look out to Cruz Alta, the highest point of the Serra de Sintra, marked by a stone cross and a statue of Baron Eschwege.

Toys, Romantic Follies and Modern Art

There are two museums worth checking out in the town centre. Housed in an old watermill, the 👬 **Museu Anjos Teixeira** exhibits paintings and sculptures by the Portuguese sculptor Artur Anjos Teixeira and Pedro, his more success-ful, better-known son. Families with kids in tow will also enjoy paying it a visit.

Explore whimsical follies, underground chambers, grottoes and fountains in the lush grounds of 19th-century **Quinta da Regaleira**, the vision of Italian set designer Luigi Manini. *Insider Tip*

Further significant sites (also managed by the "Parques de Sintra" group) include the **Convento de Capuchos**, a 16th-century Capuchin convent, and the **Chalet e Jardim**

Palácio da Pena

The Palácio da Pena came about when Prince Ferdinand (later Ferdinand II of Portugal) commissioned Wilhelm von Eschwege to design him an exceedingly eclectic palace that included a mishmash of architectural styles. The result is a marvellous mélange of Medieval, Manueline, Moorish and Far-Eastern influences.

❶ Chapel: Once part of a 16th-century monastery, this chapel was incorporated into the palace complex. The Renaissance altar was created by the French sculptor, Nicolas Chanterène.

❷ Cloister: The original monastery on the site also boasted this double-storey Manueline cloister that's clad in beautiful *azulejos* tiles.

❸ Main Tower: The main tower was built in the style of Lisbon's Torre de Belém.

❹ Sala Árabe: Step into the "Arab Room" with its striking Arabic arches and you'll feel like you've been transported to the Middle East. The walls and ceilings are covered with *trompe l'oeil* paintings by Paolo Rizzi, and the furniture, ceramics and souvenirs all add to the general stylistic effect.

❺ Salão Nobre: The impact of this ballroom and banqueting hall is somewhat hidden behind its wealth of lavish furnishings. The walls are covered with geometric Arabic ornamentation, and the lighting is provided by the chandelier and the four Turkish figures who each wield candelabras with twenty-five candles.

❻ Manuel II's Bedchamber: This oval room with luminous red walls is where the last king of Portugal slept when he visited his mother in the palace. A portrait of the king himself hangs over the fireplace.

❼ Kitchen: Housed in vaulted rooms, the palace kitchen boasts a variety of treasures, including the porcelain from Vista Alegre that Prince Ferdinand had made specially for his brand new residence.

Palácio da Pena

The main tower is the most distinctive of all the palace's variously styled high-rise edifices

The palace interior is filled with magnificent azulejos

Lisbon & Around

da **Condessa d'Edla**, a villa with a park that dates from the second half of the 19th century. Don't leave without trying *queijadas* (► 38) – sweet cheese and cinnamon pastries that have been made in Sintra since Moorish times. They sell particularly tasty ones at the **Fábrica das Queijadas da Sapa** near the Palácio de Sintra at Volta do Duche.

➕ 216 A4 ℹ️ Praça da República 23 ☎ 219 231 157; www.cm-sintra.pt
🚆 From Estação do Rossio to Sintra

Palácio Nacional de Sintra
✉️ Largo Rainha Dona Amélia ☎ 219 237 300; www.parquesdesintra.pt
🕐 March–Oct 9:30–7; Sep–Feb 9:45–6 (last entry 30 mins before closing)
💶 €9 (high season), €8.50 (low season)

Castelo dos Mouros & Convento dos Capuchos
☎ 219 237 300; www.parquesdesintra.pt
🕐 March–Oct 9:30–8; Sep–Feb 10–6 (last entry 60 mins before closing) 💶 €7

Palácio Nacional da Pena
✉️ Estrada da Pena ☎ 219 237 300; www.parquesdesintra.pt
🕐 March–Oct 9:45–7; Sep–Feb 10–6 (last entry 60 mins before closing)
💶 €13.50

Museu Anjos Teixeira
✉️ Azinhaga da Sardinha – Rio do Porto – Volta do Duche; 2710-631 Sintra
☎ 219 238 827; http://museuvirtual.cm-sintra.pt
🕐 Tue–Fri 10–6; Sat, Sun noon–6 💶 Free

Quinta da Regaleira
✉️ Rua Barbosa du Bocage ☎ 219 106 656; www.regaleira.pt
🕐 Nov–Jan 10–5:30; Feb, March, Oct 10–6:30; April–Sep 10–8
(last entry 30–60 mins before closing) 💶 €6

Chalet e Jardim da Condessa d'Edla
☎ 219 237 300; www.parquesdesintra.pt
🕐 March–Oct 9:30–8, Sep–Feb 10–6 (last entry 5) 💶 €8.50

INSIDER INFO

Insider Tip

- The most important sights (the Old Town, the Castelo dos Mouros, the Palácio Nacional da Pena) are all connected by a **bus line** that loops round the town.
- The **Sintra Festival**, which takes place in June and July, is one of Portugal's top classical music festivals. Details from Sintra tourist information office.
- Concerts and other events are held at the **Centro Cultural Olga Cadaval** (Praça Doctor Francisco Sá Carneiro; www.ccolgacadaval.pt)

In more depth Another of Portugal's elaborate royal palaces, the **Palácio de Queluz**, is an impressive Rococo edifice that's the Portuguese answer to Versailles (219 237 300; www.parquesdesintra.pt; March–Oct daily 9–7, Sep–Feb daily 9–5:30, last entry 30–60 minutes before closing; entrance fee: €8.50). It's close to the Sintra train line and can be visited on the way back to Lisbon.

⭐9 Castelo de São Jorge

Dominating the skyline above the Alfama district, the Castelo de São Jorge has a long and chequered history. Yet, despite its bloody past, this is now one of the most peaceful spots in Lisbon. The gardens make a pleasant place to escape for an hour or two, and there are fine views over the city and river from its walkways and terraces.

St George's Castle occupies the site where Phoenician traders set up their first camp when they occupied Lisbon during the eighth century BC. It was fortified by the Romans and again by the Visigoths, and the Moorish rulers built their palace here.

The castle was taken for the Christians in 1147 by Afonso Henriques, Portugal's first king, who captured it after a 17-week siege, with the help of British and French crusaders. The victorious battle saw the death of the Portuguese knight Martim Moniz, who is honoured in the name of a Metro station and a square in the Baixa.

After the Christian conquest, the Portuguese kings used the **Moorish palace** as their royal home until Dom Manuel I moved it to Terreiro do Paço, on the site of Praça do Comércio. Set aside a good amount of time to explore its historic defenses!

Climb onto the ramparts for the best views

You enter the outer walls through the Arco de São Jorge, where a niche houses an image of the saint. This leads you

Lisbon & Around

into the *bairro* of **Santa Cruz**, a village-like quarter of medieval houses around the 18th-century church of Santa Cruz do Castelo. A separate gateway leads into the castle proper, and a parade ground dominated by a **statue of Afonso Henriques**.

The superb views from Castelo de São Jorge

Wonderful **views** over the River Tagus and large parts of the town can be enjoyed from the castle terrace.

Walkways lead around the walls. In summer, peacocks strut through the gardens and various artists set up their stalls beneath the ramparts.

A permanent exhibition of discoveries from the castle's archaeological site shows off the life and culture of the area from the early Middle Ages to the 18th century. The Moorish period is particularly well represented.

The other attraction here is the fascinating 🕯**Periscópio** that's housed in the Torre de Ulisses. This device provides live 360° images of the city and the people going about their daily business on Praça do Comércio below. Families with kids will love it.

TAKING A BREAK

There's an attractive café and a restaurant inside the castle itself. The latter isn't called the **Casa do Leão** ("Lion House") for nothing – lions imported from Africa lived here in a wing of the royal palace in the late Middle Ages. Both the café and restaurant can get pretty busy during the high season.

➕ 209 E4
🚌 Bus 737; tram 12, 28

Castelo
☎ 218 800 620; http://castelodesaojorge.pt
🕐 March–Oct 9–9; Nov–Feb 9–6 (last entry 30 mins before closing)
💶 €8.50

Periscópio
🕐 Daily 10–5, depending on the weather
💶 Included in the price of entry to the castle

INSIDER INFO

- The castle can be reached by a short, steep climb from the **Miradouro de Santa Luzia**, but if you want to avoid the walk, **bus 737** goes all the way to the outer walls.
- The castle terrace is a great place to watch the **sunset**.

11 Museu Calouste Gulbenkian

The most significant art museum in Portugal is the result of one man's passionate collecting, encompassing the entire history of both Eastern and Western art. What makes it all the more enjoyable is that, although each piece is worth seeing in its own right, the clearly arranged, well presented nature of the collection means that it can be thoroughly explored in a visit of two or three hours.

The Mirror of Venus, 1870–76, by Sir Edward Burne-Jones

Calouste Gulbenkian (1869–1955) was an Armenian oil magnate who earned his nickname "Mr Five Per Cent" when he negotiated a five per cent stake in the newly discovered oilfields of Iraq. He spent much of his wealth acquiring works of art, from Roman coins to old masters. During World War II, he moved to Portugal, and bequeathed his fortune and his art collection to the Portuguese. The foundation, established after his death, is now one of the largest cultural institutions in the world, which supports museums, orchestras and charitable projects.

Treasures From Around the World
The **Museu Calouste Gulbenkian** was opened in 1969 and contains the most precious objects from Gulbenkian's collection. Your tour of the museum begins with a small room devoted to ancient Egyptian art, including funerary statues, bronze sculptures and an alabaster bowl dating from 2700BC. The next room contains superb classical art from Greece and Rome, together with an impressive

Lisbon & Around

life-size relief of an Assyrian warrior from the ninth century BC.

Some of the greatest treasures are found in the **Gallery of Islamic and Oriental Art**, which features Persian rugs, Ottoman ceramics, enamelled glassware and a beautiful late 13th-century glazed ceramic *mihrab* (a prayer niche indicating the direction of Mecca) from a Persian mosque. Also in this room is a small case of illuminated gospel manuscripts from Gulbenkian's native Armenia.

This leads into the **Far East Gallery**, which has porcelain, jade, lacquered boxes and screens.

A 14th-century mosque lamp

European Art

The largest part of the museum is devoted to **European art** from the 13th to the 20th centuries. It begins with early illuminated gospels and a 14th-century French triptych depicting scenes from the life of the Virgin. Among the paintings to look out for are *Portrait of an Old Man* by Rembrandt and *Portrait of Hélène Fourment* by Rubens (featuring his second wife). Works from the Impressionist period include a *Self-Portrait* by Degas and *Boy Blowing Bubbles* by Manet. The museum also boasts pieces by such prominent European artists as Gainsborough, Turner, Renoir and Monet and some superb sculptures by Rodin.

Don't miss the **René Lalique Gallery** at the end of the European Art section. René Lalique, a friend of Calouste Gulbenkian, created stunning art nouveau jewellery with animal and floral motifs.

The temporary exhibitions held in the **Centro de Arte Moderna** are also worth checking out. They're organized by the Gulbenkian Foundation.

TAKING A BREAK

The museum has a cafeteria and a self-service restaurant that are both good places to chill out.

➕ 208 off A5 ✉ Avenida de Berna 45
☎ 217 823 000; www.museu.gulbenkian.pt 🕐 Tue–Sun 10–5:45
Ⓜ São Sebastião or Praça de Espanha 🚌 Bus 713, 716, 726, 742, 746, 756
💶 €5; free Sun

INSIDER INFO

- The Gulbenkian Foundation has its own **orchestra and choir** and also hosts concerts by visiting musicians. Ask for a programme at the museum reception desk or contact the box office (tel: 217 823 000).
- As well as paintings and sculpture, the European art galleries contain fine examples of 18th-century **Louis XV furniture** from France and a set of gorgeous Italian tapestries.
- The atrium of the museum bookshop becomes the stage for a wide variety of **free concerts** and cultural events held on a number of Sundays throughout the year (starting at noon each time).

⏸ Alfama

The oldest quarter of Lisbon is also its most charming. Alfama sprawls across a hill between the Castelo de São Jorge and the River Tagus, a maze of cobbled lanes, alleyways, staircases and hidden courtyards.

View from Portas do Sol over the rooftops of Alfama

The streets of this city district are the perfect setting for an aimless stroll. It's a place where you'll be rewarded with endless surprises – a flower-strewn courtyard here, a little tucked-away square there, or a statue of the Virgin in a niche high on a wall. Alfama is still a typical Lisbon quarter with a special atmosphere that its inhabitants love. The life of the community goes on in artfully dilapidated houses with wrought-iron balconies and *azulejo* panels on the walls. Some of the buildings are crumbling, while others have undergone recent renovation.

Cathedral and Teatro Romano

The name Alfama probably derives from the Arabic *al hama* (fountain) and there is evidence of Roman and Moorish settlements here. The Christians built their *Sé* (cathedral) on the site of the main mosque soon after Afonso Henriques captured the city in 1147. Constructed in a Romanesque style and closely resembling a fortress, it boasts twin towers that stand either side of a rose window on the main façade. The Gothic cloisters contain the excavated remains of the Roman city.

Lisbon & Around

Just above the cathedral, the **Teatro Romano** is a partly excavated Roman theatre, built during the reign of Emperor Augustus and rebuilt under Nero in the 1st century AD. The theatre itself, which has been looked after by the Museu de Lisboa since mid-2015, is found in a shed on Rua de São Mamede, where archaeological discoveries are used to describe the Roman history of the city.

Miradouro de Santa Luzia

Walk (or take tram 28) uphill from the cathedral to reach **Miradouro de Santa Luzia**, a lookout point with fine views over Alfama and the River Tagus. Notice the tiled panels on the south wall of the nearby church, one depicting Lisbon before the earthquake, the other showing Christian soldiers with helmets, swords and shields attacking the Castelo de São Jorge (➤ 61), which is defended by turbaned Moors.

Museu de Artes Decorativas

Around the corner is the **Museu de Artes Decorativas**, containing the applied arts collection of the Portuguese banker Ricardo do Espírito Santo Silva. The collection is particularly rich in Portuguese furniture, as well as ceramics, clocks, fans and guns, all displayed in a re-creation of a 17th-century aristocratic home. Don't miss the *Giraffe Parade*, a colourful 16th-century Flemish tapestry in the main hall. The museum also has workshops where artisans reproduce traditional skills such as bookbinding and woodcarving.

There are more views over the Alfama rooftops from the terrace at **Largo das Portas do Sol**, opposite the museum. Notice here the **statue of São Vicente**, Lisbon's patron saint, bearing the city's symbol, a boat with two ravens (the relics of the saint were said to have been brought to Lisbon by Afonso Henriques in a boat piloted by ravens).

An aristocratic drawing room in the Museu de Artes Decorativas

The superb illuminated dome of Santa Engrácia

Two Churches

Looking east from the terrace, the skyline is dominated by two marble churches, the vast bulk of **São Vicente de Fora** and the domed church of **Santa Engrácia**. You can hop back on the tram to visit both of them.

São Vicente de Fora means "St Vincent Beyond the Wall" as the church was originally outside the city walls. The first church was built on this site soon after the Christian conquest, though the current one dates from 1629. Go through a side entrance to visit the monastery and cloisters. There is a fine 18th-century sacristy with walls of inlaid polychrome marble and a set of *azulejo* tiles (➤ 32) depicting the fables of the 17th-century satirist La Fontaine. The former monks' refectory is now the pantheon of the **House of Bragança** (➤ 137) containing the tombs of monarchs from Catherine of Bragança (Queen of England) to the assassinated Dom Carlos I and his son, Dom Manuel II, who died in 1932.

The baroque church of **Santa Engrácia**, which is also known as the Panteão Nacional, contains monuments to such Portuguese heroes as the *fadista* Amália Rodrigues and the explorers Vasco da Gama (➤ 16, 52, 57) and Luís de Camões. You can take the lift up to the rooftop for fabulous views out over the River Tagus and the city.

The open ground between the two churches, **Campo de Santa Clara**, is the setting for Lisbon's liveliest flea market, the Feira da Ladra (Thieves' Market), which takes place on Tuesday and Saturday from 6am to 6pm. The roots of this vibrant event date right back to the Middle Ages.

Fado

Alfama is the true home of the traditional music of *fado* (➤ 22), and there are several clubs where you can hear it performed each night. To find out more about this uniquely Portuguese music, visit the **Museu do Fado**. This museum describes the history and traditions of *fado* and of the Portuguese guitar, a mandolin-type instrument that was introduced by British traders in the 18th century. There are frequent live performances, and the shop sells *fado* books and CDs. The audio guide with its numbered stops lets you experience the sounds of *fado* as you wander around.

Lisbon & Around

TAKING A BREAK

Cafés, *fado* bars and restaurants cluster on and around Rua de São Pedro, Rua São João da Praça and Rua dos Remédios. There's a restaurant in the Fado Museum (**A Travessa do Fado**) with places to sit outside. You'll also find a café in the Museu de Artes Decorativas.

➕ 209 F3   🚌 Bus 737; tram 12, 28

Sé
➕ 209 E2   ✉ Largo da Sé   ☎ 218 876 628
🕐 Museum: 10–5. Cloisters: 10–6. Cathedral: 9–7   💶 Church: free. Cloisters: €3

Teatro Romano – Museu de Lisboa
➕ 209 E3   ✉ Rua de São Mamede 3A   ☎ 218 820 320; www.museudelisboa.pt
🕐 Tue–Sun 10–1, 2–6   💶 €1.50

Museu de Artes Decorativas
➕ 209 F3
✉ Largo das Portas do Sol 2
☎ 218 814 600; www.fress.pt
🕐 Wed–Mon 10–5   💶 €4

Narrow cobbled streets in Alfama, Lisbon's oldest quarter

São Vicente de Fora
➕ 209 off F4   ✉ Largo de São Vicente
☎ 218 810 559
🕐 Church: Tue–Sat 9–5, Sun 9–12:30.
Cloisters: Tue–Sun 10–6 (last entry 5)
💶 €5

Santa Engrácia (Panteão Nacional)
➕ 209 off F4
✉ Campo de Santa Clara
☎ 218 854 820   🕐 Tue–Sun 10–5
🚌 Bus 34   💶 €4

Museu do Fado
➕ 209 off F3
✉ Largo do Chafariz de Dentro 1
☎ 218 823 470; www.museudofado.pt
🕐 Tue–Sun 10–6   💶 €5

INSIDER INFO

Insider Tip

- Come here on **weekday mornings** when the street life is at its most lively.
- Alfama is an area with a reputation for **petty crime**, so avoid flaunting anything valuable and take care when wandering at night. One particularly charming spot is the **courtyard** at the top of **Escadinhas de Santo Estêvão**, between Rua dos Remédios and Santo Estêvão.
- **Igreja de Santo André e Santa Marinha** is one of the oldest convents in Lisbon. Parts of the convent are closed to the public, but the church is open and the views over the city and river from the courtyard are stunning.

⓭ Parque das Nações

The former Expo'98 site has become an open-air playground where *Lisboetas* flock at the weekend to enjoy its many restaurants, bars, gardens and riverside walks. With stunning modern architecture and a range of contemporary attractions, a day out in the "Park of Nations" offers a completely different experience of Lisbon.

The waterfront area is a pleasant place to relax

Hosting the World Exposition in 1998 gave Lisbon the opportunity for a major project in urban renewal. A derelict area of warehouses and oil refineries, 5km (3mi) east of the city, was transformed into a riverside park. When Expo'98 closed, the site was renamed **Parque das Nações** and turned into a business and residential zone – in effect, a new city with cultural and sporting facilities. There are now more visitors than there were when Expo'98 was in full swing.

Most visitors arrive at the concertina-like **Estação do Oriente**, a strikingly vaulted steel-and-glass Metro station, designed by much-lauded Spanish architect Santiago Calatrava. This leads into the Vasco da Gama **shopping mall**. Walk through the mall to emerge on the waterfront.

🚺 Underwater World

The **Oceanário**, a top-quality family destination, is one of Europe's largest oceanariums. It's based around a huge tank with windows at two levels that let you watch the sharks near the surface and the flatfish on the seabed.

Gathered around this are four separate tanks devoted to the ecosystems of the North Atlantic, South Atlantic, Pacific and Indian oceans. More than 15,000 marine animals and birds are on show, including puffins, penguins, sea otters and spider crabs, together with some superb examples of coral reefs.

From here you can walk along the banks of the River Tagus to the sail-shaped **Torre Vasco da Gama**, a skeletal concrete-and-steel structure. Following years of work and a lot of investment, the tower has been transformed into a luxury hotel that makes the area feel a little bit like an exclusive part of Dubai.

The extraordinary 18km (11-mile) bridge, the **Ponte Vasco da Gama**, spans the River Tagus; it passes over water for 10km (6mi) of its length and almost seems to be floating.

TAKING A BREAK

There are dozens of restaurants of different kinds to choose from in the area, including pizza houses, *tapas* bars and traditional restaurants serving Portuguese specialities.

➕ 216 B4
ℹ️ www.portaldasnacoes.pt
🚇 Oriente

The ultra-modern and extraordinary Wall of Water Fountain

Oceanário
☎ 218 917 000; www.oceanario.pt
🕐 June–Sep daily 10–8; Nov–March 10–7
(last entry one hour before closing)
💶 €14 (€17 incl. the temporary exhibitions)

Teleférico (cable-car)
☎ 218 956 143; www.telecabinelisboa.pt
🕐 Daily Nov–Feb 11–6; March–May 11–7; June–Sep 10:30–8, Oct 11–7
💶 €3.95 (single), €5.90 (return)

INSIDER INFO

- The Parque das Nações is home to the **Vasco da Gama Shopping Center**, where you can shop 'til you drop and eat to your heart's content.
- If you want to learn more about the Oceanário, splash out an extra €2.50 to rent an English **audio guide**.
- Ask at the ticket desk in the Oceanário to get a **reduced family ticket** for just €44 (valid for 2 adults & 2 children aged 12 and under).

In more depth Take a botanical stroll through Portugal's former colonies at the riverside **Jardim Garcia de Orta**. Flame-like birds of paradise flowers, pepper trees and frangipani all flourish here. If the weather is unfavourable, head to the 🏛 **Pavilhão do Conhecimento** (Tue–Fri 10–6, Sat, Sun 11–7, entrance fee: €9; kids/young people €5/€6), an interactive science museum (www.pavconhecimento.pt).

At Your Leisure

🔢 Museu Nacional de Arte Antiga

The National Museum of Ancient Art does have the most complete collection of Portuguese art, together with the cultures that influenced it. Among the items to look for are Indo-Portuguese furniture, Sino-Portuguese ceramics, a carved-ivory salt cellar from Africa, and 16th-century lacquer screens showing the arrival of Portuguese explorers in Japan. Many of the religious paintings, such as Nuno Gonçalves' 15th-century *St Vincent Altarpiece*, were confiscated from churches following the dissolution of the monasteries in 1834. The museum also contains a complete baroque chapel from the Carmelite convent that once stood on this site, with gilded woodwork and outstanding *azulejo* tiles (➤ 32).

🔲 208 off A1
✉ Rua das Janelas Verdes, Lapa
☎ 213 912 800; www.museudearteantiga.pt
🕙 Wed–Sun 10–6, Tue 2–6
🚌 Bus 713, 714, 732; tram 15E, 18E, 25E
💶 €6; free 1st Sun of the month

Gilt baroque silverwork

🚼 FOR LITTLE EXPLORERS

- **Planetário Calouste Gulbenkian**: this planetarium next to the Museu de Marinha (➤ 52) has children's shows at weekends (http://planetario.marinha.pt; €5 for adults, €2.50 for young people and kids.)
- **Museu da Carris**: tram museum at Rua 1° de Maio 101–103 (Mon–Sat 10–6; http://museu.carris.pt; entry €4; young people and kids €2).
- **Jardim Zoológico**: take the Metro to Jardim Zoológico to visit Lisbon's zoo (mid-Sep to mid-March 10–6 (last entry 5:15), mid-March to mid-Sep 10–8 (last entry 6:45); tel: 217 232 900; www.zoo.pt; entrance fee: €19.50, children €14).

🔢 Estrela

Estrela, a well-to-do neighbourhood some 2km (1.2mi) west of Bairro Alto, is dominated by its late-18th-century baroque **Basílica**, whose graceful white dome is visible across the city. The **Jardim da Estrela** opposite is one of Lisbon's prettiest public gardens, with a bandstand, a play area and a duck pond. Around 15 minutes away on foot, you'll reach the **Cemitério dos Prazeres**, a gigantic cemetery with impressive monuments that's well worth paying a visit.

🔲 208 off A3 🚃 Tram 25E, 28

Insider Tip

Basílica da Estrela
✉ Praça da Estrela ☎ 213 960 915
🕙 Daily 9–8 💶 Free (view from the dome, €2)

🔢 Bairro Alto

The grid of 16th-century lanes that makes up the Bairro Alto (upper town) is best known as Lisbon's nightlife quarter, where the plaintive strains of *fado* compete with African and Latin vibes.

Traditionally a working-class area, Bairro Alto has been given a new lease of life, with cocktail bars and a glut of live music venues, bars, pubs and discos. It is also a great spot for shopping, where the shops sell everything from alternative fashion to vintage accessories, cutting-edge art to designer garb.

Near here is the Jesuit **Igreja de São Roque**, whose plain façade belies the richness of its interior, especially its lavish side chapels. The Capela de São João Baptista, fourth on the left, is a riot of marble, alabaster, lapis lazuli, amethyst, mosaic, silver and gold that was built in Rome and taken to Lisbon on the orders of Dom João V.

Just down the hill, on the edge of the chic shopping district of Chiado, the **Museu Arqueológico do Carmo** occupies the old Carmelite convent, destroyed in the earthquake of 1755 and now a Gothic shell. Among the items on display are Egyptian and Peruvian mummies, Roman mosaics and a stone bust of Afonso Henriques dating from the 12th century.

The atmospheric streets of the Barrio Alto area at night

➕ 208A3 🚊 Tram 28, Elevador da Glória

Igreja de São Roque
➕ 208 A4 ✉ Largo Trindade Coelho
☎ 213 235 444; www.museu-saoroque.com
🕐 April–Sep Mon 2–7, Tue–Sun 10–7;
Oct–March Mon 2–6, Tue–Sun 10–6
🎫 Museum: €2.50

Museu Arqueológico do Carmo
➕ 208 B3
✉ Largo do Carmo ☎ 213 478 629;
www.museuarqueologicodocarmo.pt
🕐 June–Sep Mon–Sat 10–7; Oct–May 10–6
🎫 €5

THE FIVE BEST VIEWPOINTS

- **Castelo de São Jorge** (▶ 61): standing at the top of Alfama, there are fine views from the castle ramparts.
- **Miradouro de Santa Luzia**, Alfama (▶ 66): views over the River Tagus and Alfama.
- **Miradouro de São Pedro de Alcântara**, Bairro Alto (▶ 71, 186): views from the top of the Elevador da Glória over the Baixa and River Tagus.
- **Ponte 25 de Abril**: stretching across the River Tagus, the views from the bridge are breathtaking.
- **Santuário Nacional de Cristo Rei**: The gigantic statue of Christ rises up on the other bank of the Tejo; you'll get some fantastic views of the city from the promenade!

🔟 Parque Eduardo VII

This large, formal park was laid out at the end of the 19th century and named after the English king, Edward VII. The best reason for coming here is the **magnificent view** from the terrace at the top of the park, where a stone monument commemorates the 1974 revolution. From here you look down over sweeping lawns and along the broad Avenida da Liberdade all the way to the River Tagus. Near here is a garden dedicated to the *fado* singer Amália Rodrigues.
➕ 208 off A5 🚇 Marquês de Pombal,
Parque, São Sebastião 🕐 Daily 9–sunset

🔟 Museu Nacional do Azulejo

It's worth making the short trek out of the centre of Lisbon to visit the

Walkways intersect lengths of grass with manicured hedges at Parque Eduardo VII

National Tile Museum, housed in the former convent of Madre de Deus. The museum traces the development of *azulejo* tiles (▶ 32) from the 15th century onwards, in the setting of a lovely baroque church with Manueline cloisters and tiled walls. The highlight is an 18th-century panel of more than 1,300 tiles, which gives a panoramic view of pre-earthquake Lisbon. The 20th-century galleries show how *azulejos* have moved out of monasteries and into shopping malls, Metro stations and the realms of abstract art.

🚇 209 off F2 ✉ Rua Madre de Deus 4 ☎ 218 100 340; hwww.museudoazulejo.pt 🕐 Tue–Sun 10–6 (last entry 30 mins before closing) 🚌 Bus 718, 742, 794 💶 €5; free 1st Sun of the month

🔟 Estoril & Cascais

These twin resorts, linked by an attractive seafront promenade, lie at the heart of the Lisbon coast. Estoril is more cosmopolitan and chic, with a casino, golf course, racetrack and a mock castle on the beach. During World War II, when Portugal remained neutral, Estoril was a refuge for diplomats, spies and exiled royalty – King Juan Carlos of Spain spent his childhood here.

Cascais, a former fishing village, is now a holiday resort with added cultural extras. It boasts several museums, including the Museu Condes de Castro Guimarães, the Casa das Histórias Paula Rego and the **Farol Museu de Santa Marta** (Lighthouse Museum).

The square in front of Cascais Town Hall is decorated with a lovely mosaic of black-and-white waves

A corridor in the spectacular Palácio-Convento de Mafra

Beyond Cascais, a coastal corniche leads past **Boca do Inferno** (Hell's Mouth), where waves crash against the cliffs, to the dunes at Praia do Guincho, a popular windsurfing beach, and the 🔢 **Cabo da Roca**, mainland Europe's westernmost point. The Cape is an bracing place to experience the spray of the sea and the wind in your face. Families with kids will enjoy it, too (but stay away from the edge!)

Insider Tip This area makes a good base for a short stay near Lisbon, combining a beach holiday with a city break. Trains to Lisbon follow a scenic line along the coast, via the resorts of São Pedro do Estoril and Carcavelos.

➕ 216 A4 🚉 From Cais do Sodré

🔟 Palácio de Mafra

The pink marble Palácio-Convento de Mafra, 40km (25mi) northwest of Lisbon, was built by Dom João V in 1717 to give thanks to God for the birth of a royal heir. Like El Escorial in Madrid, it served both as a royal palace and a monastery.

Financed by profits from Brazilian gold, the palace employed 50,000 workers in its construction; originally intended to hold 13 monks, it ended up accommodating 300 monks and the entire royal family. You can visit the basilica and the palace, including the monks' cells, the pharmacy, and the baroque library, on guided tours. There are also tours of the royal hunting ground, now a wild-life park.

➕ 216 A5

☎ 261 817 550; www.palaciomafra.pt

🕐 Summer: Wed–Mon 10–6 (last entry 5), Wed–Mon 9:30–5:30 rest of year (last entry 6:30)

🚌 Mafrense bus (www.mafrense.pt) links palace to Lisbon and Ericeira

💷 €6; free 1st Sun of the month

LISBON RIDES

It's fun (and quite a lot cheaper) to join the locals and travel on the city's public transport.

- **Ferries**: Commuter ferries cross the Tagus to Barreiro and Cacilhas. The boats for Barreiro depart from Terreiro do Paço, with superb views of the city.
- **Trams**: A ride on one of Lisbon's bright yellow, wood-panelled vintage trams is an experience in itself. The most enjoyable route is No 28, which rattles up and down the steep streets to Estrela. *Insider Tip*
- **Elevadores**: These ancient lifts and funiculars are part of Lisbon's public transport system. Take Elevador da Glória from Praça dos Restauradores to Bairro Alto, or Elevador de Santa Justa for views over Baixa.

Where to...
Stay

Prices
Expect to pay for a double room per night in high season
€ under €80   €€ €80–€110   €€€ €110–€150   €€€€ over €150

LISBON

Albergaria Senhora do Monte €€
The gorgeous pink and white décor and marble bathrooms in this hotel complement its romantic location, high up in the quiet *bairro* of Graça. It has 28 modern rooms and a bar with a terrace that enjoys sweeping views of the city and the river below (open to non-guests for drinks). The more expensive rooms with south-facing terraces have air conditioning – ask for one when booking. It's a short tram ride to downtown Lisbon.

➕ 209 E5
✉ Calçada do Monte 39
☎ 218 866 002;
www.albergariasenhoradomonte.com
🚇 Martim Moniz 🚋 Tram 28

Britania Hotel €€€–€€€€
Tucked down a quiet street near the boutique-lined Avenida da Liberdade boulevard, this art deco boutique hotel by architect Cassiano Branco gets rave reviews. Polished marble, geometric cork floors and chrome lighting whisk you back to the 1940s. However, the plush rooms come with modern creature comforts such as free WiFi internet, DVD players and bathrobes. Head down to the shipshape bar to watch the world go by over a coffee and the daily papers or a cocktail.

➕ 208 off A5
✉ Rua Rodrigues Sampaio 17
☎ 213 155 016; www.hotel-britania.com
🚇 Avenida

Casa do Bairro €€
This B&B in a converted 19th-century town house in Lisbon's hilltop district of Santa Catarina is just five minutes' walk from Bairro Alto. Wood floors and bold colours contrast strikingly with such original features as stucco and *azulejos* in rooms with WiFi and cable TV. It's one of just six "Shiadu Boutique Guesthouses" in Portugal.

➕ 208 off A2
✉ Beco do Caldeira 1
☎ 914 176 969; http://shiadu.com/Portugal/Lisbon/Casa-do-Bairro
🚇 Baixa-Chiado

Hotel Bairro Alto €€€
Chic, luxurious and in a great neighbourhood, this restored 18th-century townhouse makes for a memorable stay in Lisbon. Every detail has been thought about here – generous beds in sleekly designed bedrooms, 24-hour concierge, a good café-bar, a small gym and spa. The sixth-floor terrace offers views over the rooftops of Bairro Alto and down to the River Tagus. Everything suggests understated luxury, but it can all get rather expensive. If you want to experience the hotel without quite the same price tag, the loft rooms are smaller, with sloping roofs, but are well designed and offer excellent value.

➕ 208 A3
✉ 8 Praça Luís de Camões
☎ 213 408 288; www.bairroaltohotel.com
🚇 Baixa-Chiado

Lisbon & Around

Hotel Heritage Av Liberdade €€€–€€€€

This hotel belongs to a small chain of renovated historic buildings that have been turned into luxury boutique hotels. Renovated by Portuguese architect Miguel Câncio Martins, this 18th-century townhouse was the winner of the Historic Rehabilitation Prize 2008 of the Portuguese Real State Oscars. The hotel feels chic and intimate, with good-sized bedrooms, large marble bathrooms and a heated lap pool in the basement, and there's WiFi in all rooms. There's a cosy, well-decorated bar downstairs, where breakfast is served and bar snacks in the evenings. Even better, it's an easy walk into the centre of town.

🞢 208 A5
✉ Avenida da Liberdade 28
☎ 213 404 040; www.heritageavliberdade.com
🜚 Restauradores

Hotel Myriad €€€€

An outstanding hotel in the Torre Vasco da Gama (▶ 70) which towers over the riverbank at a height of more than 140m (460ft). It's home to various grades of room, as well as the River Lounge Restaurant, the River Lounge Bar and a spa on the 23rd floor. The modern fitness studio is open 24/7.

🞢 216 B4
✉ Parque das Nações, Cais das Naus
☎ 211 107 600, http://myriad.pt

Hotel Olissippo Oriente €€–€€€

This modern, four-star hotel in the city's new financial district has a restaurant and 182 comfortable rooms. The Parque das Nações (▶ 69) with its eateries, shops and various diversions lies just outside the door. All of the rooms enjoy dazzling views of the park's futuristic buildings, the Tejo river and the Ponte Vasco da Gama (▶ 70).

🞢 216 B4
✉ Avenida Dom João II, Parque das Nações
☎ 218 929 100; www.hotelolissippo-oriente.com
🜚 Oriente

Jerónimos 8 €€–€€€

Situated opposite the magnificent Jerónimos monastery (▶ 52), this contemporary, cleverly designed hotel is perfectly placed for exploring Belém. Its public areas are sleek and modern, with low-level sofas in bright colours and large artworks hanging on the walls. There are several terraces on the upper floors that are great for enjoying a drink on warm days. The bedrooms are reasonably sized, uncluttered and comfortable. The lively, popular Bussaco Wine Bar serves a range of drinks and cocktails, together with a selection of simple, well-cooked bar food.

🞢 208 off A1
✉ Rua dos Jerónimos 8
☎ 213 600 900; www.jeronimos8.com
🚋 Tram 15

Pensão Londres €

A simple, reliable *pensão* in Bairro Alto. Many of the rooms command fabulous views across the rooftops to the Ponte 25 de Abril or the Castelo São Jorge (▶ 61). The 36 rooms, ranging from well-appointed singles to doubles, triples and suites, all have their own bathrooms. Some boast delightful stucco ceilings, and the largest doubles come with attractive period furniture. A full breakfast is served in a charming dining room with a fine view. Gay and lesbian couples are most welcome.

🞢 208 off A4   ✉ Rua Pedro V 53/1-
☎ 213 462 203; www.pensaolondres.com.pt
🚌 Bus 91; Elevador da Glória

Zuzabed & Breakfast €€

It's well worth the stiff climb up the Calçada do Duque to reach this homely B&B in the Chiado district that's run by Luís Zuzarte, an affable and knowledgeable host. He's put his artistic stamp on the individually decorated rooms, all of which have balconies.

Head to the terrace for dreamy views over Lisbon and the castle. Free WiFi and home-made cakes at breakfast sweeten the deal.

➕ 208 B4
✉ Calçada do Duque 29
☎ 936 991 223; www.zuzabed.com
🚇 Rossio 🚠 Elevador da Glória

SINTRA

Cinco B&B €€

High on a hill, this is one of Sintra's most charming retreats. You'll receive the warmest of welcomes from Carole and Stuart the minute you arrive at their family's attractive stone cottage. The spacious, tastefully decorated one-bedroom apartment features a well-equipped kitchenette, a bright living room with a DVD player and a terrace with tremendous views across the valley to the Atlantic. Guests are also welcome to use the family's swimming pool. Rates apply to one to two people in the apartment, with an additional charge per extra adult or child.

➕ 216 A4 ✉ Largo da Caracota 5
☎ 914 502 255; www.stayatcinco.com
🚉 From Estação do Rossio

Lawrence's Hotel €€€€

This beautiful place near the centre of Sintra claims to be the oldest hotel in Iberia, and boasts a history reaching right back into the 18th century. The 11 exquisitely decorated rooms and 6 suites have the latest facilities, including air conditioning and satellite TV; some also have open fireplaces and jacuzzis in their huge bathrooms. Even if you're not a hotel guest, you can sample some of the best cooking in Sintra at the top-class restaurant. A refined cellar backs up the Portuguese-influenced cuisine.

➕ 216 A4
✉ Rua Consiglieri Pedroso 38–40
☎ 219 105 500; www.lawrenceshotel.com
🚉 From Estação do Rossio

Where to...
Eat and Drink

Prices
Expect to pay per person for a three-course meal, excluding drinks and tips.
€ under €20   €€ €21–€30   €€€ €31–€40   €€€€ over €40

LISBON

100 Maneiras €€€€

This is *the* place for imaginative food made from market-fresh ingredients. The service is attentive, the setting arty yet unpretentious. There's only one tasting menu, but come with an open mind and an empty stomach and you won't be disappointed. Dishes such as marinated sardines with toasted basil and passion fruit, tender loin of lamb in a pistachio crust and palate-cleansing ginger sorbet strike a perfect balance. The menu features a changing selection of dishes. Book ahead.

➕ 208 A4
✉ Rua do Teixeira 35
☎ 910 307 575;
www.restaurante100maneiras.com
🕐 7:30pm–11pm, bar until 2am
🚌 Bus 202, 758, 790; Elevador da Glória

Antiga Confeitaria de Belém €

Although you can order a range of delicious sandwiches and cakes, most people come here for the *pastéis de nata* (►42). These crisp tartlets filled with egg-custard are sold in *pastelarias* across the country, but the ones sold here are unanimously regarded as the very best. Around 200,000 of them are bought here each and every week. A lot of people visit to have a tartlet and a drink.

Insider Tip

🚩 208 off A1
✉ Rua de Belém 84–92
☎ 213 637 423; www.pasteisdebelem.pt
🕐 July–Sep 8am–midnight;
Oct–June, 8am–11pm
🚌 Bus 714, 729, 751 🚊 Tram 15E

Belcanto €€€€

Since reopening a few years ago, this restaurant run by TV chef José Avillez has become known as one of the capital's most distinguished gastronomic destinations. Sophisticated culinary creations served in a refined setting.

🚩 208 off A3
✉ Largo de São Carlos 10 ☎ 213 420 607;
www.joseavillez.pt, www.belcanto.pt
🕐 Tue–Sat 12:30–3 and 7:30–11,
closed first two weeks in Aug
🚊 Baixa-Chiado

A Bica do Sapato €€€€

Right on the waterfront, this three-in-one temple to good food is currently the place to eat and be seen, whether in the stylish café-bar, the sushi section or the restaurant. In the latter you can sample clever concoctions such as soft-shell crab tempura, salmon *temaki* and spicy *hosomaki*.

Insider Tip

The restaurant is one of the few places in Lisbon with a dedicated vegetarian menu.

🚩 209 E2 ✉ Avenida Infante Dom Henrique,
Armazém B, Cais da Pedra, Santa Apolónia
☎ 218 810 320; www.bicadosapato.com
🕐 Restaurant: Mon 5pm–11:30pm,
Tue–Sun 12:30–2:30, 8–11:30. Sushi Bar:
Mon–Sat 7:30–1:30. Café: Mon 5pm–1am,
Tue–Sun noon–3:30, 7:30–1am
🚊 Santa Apolónia
🚌 Bus 9, 28, 35, 81, 82, 90

A Brasileira €–€€

Few old-style cafés have survived in Lisbon, but this one has – the timeless atmosphere is enhanced by a handless clock at the far end of the mirrored salon. It's a meeting place for students, intellectuals and other regulars drawn by the excellent coffee and *pastéis* (►42), and also a shrine to Fernando Pessoa who frequented it – witness the bronze statue on the small *esplanada,* next to which many tourists have their picture taken, often having never heard of the great 20th-century poet. It is a bit touristy, and not the cheapest place, but a real institution.

🚩 208 B3 ✉ Rua Garrett 120 ☎ 213 469 541
🕐 Daily 8am–2am 🚊 Baixa-Chiado

Café Martinho da Arcada €€€

One of Portugal's oldest cafés with more than 230 years of service under its belt. It sits in a superb location at the foot of the Alfama under the arcades on one of the city's main squares. They serve a wide selection of dishes, from gilt-head seabream to grilled rabbit, all made using ingredients sourced at local markets. If you can't decide, the friendly waiters are happy to help. The wine list is excellent.

🚩 209 D2 ✉ Praça do Comércio 3
☎ 218 879 259; www.martinhodaarcada.pt
🕐 Mon–Sat 7am–11pm 🚊 Tram 15, 28

Casa da Comida €€€€

Tucked away in a side street just above the Rato, this is one of Lisbon's finest restaurants, with prices to match. Inside it has the sophisticated décor of a noble mansion and a beautiful patio. The superb cuisine puts a French twist on traditional Portuguese dishes, using local crab and clams, pheasant and partridge. The desserts are as fabulous as the wine cellar. It's the perfect place for a celebration or expensive treat.

🚩 208 off A5 ✉ Travessa das Amoreiras
☎ 213 860 889; www.casadacomida.pt
🕐 Mon–Sat 9am–midnight
🚊 Rato 🚌 Bus 706, 713, 727

Casa do Alentejo €–€€

Behind a run-of-the-mill façade, there's a fantastic, if slightly decadent, patrician mansion, with Moorish patios and beautiful skylights, decorated with carved wood, gleaming *azulejos* and huge palms. The reliably good and well-priced food served in two dining rooms, one more subdued, the other lined with bright tiles, gives you a taste of the Alentejo, with classic dishes such as *carne de porco à alentejana* (pork with coriander and clams).

🗺 208 B5
✉ Rua das Portas de Santo Antão 58
☎ 213 405 140; www.casadoalentejo.com.pt
🕐 Daily noon–3, 6:30–10   🚇 Restauradores

Cerverjaria Trindade €–€€

This boisterous but cheerful beerhouse (*cerverjaria*, ➤ 41) also serves seafood, and is popular with artists and locals. Once a convent, the Trindade has beautiful vaulted ceilings and a splendid display of *azulejos*, which make it an atmospheric place to eat. Draught Portuguese beer served ice-cold is the perfect accompaniment to the simple delicious, seafood dishes.

🗺 208 B3   ✉ Rua Nova da Trinidade 20
☎ 213 423 506; www.cervejariatrindade.pt
🕐 Daily noon–midnight
🚇 Rossio   🚌 Bus 202, 758, 790

Chafariz do Vinho €–€€

A good selection of Portuguese and international wines is served at this very attractive, traditional building that used to play a key role in providing the city with water. They also serve some nice food, including various types of *tapas* and other tasting plates to accompany their drinks.

🗺 208 off A5   ✉ Chafariz da Mãe d'Água, Rua da Mãe d'Água à Praça da Alegria
☎ 213 422 079; www.chafarizdovinho.com
🕐 Tue–Sun 6–2am
🚇 Avenida   🚌 Bus 202, 758, 773

Comida de Santo €€€

Of Lisbon's many Brazilian restaurants, this one has the most reliably good food, all served with a smile amid tropical surroundings. It can get very busy, especially on Sundays, so book in advance. The delicious Bahia-dominated cuisine includes generous portions of such dishes as thick *vatapás* (spicy shrimp purée) and succulent chicken *muquecas* (cooked in coconut milk). They also have vegetarian options. Round off your meal with fresh mango and papaya or papaya mousse with coconut milk pudding.

🗺 208 off A4
✉ Calçada Engenheiro Miguel Pais 39
☎ 213 963 339; www.comidadesanto.pt
🕐 Wed–Mon 12:30–3:30 and 7:30–1am
🚇 Rato   🚌 Bus 202, 758, 773

Cruzes Credo €

Sit outside or in the cosy interior at this nice café-restaurant with a relaxed atmosphere behind the Sé (cathedral). Serves a selection of delicious light bites, ranging from toasted sandwiches to Portuguese specialities. The bar becomes a favourite haunt of students and young party animals later in the evening.

🗺 208 E2   ✉ Cruzes da Sé 29, Alfama
☎ 218 822 296
🕐 Daily 10–2am   🚊 Tram 28

Pap'Açorda €€€–€€€€

This Bairro Alto haunt of the rich, famous and glamorous never seems to go out of fashion. Although the service can receive mixed reviews, the lavish crystal chandeliers, plentiful plants, lively atmosphere and expertly prepared food all explain the restaurant's popularity. The emphasis is on mussels, clams and other seafood. The house speciality is the Lisbon delicacy, *açorda*, a concoction of bread, oil, egg and coriander that tastes far better than it sounds (or looks!). The *açorda real*, with lobster and prawns, is truly "regal". We recommend the chocolate mousse for dessert.

🗺 208 A3   ✉ Rua da Atalaia 57–59
☎ 213 464 811   🕐 Mon–Sat 8pm–10:30pm
🚇 Rossio   🚌 Bus 92

Pavilhão Chinês €

Located on the edge of the Bairro Alto, the Chinese Pavilion is a classy tea room and cocktail bar combined, popular with tourists and locals alike (though there are more locals from around 11pm). It must be among the world's most eccentric bars. The walls, cabinets and ceilings of its three red lacquer salons are crammed with ornaments, including fans and oriental porcelain, statues and dolls, lead soldiers and iron helmets, all of which have been collected by Lisbon artist Luís Pinto Coelho. Both are unusual places for an aperitif.

➕ 208 off A4 **✉** Rua Dom Pedro V 89
☎ 213 424 729
⊙ Mon–Sat 6–2am, Sun 9–2am **🚌** Bus 92

Solar do Vinho do Porto €

A cosy but modern place, furnished with comfortable sofas and a dimly lit bar, Solar do Vinho do Porto is the perfect place to taste your way through a bewildering list of more than 300 ports, with the help of the expert staff.

➕ 208 A4
✉ Rua de São Pedro de Alcântara 45
☎ 213 475 707; www.ivdp.pt
⊙ Mon–Fri 11am–midnight, Sat 3pm–midnight
🚌 Bus 202, 758, 790; Elevador da Glória

Tágide €€€€

Highly acclaimed, state-of-the-art cuisine served by helpful staff. If you can get a window seat (book well ahead and ask for one specifically!) you'll also be treated to incredible views of the city and the river that would distract you from the food if it weren't so delicious. Not surprisingly, the cellar is one of the most refined in Lisbon, and you can choose a suitable wine to accompany different regional dishes. Their weekday lunch menu is much more affordable (€€).

➕ 208 B2
✉ Largo da Academia Nacional de Belas Artes 18
☎ 213 404 010; www.restaurantetagide.com
⊙ Tue–Sat 12:30–3, 8–midnight **🚋** Tram 28

Wine Bar do Castelo €

If you are not in the mood for a formal dinner, this inviting little wine bar near the castle is great for a light supper. Exposed brick and warm wood set the scene for some of Portugal's best wines – ask the friendly manager Nuno for his recommendations. Wines from crisp Alentejo whites to full-bodied Douro reds pair well with *tapas* such as olives, cheese, cured ham, chutney and crusty bread.

➕ 209 E3
✉ Rua Bartolomeu de Gusmão 11–13
☎ 218 879 093
⊙ Daily noon–10 **🚌** Bus 737 **🚋** Tram 28

SINTRA

Tulhas €€

A charming restaurant located right in the centre of Sintra (➤ 56), The food is varied, with both fish and meat dishes, and you should certainly try the house special, *lombos de vitela com vinho de Madeira* (medallions of veal in Madeira sauce). Tulhas is the ideal place for a quiet and relaxing authentic lunch during a day's sightseeing in Sintra.

➕ 216 A4 **✉** Rua Gil Vicente 4–6
☎ 219 232 378 **⊙** Thu–Tue noon–3:30, 7–10
🚉 From Estação do Rossio

Where to...
Shop

MARKETS & SHOPPING MALLS

The Feira da Ladra (Campo de Santa Clara, São Vicente, Tues and Sat from around 6am–5pm) is Lisbon's flea market. You'll also find weekly markets in around 30 different parts of the city.

The most interesting traditional market is the **Mercado da Ribeira**

(Cais do Sodré, Avenida 24 de Julho, Mon–Sat 6am–2pm, Food Court daily 10am–2pm). A modern food court with 35 stands selling high-class Portuguese treats opened in one of the two halls there in 2014.

The traditional **Mercado de Campo de Ourique** (Rua Coelho da Rocha; Mon–Fri 10am–11pm, Sat 10am–1am) has also been extended by the addition of a hip food court.

Visit the modern mall of **Armazéns do Chiado** (Rua do Carmo 2; www.armazensdochiado. com) for independent shops and international chain stores.

The landmark towers of **Amoreiras** (Avenida Engenheiro Duarte Pacheco), **Centro Comercial Colombo** (Avenida Lusíada, Benfica) and **Centro Comercial Vasco da Gama** (Avenida Dom João II, out at the Parque das Nações) are all great places to window shop. The latter is particularly well-stocked with various stores and eateries.

SHOPPING CARD

If you want to shop 'til you drop in Lisbon, it's worth getting your hands on a **Lisboa Shopping Card**. Available at tourist offices, they're valid for 24 hours (€3.70) or 72 hours (€5.80). The cards give you discounts of 5 to 15% at around 200 participating stores in the heart of the city (not for use in conjunction with clearance sales or other offers).

CLOTHES & FOOTWEAR

Baixa and Chiado are both popular shopping districts for lovers of fashion. The most reliable addresses for ready-to-wear in Baixa include **Ciola** (Rua dos Fanqueiros 87), **Jovanel** (Figueira 6-B), **Ankita** (Rua dos Fanqueiros 123), **Le Tailleur Moderne** (Rua Augusta 213), **Mister Man** (Rua São Nicolao 1) and **Figurino d'Ouro** (Rua dos Fanqueiros 237).

If you're in Chiado, head to **Carmus** (Rua do Carmo 83) and **Vitrine** (Rua Garrett 28).

A Gardenia (Rua Garrett 54) sells popular labels (you'll also find them at Galerias Chiado Plaza 38).

Tiny **Luvaria Ulisses** (Rua do Carmo 87A) carries exquisite hand-made kid gloves.

For vintage fashion, try **A Outra Face da Lua** (Avenida Almirante Reis 94 A), which sells items ranging from 1960s platform shoes to glittery ballgowns.

CRAFTS

Alma Lusa (363 Rua de Sao Bento) is an excellent Portuguese design shop with branches in Lisbon and at Lisbon Airport.

If you want some reproduction *azulejos*, visit **Sant'Ana** (Rua do Alecrim 95, Chiado; there's another showroom at Calçada da Boa-Hora 94 B).

If you've still got a thousand euros left, **Casa dos Tapetes Arraiolos** (Rua da Imprensa Nacional 116) sells hand-made carpets from **Arraiolos** (▶ 158).

FOOD & DRINK

You can buy the city's best *bacalhau* (▶ 31, 41), cheese, cured hams and wines at **Manteigaria Silva** (Rua Dom Antão de Almada 1C-D).

Manuel Tavares (Rua da Betesga 1A-B) sells wines and a diverse selection of fancy foods.

Garrafeira Nacional (Rua de Santa Justa 18) stands out thanks to its beautifully arranged spirits.

You'll find breads and pastries at **Pasteleria San Roque** in Bairro Alto (57 Rua Dom Pedro V), and fresh *pastéis* (▶ 42) at the **Antiga Confeitaria de Belém** (Rua de Belém 84–88, ▶ 77).

Where to...
Go Out

INFORMATION

Blue Ticket (www.blueticket.pt) sells tickets for sports fixtures, concerts and other events. You can also buy them from FNAC stores in shopping malls when you arrive.

ARTS & CULTURE

The **CCB** (short for **Centro Cultural de Belém**, ►51) stages a selection of exhibitions, theatrical performances and dance events.

The Expo pavilions in the **Parque das Nações** (►69) are now successfully used as venues for cultural projects. See the superb Companhia Nacional de Bailado (National Ballet) at **Teatro Camões** (tel: 218 923 470; www.cnb.pt).

The **Teatro Polietama** is a reliable theatre destination in the city centre (Rua das Portas de Santo Antão 109, tel: 213 405 700; www.teatro-politeama.com).

FOOTBALL

Watch a match at either **Sporting** (Estádio de Alvalade, Edifício Visconde de Alvalade, Rua Professor Fernando da Fonseca; www.sporting.pt) or **Benfica** (Estádio da Luz, Avenida General Norton de Matos; www.slbenfica.pt).

MUSIC

Clube de Fado (Rua São João da Praça 94; tel: 218 852 704; www.clube-de-fado.com) is one of Lisbon's top *fado* venues.

Café Luso (Travessa da Queimada 10, tel: 213 422 281; www.cafeluso.pt) is also extreme-

ly popular. Large concerts take place in the **MEO Arena** (formerly called the Pavilhão Atlântico) in the Parque das Nações.

The **Teatro Nacional de São Carlos** (Rua Serpa Pinto 9; tel: 213 253 045; http://tnsc.pt) stages operas.

FAMILY FUN

The best **beaches** are at Caparica, across the River Tagus or between Carcavelos and Guincho on the city side of the Tagus.

Puppets, marionettes, shows and guided visits amuse the little ones at the 🔢 **Museu da Marioneta** (Convento das Bernardas, Rua da Esperança 146; tel: 213 942 810; www.museudamarioneta.pt; closed Mon).

NIGHTLIFE

For a noisy night, visit the **Bairro Alto** (►71). For a more relaxed evening, head for **Baixa**. **Alfama** is the place to go for authentic *fado* (►22). If you want to sample Lisbon's pulsating club scene (go late!), check out **Avenida 24 de Julho** and the **Docas de Santos**.

Lux has a packed calendar of events (Avenida Infante Dom Henrique, Armazém A, Santa Apolónia; www.luxfragil.com).

Club Noir (Rua da Madalena 201; Fri–Sat 11pm–4am) resounds to the thumping sounds of hard rock, heavy metal, post-punk and gothic rock.

For gay venues, visit the **Principe Real district**.

Etilico (Rua Grémio Lusitano 8) is a popular gay bar in Bairro Alto.

Visit www.lisbongaycircuit.com for more information on Lisbon's scene.

Gay, lesbian and straight people all hang out in the avant-garde **Purex** (Rua das Salgadeiras 28).

Northern Portugal

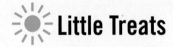 **Little Treats**

Sailing from Port(o) to Port(o)
Experience Porto from the water by taking a boat tour along the river Douro. Families with kids will enjoy it, too (▶93).

Enchanting Embellishments
Porto's Palácio da Bolsa (Stock Exchange Palace, ▶92) is filled with ostentatious décor, particularly in the "Arab Room".

Unspoilt Nature
Get right back to nature in the **Parque Nacional da Peneda-Gerês** (▶99) – it's best experienced along its hiking trails.

Getting Your Bearings

The north is the cradle of Portugal, and Guimarães – a former European Capital of Culture – was its first kingdom. Portugal's first king, Afonso I (the Conqueror), was born here in 1109 and extended the city south with land wrested back from the Moors. It was the north, too, that produced Portugal's last and longest ruling dynasty, the dukes of the House of Bragança, who came to power in 1640 and ruled until the foundation of the republic in 1910.

The aristocratic manor house of Casa de Mateus

Porto, the biggest city of the north, grew rich when merchants travelled to Brazil, returning with gold and diamonds, which financed the city's extravagant churches and palaces.
Later, it profited from the port wine trade, which still dominates Vila Nova de Gaia and the valleys of the Upper Douro.

The north is divided into two contrasting regions. The Minho, which occupies the historic boundaries of Portucale between the Douro and Minho rivers, is a land of lush, green countryside fed by the highest rainfall in Portugal. Much of it is given over to smallholdings, though there are also manor houses, many of which take in guests. This densely populated region hosts some of Portugal's biggest country markets and fairs. It also contains two important historical towns – Portugal's first capital, Guimarães, which has a medieval centre that is a UNESCO World Heritage site, and its religious centre, Braga.

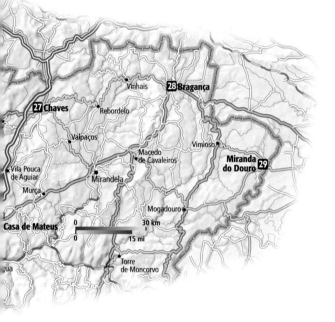

Trás-os-Montes is a wild and rugged region of mountains and remote villages with a harsh climate. Few crops survive except the hardiest vines, and the region grows some of the grapes for Mateus Rosé, as well as for port wine production.

The decorated interior of Braga Cathedral

Northern Portugal

Three Perfect Days

If you don't have much time to explore the northern part of Portugal, try our three-day itinerary for size. We'll make sure you don't miss any of the region's highlights. For more information see the main entries (➤ 88–103).

Day 1

Morning
Start exploring the Old Town of **㉑ Porto** (➤ 90) by climbing Torre dos Clérigos for views over the city's red rooftops and spires to the River Douro Then visit the Bolhão market and have a coffee at **Café Majestic** (➤ 106) before walking uphill to the cathedral. Go down to the Ribeira district (above) to admire the neoclassical Bolsa (Stock Exchange) and lavishly gilded São Francisco church before lunch in one of the riverside cafés.

Afternoon and Evening
Walk across the Ponte Dom Luís I to ☆ **Vila Nova de Gaia** (➤ 88). Spend the afternoon touring the wine lodges and tasting port. In summer, you can take a boat cruise on the River Douro. Return to the north bank for dinner on Cais da Ribeira at one of the restaurants overlooking the quayside.

Day 2

Morning
Leave Porto and head east (on the IP4/A4 to Amarante and Vila Real) to the **㉒ Casa de Mateus** (➤ 94). After a stroll around the manicured formal gardens, take the N2 south to vine-strewn **Peso da Régua** for lunch by the river.

Afternoon and Evening

From here, you can do a shortened version of the Port Country tour (► 188), travelling through the steeply terraced vineyards between Peso da Régua and Pinhão on a beautiful stretch of the Douro Valley. Returning to Vila Real, take the IP4 to Amarante and head north on the N101 to **25 Guimarães** (► 101). Follow the signs to the castle (castle statue, right), then wander down to the Old Town for a drink at one of the cafés on Largo da Oliveira. For a treat, stay at **Pousada Mosteiro de Guimarães** (► 105), in a 12th-century convent. One of the finest of all the *pousadas* (► 39), this one has fountains and *azulejo*-tiled cloisters.

Day 3

Morning

Start early to visit the magnificent 11th-century **23 Braga** (► 96) and the hilltop sanctuary at **23 Bom Jesus** (► 97). From here, drive north on the IP1/A3 to the picture-perfect town of Ponte da Lima for a walk along the River Lima and a drink in a café by the Roman bridge. Follow the N203 along the Lima Valley to enter the granite wilderness of the **24 Parque Nacional da Peneda-Gerês** (below, ► 99).

Afternoon and Evening

Allow plenty of time to explore the mountainous national park. Tour the villages of Soajo and Lindoso before entering Spain on the way to Caldas do Gerês (► 100). Take the N103 to **27 Chaves** (► 102). If you have time, visit **28 Bragança** (► 102). Take the motorway back to Porto for dinner.

✰ 10 Vila Nova de Gaia

The names of famous port shippers, Sandeman, Ferreira and Taylor, spelled out in neon letters on the hillside, draw you irresistibly across the water to Vila Nova de Gaia, the home of the port wine trade. Here, barrels of port mature in cool cellars and lodges, many of which can be visited.

Although the grapes for port are grown in the Douro Valley, the ageing process takes place at the river mouth, in Vila Nova de Gaia, which was chosen in the 18th century by British traders for its north-facing position, cool ocean breeze and high levels of humidity. These days, however, the port houses are, increasingly, moving their warehouse facilities out of town and converting their lodges (a corruption of the Portuguese word *loja*, meaning "warehouse") into restaurants, hotels and open houses with guided tours.

Kick off your visit with a tour and a tasting session at the **Espaço Porto Cruz**, a multimedia centre which boasts beautiful views from its roof terrace (Largo Miguel Bombarda 23; wine shop Tue–Sun 11–7; Restaurant Tue–Sat 12:30–3 and 7:30–11, Sun 12:30–3, Terrasse Lounge 360° Tue–Thu 12:30–0:30, Fri, Sat until 1:30, Sun until 7; http://myportocruz.com).

Look along the Douro to spot *barcos rabelos*, the traditional flat-bottomed boats that are used to transport port wine downriver from the Douro Valley. You can still see them moored outside many port houses (▶ 189) or watch them being sailed once a year during the annual regatta on 24th June (▶ 108).

View from the Dom Luís I bridge over the port wine warehouses on the steep, rocky banks of the river Douro

The **teleférico de Gaia** has given the neighbourhood a huge boost. This 562m (1,844ft) cable car links the Cais de Gaia to the Jardim do Morro on Avenida da República and affords some wonderful views of the city (daily 10–8 in summer; varies from 10–6/7 at other times of the year; single ticket: €5, return: €8; www.gaiacablecar.com). Other projects for increasing tourism are still in the pipeline. Another way to get to Vila Nova de Gaia from Porto (▶ 90) is by heading across the **Ponte Dom Luís I**. Walk along the lower deck for direct access to the riverbank, or climb to the upper deck to enjoy some spectacular views.

Insider Tip

To visit the **port lodges**, get a list and a map from the tourist office or visit www.cavesvinhodoporto.com. Most

THE DOURO BY TRAIN

Take a train journey through the Douro Valley, from Porto to Pocinho by the Spanish border. It runs for 100km (62mi) by the River Douro, through seemingly endless stretches of beautiful scenery. There's a steam train on Saturdays from Regua to Tua (www.cp.pt).

The tasting terrace at Taylor's

people start with top producer **Sandeman** (Largo Miguel Bombarda 3; tel: 223 740 500; www.sandeman.eu; March–Oct daily 10–12:30, 2–6, 9:30–12:30 2–5:30 rest of year), which was founded by Briton George Sandeman with a £300 loan from his father back in 1790. They run the shortest and most commercialized of all the cellar tours.

It is interesting to compare Sandeman with a smaller firm, such as **Ferreira** (Avenida Ramos Pinto 70; tel: 223 746 107, inexpensive), which was founded in 1751 and is still Portuguese owned.

Other lodges include **Cálem** (tel: 223 746 660; www.calem.pt; May–Oct daily 10–7, until 6 rest of year; *fado* concerts are held in the lovely visitor centre) and **Ramos Pinto** (Avenida Ramos Pinto 400; tel: 936 809 283; www.ramospinto.pt; June–Sep Mon–Sat 10–6; 9–5 rest of year).

TAKING A BREAK

There are several restaurants and cafés by the waterfront, or book at **Barão de Fladgate** (➤ 106), housed in the Taylor's Lodge (see panel below), for superb seafood and port wine.

➕ 210 A2 🛈 Avenida Diogo Leite ☎ 223 758 288

INSIDER INFO

■ Let your taste buds explore the many **different styles** of port: the aperitif, dry white, amber-coloured tawny, rich ruby and vintage varieties (➤ 14). You don't usually have to book ahead for tours – they'll get things underway as soon as a sufficient group of visitors has arrived.

Insider Tip

■ It's worth making the steep climb up to **Taylor's** (Rua do Choupelo 250; tel: 223 772 956; www.taylor.pt), where you'll find a warm welcome at their old-style lodge. The long, eventful history of this port house dates back to 1692. A guided tour and tasting session costs €12 per person. Tours are available Mon–Fri 10–6 and Sat, Sun 10–5. Relax on the terrace afterwards and enjoy the wonderful views of the Douro and the Ponte Dom Luís I.

Northern Portugal

㉑ Porto

Portugal's second city enjoys a magnificent position, tumbling down the steep slopes on the north bank of the River Douro. A workaday, rough-and-ready port city, frayed at the edges but wonderfully charismatic, Porto makes a good introduction to the many delights of northern Portugal.

Porto (the English name, Oporto, derives from *o porto*, "the port") has been occupied for at least 3,000 years. The Romans built a harbour here at *Portus*, an important river-crossing on the route from Lisbon to Braga. The settlement on the south bank (now Vila Nova de Gaia) was called *Cale*. These gave their names to the county of "Portucale", part of the dowry of Teresa of Castile when she married Henry of Burgundy in 1095. When their son, Afonso Henriques, ousted the Moors from the rest of the country, he named his kingdom Portugal.

Relations between Portugal and England had been cordial for 150 years when, in 1387, Porto celebrated the marriage of João I (➤ 114) and Philippa of Lancaster, forging a military alliance between Portugal and England that still exists to this day. Their son was Henry the Navigator (1394–1460, ➤ 16), a pioneer of the Age of Discovery and a driving force behind Portugal's territorial gains in Africa.

View of the Ribeira area of Porto

The Modern City
The heart of Porto is **Avenida dos Aliados**, whose central promenade, with flowerbeds and a mosaic pavement, leads to the town hall. From the foot of the avenue, on Praça da Liberdade, you can see the baroque church of **Clérigos** to the west. Designed by the Italian architect Nicolau Nasoni, this was the first oval church in Portugal. You can climb its 75m (246ft) tower, one of the tallest in the country, for views over the city and Vila Nova da Gaia (➤ 88).

East of Avenida dos Aliados, **Baixa** is the main shopping district, centred around the covered Bolhão market. Vegetables are sold

A cabin on the Teleférico de Gaia passes the Dom Luís I bridge between Porto and Vila Nova de Gaia

upstairs, while stalls downstairs offer maize bread, fish, meat and tripe. Across the road are several tempting *confeitarias* and shops featuring Porto's other speciality, *bacalhau*. These large pieces of salted cod – which look like cardboard and smell even less appetising (➤ 31) – are ubiquitous components of Portuguese cuisine.

Rua de Santa Catarina is lined with leather and jewellery shops and the old-world Café Majestic (➤ 106), and leads to Praça da Batalha.

The **Sé** (cathedral) is visible, built on a rocky outcrop above the Douro. Begun as a Romanesque fortress church in the 12th century, it was remodelled in Gothic style. The 14th-century cloisters are decorated with *azulejos* (➤ 18) showing the life of the Virgin. A grand staircase leads to the chapter house and an upper gallery that has fine views.

The area known as the **Bairro da Sé** – a warren of narrow alleyways, steep staircases and candy-coloured houses between the Sé and the waterfront – became a UNESCO World Heritage Site in 1996. It's the oldest of Porto, and bears similarity to Alfama (➤ 65) in Lisbon. The life of the district mingles with ancient churches and *azulejo*-tiled walls. Come here to get a glimpse of day-to-day life in Portugal!

AN EYE FOR ART AND STYLISH LIVING

The **Museu Nacional Soares dos Reis** in Palácio dos Carrancas (Rua Dom Manuel II; tel: 223 393 770, www.museusoaresdosreis.pt, Tue–Sun 10–6:30, entrance fee: €5, free 1st Sun of the month) is Portugal's oldest national museum. It's dedicated to Portuguese art, including the work of 19th-century sculptor António Soares dos Reis. The **Museu Romântico** (Quinta da Macieirinha, Rua de Entrequintas 220; tel: 226 057 033, Mon–Sat 10–5:30, Sun 10–12:30, 2–5:30; entrance fee: €2.50, free Sat, Sun), is a re-creation of a 19th-century aristocratic home with a romantic garden.

Northern Portugal

ART, MUSIC AND BEACHES

Check out Porto's striking **Casa da Música** (Avenida da Boavista 610, Tel. 22 01 20 02 20, www.casadamusica.com; Mon–Sat 10–7, Sun 10–6). Buses 201 and 502 run from here to the **Museu de Arte Contemporânea** (Rua Dom João de Castro 210; tel: 226 156 500; www. serral ves.pt; April–Sep Tue–Fri 10–7, Sat, Sun 10–8; Oct–March, Tue–Fri 10–5, Sat, Sun 10–7; entrance fee museum €10, park only €5, free 10–1 on the 1st Sun of the month). It's situated in the gardens of the art deco Casa de Serralves, designed by Álvaro Siza Vieira. Enjoy the rose garden, arboretum, teahouse, lake and sculpture park. Continue on the bus to **Foz** where the main Avenida da Boavista, which runs from the centre to the waterfront promenade at Foz do Douro, has been given a cutting-edge makeover with eye-catching architecture.

A statue of Henry the Navigator (►16, 90) stands near the former customs house on **Praça do Infante** where it's thought he was born. The square is also home to the **Palácio da Bolsa**, the Stock Exchange that was built in 1834 on the ruins of the São Francisco convent. Its interior is filled with a heady mix of excessively lavish décor.

Statue of Henry the Navigator on Praça do Infante

Behind the building, the **Igreja de São Francisco** is richly ornamented with gilded baroque carvings. Before the church was ransacked by Napoleon's troops, there were more than 400kg (880lbs) of gold covering the chestnut-wood walls. The church authorities were so shocked at this blatant display of extravagance that they ordered the church to be deconsecrated. Notice the **Tree of Jesse**, in carved and gilded wood, adorning the north wall. The visit takes in the **catacombs,** where there is an ossuary of human bones.

A traditional grocer's shopfront in Porto

Ribeira, the fishermen's district with its narrow streets and painted houses rising above riverside arcades, is Porto's most atmospheric quarter. The area comes alive at night, with busy restaurants and bars in the shadow of the **Ponte Dom Luís I**, the bridge that links Porto to Vila Nova de Gaia (➤ 88).

TAKING A BREAK

Café Majestic (➤ 106) is a belle époque beauty with oak-framed mirrors and leather banquettes, serving delicious breakfasts, pastries, cakes and a selection of hot meals.

🔢 210 A2
ℹ️ Rua Clube dos Fenianos 25 (top of Avenida dos Aliados)
☎ 223 393 472; www.portoturismo.pt

Torre dos Clérigos
✉️ Rua de São Felipe Néry
☎ 222 001 729; www.torredosclerigos.pt
🕐 Daily 9–7 💰 Church: free. Tower: €3 (with audio guide €5)

Sé
✉️ Terreiro da Sé ☎ 222 059 028
🕐 Church: April–June, Oct 9–12:30, 2:30–7; July–Sep Mon–Sat 9–7, Sun 9–12:30 and 2:30–7; Nov–March 9–12:30, 2:30–6.
Cloisters: April–June, Oct daily 9–12:15, 2:30–6:30; July–Sep Mon–Sat 9–12:30, Sun 2:30–6:30; Nov–March, Mon–Sat 9–12:15, 2:30–5:30, Sun 2:30–5:30
💰 Church: free. Cloisters: €3

Palácio da Bolsa
✉️ Rua Ferreira Borges ☎ 223 399 000; www.palaciodabolsa.com
🕐 April–Oct daily 9–6:30; Nov–March 9–12:30, 2–5:30
💰 €8 (guided tour)

Igreja de São Francisco
✉️ Rua do Infante Dom Henrique ☎ 222 062 125; www.ordemsaofrancisco.pt
🕐 July–Sep daily 9–8; March–June, Oct daily 9–7; Nov–Feb daily 9–5:30
💰 €3.50

INSIDER INFO

- The best way to get around Porto is **on foot**, but you will need a good pair of shoes for all the steep hills and cobbled streets. The **Porto Card** is a very helpful tool for exploring the city. It comes in two varieties: one including transport (one day: €13, two days: €20, three days: €25) and the "walker" pass (one day: €6, two days: €10, three days: €13). You can buy the cards from tourist information offices and at the airport.
- Take one of the 🚢 **river cruises** that depart regularly in summer from the quayside at Cais da Ribeira or from the waterfront at Vila Nova de Gaia. Just turn up and buy a ticket. Tours last a maximum of one hour. Younger visitors will love them, too.
- For the **best views of Porto**, cross the upper level of the Dom Luís I bridge to reach the terrace of Nossa Senhora da Serra do Pilar on the south bank.

Insider Tip

㉒ Casa de Mateus

The building that graces the label of every bottle of Mateus Rosé is as perfect a Portuguese manor house as you can find. With fine furniture, paintings, formal gardens and family chapel, a visit to the Casa de Mateus offers a rare glimpse into the lives of the Portuguese aristocracy.

It was built in 1745 by the third *Morgado* de Mateus. His descendants, the counts of Vila Real, still live in a wing of the house. The architect is unknown, but it is attributed to Nicolau Nasoni, the Italian who designed the Clérigos church and tower in Porto (▶ 90) and was a major influence on the development of Portuguese baroque.

The façade of the house is immediately impressive, a contrast of whitewash and granite reflected in a pool that was added when the gardens were extensively remodelled in the 1930s. The forecourt is dominated by an immense double stairway, whose balustrades lead the eye up towards the pediment, flanked by classical statues and crowned by a family escutcheon.

The lovely gardens of the Casa de Mateus

INSIDER INFO

- **Classical music concerts** are sometimes held in the grounds on summer weekends. They're not advertised very far in advance.
- They do produce their own wine on the estate, called **Alvarelhão**, which you can buy in the shop. It has nothing to do with Mateus Rosé, however (and they don't stock it, either). The name "Casa de Mateus" appears on the jams and preserves, etc., they sell here.
- The nearby town of **Vila Real** (Royal Town), dramatically perched above a gorge at the confluence of the Corgo and Cabril rivers, is the capital of the Upper Douro. The best sights are the Gothic cathedral and the house on the main street where the explorer Diogo Cão, who "discovered" the mouth of the Congo in 1482, was born.

The house can only be visited on guided tours. You begin in the entrance hall, with its carved chestnut ceiling, 18th-century sedan chairs and family coat of arms on the wall. This leads into the **Four Seasons Room**, which takes its name from the strange paintings of seasonal vegetables in human form. On the table in the centre stands a 16th-century Hispano-Arab plate, the oldest item on display.

The neighbouring **Blue Room** features Chinese porcelain in a 17th-century Chinese cabinet, while the **Dining Room** has a Brazilian jacaranda wood dresser containing stunning Portuguese china and silver.

The highlight of the **Four Corners Room**, where ladies gathered after dinner while the men smoked and drank port, is a fine, hand-carved Indo-Portuguese ivory and wood travelling desk.

The family **museum** has several rare treasures, including the original copperplates by Jean Fragonard for a limited edition of *Os Lusíadas* (*The Lusiads*) by Portuguese poet Luís de Camões, produced in 1817 and sent by the Morgado de Mateus to 250 libraries and noble families in Europe to promote Portuguese history and culture. Some of the letters of thanks are displayed, along with religious vestments and chalices, relics of saints and martyrs, a 17th-century ivory crucifix and a statue of the Virgin carved from a single piece of ivory.

Be sure to walk around the **gardens**, with their dark avenue of cedar trees, neatly clipped box hedges and peaceful views over the surrounding countryside. *Insider Tip*

TAKING A BREAK
There is a small **café** in the gardens for snacks and refreshments, which is open in summer.

✚ 211 D3
✉ 4km (2.5mi) east of Vila Real
☎ 259 323 121; www.casademateus.com
🕙 May–Oct 9–7; Nov–April 9–5
🎟 House & Gardens: €11. Gardens only: €7.50

㉓ Braga & Bom Jesus

Braga likes to describe itself as the Portuguese Rome. Although that's a bit of an exaggeration, the largest city in the Minho has a long history as a religious capital that has left it with a number of churches, Renaissance mansions and the Bom Jesus sanctuary.

Braga

A saying has it that "while Coimbra studies and Lisbon plays, Porto works and Braga prays". The Roman bishop St Martin of Braga converted the local Swabian tribe to Christianity in the sixth century AD and established the custom, still used in Portugal, of naming the days of the week in numerical order rather than after pagan gods (Monday, *segunda-feira*, is "second day", Tuesday, *terça-feira*, "third day", etc.). In the 12th century, following the Christian conquest, Braga became, and remains, the seat of the Portuguese archbishops.

Start your visit at **Praça da República**, an arcaded square at the end of a long public garden with fountains and playgrounds. There are old-fashioned cafés under the arches close to the 14th-century town keep. From here, walk down Rua do Souto, a pedestrianized shopping street, passing the former bishop's palace on your way to the Sé (cathedral).

The exquisitely ornate **cathedral** was begun in 1070 on the site of a mosque and is Portugal's oldest cathedral. Originally built in Romanesque style, the subsequent

Leisurely outdoor dining at the Café Vianna, Praça de República

The hilltop sanctuary of the Church of Bom Jesus

Gothic, Renaissance and baroque additions give it an eclectic feel. The main Romanesque doorway survives at the western end, though it is covered by a Gothic porch that was added in the late 15th century. Among the artists who worked on the cathedral are Manueline master João de Castilho, one of the architects of the Mosteiro dos Jerónimos in Lisbon (▶ 48), and the French sculptor Nicolas Chanterene, whose statue of **Nossa Senhora da Leite** (Our Lady of the Milk) is sheltered beneath a Gothic canopy at the cathedral's eastern end.

The cloister leads through to the **Museu de Arte Sacra**, which boasts exhibits from the cathedral treasury that span a period of approximately 1,500 years. The collection's most valuable pieces include the chalice and paten of St Gerald (10th/11th century) and a Hispano-Arab casket made from wood and ivory (11th century). You'll also see oil paintings, liturgical objects and a sarcophagus from the late Roman period.

The tour of the museum also includes the **Capela dos Reis**, where Henry of Burgundy and Teresa of Castile (▶ 90), parents of Portugal's first king, are buried in 16th-century tombs. A more expensive ticket also gives you entry to the **Coro Alto** (upper choir), which has gilded baroque organs and carved choir stalls.

Bom Jesus

At weekends, pilgrims and tourists flock to Bom Jesus do Monte, a hilltop sanctuary 5km (3mi) east of Braga. It's Portugal's most important religious site (after Fátima). Although primarily a place for prayer and quiet contemplation, it's also a popular picnic spot, with gardens, woodland and a lake.

The spectacular centrepiece is the 🔁 **baroque stairway** with more than 1,000 steps, which was begun by the archbishop of Braga in 1722 but not finished until the 19th century. True pilgrims ascend on their knees, especially during *Semana Santa* (Holy Week, the week before Easter), but most people walk or take the old-fashioned 🔁 **funicular** (Elevador; daily 8–8, winter 9–12:30

and 1–6; every 30 minutes). It's best to make the climb on foot to appreciate the architecture.

Via Sacra (Holy Way) begins with a winding path lined with chapels depicting the Stations of the Cross. Each chapel, dripping with wax from pilgrims' candles, is filled with life-size terracotta figures evoking scenes from Christ's Passion. As you near the summit, you reach a magnificent ornamental double stairway. Fountains depict the five senses, with water gushing out of ears, eyes, nose and mouth, while further up, the **Staircase of the Three Virtues** features the allegorical figures of Faith, Hope and Charity.

The stairway is lined with statues of biblical figures

TAKING A BREAK

You can get some refreshments near the sanctuary at the panoramic restaurant of the **Hotel do Elevador** (www. hotelsbomjesus.com). They sell such regional dishes as cabbage soup with bread and duck with rice.

✚ 210 B4
🏛 Avenida da Liberdade 1
☎ 253 262 550

Sé/Museu de Arte Sacra
✉ Rua Dom Paio Mendes
☎ 253 263 317; www.se-braga.pt
🕐 June–Sep Tue–Sun 9–12:30, 2–6:30;
Oct–May Tue–Sun 9–12:30, 2–5:30
💶 Entry to the cathedral museum's permanent collection €3; entry to the chapels and upper choir €2

INSIDER INFO

- Leave your car in the **underground car park** beneath Praça da República, from where everything of interest can be reached in a short walk.
- There are **regular buses** from Braga to the foot of Bom Jesus do Monte, or you can drive your car right up to the summit.
- The **Palácio dos Biscainhos** (near the Arco da Porta Nova gateway, Tue–Sun 10–12:15, 2–5:30; entrance fee: €5; free 1st Sun of the month) is a 17th-century mansion with stucco ceilings and *azulejo* tiles (➤ 32) that's been turned into a decorative arts museum featuring Portuguese furniture, silverware and ornamental gardens.

㉔ Parque Nacional da Peneda-Gerês

Covering an area of 700km² (270mi²), this magnificent national park is a wild, dramatic landscape filled with windswept peaks, granite crags, deep river valleys and pretty rural villages. It's the kind of place where shepherds still migrate to higher ground each spring in search of fresh pasture for their flock. The park consists of two main mountain ranges, Serra da Peneda and Serra do Gerês, which are divided by the River Lima.

With few clear entry points and villages scattered around, most of the time it doesn't seem as if you are in a national park at all. Despite the presence of wildlife, such as golden eagles, wild horses and wolves, and rare varieties of Gerês lilies and ferns, it is a way of life as much as anything that is preserved here.

You can visit the park by car on a day trip from Braga or the Minho coast. The easiest approach is along the Lima Valley from Ponte da Barca. This brings you to **Soajo** and **Lindoso**, both of which have some village houses for rent (Aldeias de Portugal; tel: 258 931 750; www.aldeiasdeportugal.pt).

The Rio Cávado runs through a picturesque landscape

Both villages are known for their *espigueiros*, communal stone granaries topped with a cross and raised above the ground as a precaution against pests. At Lindoso, a group

Northern Portugal

Insider Tip

WALKING IN THE PARK
Pick up a walking map from the information centres in Braga, Ponte da Barca or Caldas do Gerês to tackle some of the *trilhos* (walking trails) in the park. Two of the best are the Trilho da Peneda, around the village of the same name, and the Trilho Castrejo from the village of Castro Laboreiro, known for its special breed of mountain dogs.

of 60 *espigueiros* are huddled beneath the castle, resembling tombstones in a cemetery. The castle here, right next to the Spanish border, has been attacked many times. Nowadays it is a peaceful spot, with long-horned Minho cattle grazing beneath its walls.

A minor road runs north between the two villages, with views over the Lima Valley on the way to **Peneda**. This small village contains a remarkable sanctuary, **Nossa Senhora da Peneda**, modelled on Bom Jesus (►98) and reached by a similarly long staircase. The chapel, which from below seems almost to be built into the cliff, is the focus for a huge pilgrimage each September.

The most direct route between the two sections of the park means crossing the Spanish border at Lindoso and re-entering Portugal at Portela do Homem. The road dips down through a delightful wooded glade to the spa resort of **Caldas do Gerês**, where wild herbs, wildflower honey and chunky woollen sweaters are for sale and the main street is lined with spa hotels. Just outside town, a *miradouro* (viewpoint) offers fabulous panoramas over the reservoir of Caniçada.

Long-horned Minho cattle

TAKING A BREAK
There are **cafés and bars** in the villages of Soajo, Lindoso and Caldas do Gerês. Apart from that, a good option would be to stock up on **picnic** provisions in any of the nearby towns.

➕ 210 C4

Park Office
✉ Avenida António Macedo, Braga
☎ 253 203 480; www.icnf.pt
🕐 Mon–Fri 9–12:30, 2–5:30

INSIDER INFO

Insider Tip

- Allow **plenty of time** for driving within the park – the roads are steep and narrow, and the distances are greater than they look on the map.
- Visit the park's website (www.icnf.pt/portal/naturaclas/ap/pnpg/tn-pnpg) to download some free **hiking brochures** that come complete with maps (some are only available in Portuguese).
- This is Portugal's wettest area so don't forget to take **waterproofs**.

At Your Leisure

25 Guimarães

Becoming European Capital of Culture in 2012 has put Guimarães firmly on the tourist map. As well as the medieval sights of its lovely, car-free old town centre (a UNESCO World Heritage Site), visitors will now also get to see such exciting new developments as the **Platform for Arts and Creativity** in the former old market and the Design Institute that's reviving the fortunes of a converted factory.

The first capital of Portugal and the birthplace of its first king, Afonso Henriques (1109–85, ➤ 90), Guimarães has a special place in the hearts of the Portuguese nation. Most of the sights are situated in the Old Town beneath the castle. Climb over the ramparts of the 10th-century fortress and visit the Romanesque chapel at **São Miguel do Castelo** where Afonso Henriques was baptized.

The nearby palace known as the **Paço dos Duques de Bragança** was built by the first Duke of Bragança in the fifteenth century and transformed into a presidential residence during the Salazar dictatorship. It boasts a selection of Flemish tapestries, Persian carpets, Portuguese furniture and historic weapons from the Age of Chivalry. **Insider Tip** The castle and the palace are both fantastic destinations for inquisitive minds of all ages!

A short walk along the cobbled Rua de Santa Maria reveals an area that has remained unchanged for centuries. **Insider Tip** Leading from the castle to the Old Town, the street is lined by a number of restored medieval houses and ends in a pair of delightful squares, Praça de São Tiago and Largo da Oliveira, where markets sometimes take place.

Praça de São Tiago is surrounded by wooden-balconied houses, while

The commanding position of the Santa Luzia overlooking Viana do Castelo (➤ 102)

Largo da Oliveira has a Gothic shrine outside Nossa Senhora da Oliveira (Our Lady of the Olive Tree), whose cloisters house a museum of sacred art. The remains of the old city walls are also worth exploring.

➕ 210 B3
ℹ️ Largo Cónego José Maria Gomes
☎ 253 421 221; www.guimaraesturismo.com

Paço dos Duques de Bragança
✉ Rua Conde Dom Henrique
☎ 253 412 273; http://pduques.culturanorte.pt
🕘 9:30–6 (last entry 30 mins before closing)
💶 €5; free 1st Sun of the month

Castelo
🕘 Daily 9:30–6 💶 Free

Plataforma das Artes e Criatividade
✉ Avenida Conde Margaride175
☎ 253 424 715
🕘 Tue–Sun 10–7 (last entry 6:30)
💶 €5; free 1st Sun of the month

Northern Portugal

BARCELOS

The largest weekly market in Portugal takes place on Thursday mornings on a vast open square in the centre of Barcelos. 🏵 Look out for the local Barcelos pottery and brightly coloured *galos de Barcelos* "Barcelos roosters", which recall the legend of an innocent Galician pilgrim, miraculously saved from the gallows when a roast cockerel, on a plate at the time, began to crow. He invoked the help of St James, saying that if he were innocent the cockerel being prepared for the judge's dinner would sit up and crow.

26 Viana do Castelo

The capital of the Costa Verde enjoys a perfect setting on the north bank of the Lima estuary, overlooked by the pinewoods of Monte de Santa Luzia. Once a small fishing port, Viana supplied many of the seafarers who set sail during the Age of Discovery and returned to the town to build some beautiful mansions. It's a busy summer resort today.

The main square, Praça da República, is the focus of daily life with its old fountain and gorgeous Renaissance palace.

Insider Tip

🏵 Walk or – if you're feeling less energetic – take the funicular through the pinewoods to reach a lovely basilica and the ruins of a Celto-Iberian settlement (single ticket: €2, return: €3). It's a pleasant trip that kids will enjoy, too. Alternatively, cross the river to **Praia do Cabedelo**, the town's splendid beach.

✚ 210 A4
🛈 Praça da Liberdade
☎ 258 098 415; www.cm-viana-castelo.pt

27 Chaves

A drive from Braga on the N103 threads through the Gerês and Barroso mountains to Chaves, which sits prettily on the banks of the Tâmega River 10km (6mi) south of the Spanish border. It's famous for its smoked hams and red wine. The route from Braga to Chaves is around 130km (80mi) long and leads through one of the richest selections of landscapes in Portugal. Idyllic views of mountains and valleys, reservoirs, pastures, old storehouses, scattered villages and secluded farmsteads all accompany you along the way.

A statue of the first Duke of Bragança, who lived in the castle, stands on Praça de Camões, the main square of the Old Town. Also here is the Misericórdia church, with its gilded altarpiece, painted ceiling and *azulejo*-tiled walls.

✚ 211 E4
🛈 Terreiro de Cavaleria
☎ 276 340 661

28 Bragança

The remote capital of Trás-os-Montes is closely identified with Portugal's last ruling dynasty, descendants of an illegitimate son of João I who became the first Duke of Bragança – though later dukes preferred to live in their palace at Vila Viçosa (► 148).

Head outside the city centre to find a fortified 12th-century citadel that's home to some lovely white-washes houses and cobbled streets. The **castle** contains a small **military museum** and there are great views from the tower (Torre de Menagem). Nearby there's a medieval pillory, an ancient stone pig on a pedestal, and the five-sided **Domus Municipalis**, Portugal's only surviving example of Romanesque civic architecture, where public meetings were held and the *homens bons* (good men) would gather to settle disputes.

Just beneath the citadel, on the way to the cathedral, the **Igreja de São Vicente** is where Dom Pedro is believed to have secretly married Inês de Castro (➤ 126).

Bragança is a good base for excursions into the Montesinho natural park (➤ 24).

🚩 212 B4 🅷 Avenida Cidade de Zamora
☎ 273 381 273

Castelo & Museu Militar
☎ 273 322 378 🕒 Tue–Sun 9–noon and Tue–Thu, Sat, Sun 2–5 ✋ Free

29 Miranda do Douro

Set on a cliff overlooking a deep gorge in the River Douro, Miranda is a medieval border town whose inhabitants speak their own particular dialect, *mirandês*. The 16th-century Sé (cathedral) includes the Menino Jesus da Cartolinha, a statue of the child Jesus in 17th-century costume and a top hat, who is said to have appeared to rally the Portuguese forces during a Spanish siege in 1711.

The **Museu da Terra de Miranda** features a reconstruction of a farmhouse kitchen and folk costumes such as those worn by the *pauliteiros* (stick dancers) at festivals.

🚩 212 C3
🅷 Largo do Menino Jesus da Cartolinha
☎ 273 431 132; www.cm-mdouro.pt

Museu da Terra de Miranda
✉ Largo Dom João III
☎ 273 431 164
🕒 Tue 2–6, Wed–Sun 9–5:30 (6 in summer)
✋ €2

The mighty citadel that rises up above the city of Bragança

Where to...
Stay

Prices
Expect to pay for a double room per night in high season

€ under €80   €€ €80–€110   €€€ €110–€150   €€€€ over €150

PORTO

Hotel da Bolsa €€
Close to the Stock Exchange building and 50m from the Port Wine Institute, this well-located, three-star hotel (with a car park next door) is built on the site of the São Francisco monastery. Its 19th-century façade conceals a modern interior. The rooms are a little dated, but it's still a pleasant base from which to explore the city.

✚ 210 B2
✉ Rue Ferreira Borges 101
☎ 222 026 768; www.hoteldabolsa.com

Hotel Infante de Sagres €€€€
If you love living life in a wonderfully old-fashioned style, you'll adore this exquisite five-star hotel in a convenient, central location. Its attractive, renovated rooms are kept up-to-date.

✚ 210 B2
✉ Praça Filipa de Lencastre 62
☎ 223 398 500; www.hotelinfantesagres.pt

Pensão Favorita €€
You'll quickly feel at home in this stylish, restored villa that's surrounded by a garden. It's situated close to several art galleries, some good places to shop and the Museu Nacional Soares dos Reis. The 12 rooms (which include a junior suite with a balcony and two family rooms) are modern and tastefully decorated. They've preserved the traditional tiled flooring on the lower storey. Guests can eat breakfast and relax in the garden during the summer months.

✚ 210 B2
✉ Rua Miguel Bombarda 267
☎ 220 134 157; www.pensaofavorita.pt

Pestana Vintage Porto €€€
Located on the riverfront in Ribeira with views to Vila Nova de Gaia (➤88) and the Dom Luís I Bridge, this luxury boutique hotel interconnects six former town houses (all UNESCO World Heritage sites) from the 16th, 17th and 18th centuries, which have been restored and converted to the highest standards. The rooms are well appointed and comfortable. The emphasis of the restaurant and bar is on regional food and wine. Ask for a room with river views.

✚ 210 B2   ✉ Praça da Ribeira 1
☎ 223 402 300; www.pestana.com

BRAGA

Hotel Bracara Augusta €€
This is a cheerful, well-decorated and perfectly located guesthouse in the pedestrianized centre of town? Some of the rooms have views over the attractive cathedral (➤96), all are cosily decorated. The well-regarded Centurium restaurant is elegant, with stone walls and columns, and crisp white tablecloths. There is also a terrace for eating outside when the weather is warm – make use of this, if possible, for afternoon tea in the garden.

✚ 210 B4   ✉ Avenida Central 134
☎ 253 206 260; www.bracaraaugusta.com

Dona Sofia €–€€

A five-minute stroll from the main square, this welcoming guesthouse is an excellent deal. The affable English-speaking staff will help you make the most of Braga. The rooms are spotless and modern with flat-screen TVs, minibars and free WiFi. Relax in the living room, complete with a grand piano, or enjoy some drinks at the bar. Room rates include a generous breakfast buffet. Check out the offers on their website!

🔡 210 B4
✉ Largo São João do Souto 131
☎ 253 263 160; www.hoteldonasofia.com

GUIMARÃES

Pousada Mosteiro de Guimarães €€€–€€€€

One of the most impressive *pousadas* in Portugal. The highly atmospheric accommodation is set in a former 12th-century monastery on a hill overlooking the city of Guimarães and the surrounding area. The 51 bedrooms are large and stately; many boast four-poster beds and ornate bathrooms. You can relax in the large gardens with fountains and a stream, a lovely outdoor swimming pool and underground caves. The restaurant is also excellent.

🔡 210 C3
✉ Largo Domingos Leite de Castro
☎ 253 511 249; www.pousadas.pt

VIANA DO CASTELO

Casa Melo Alvim €€€

This delightful Manueline *solar* (▶ 16) next to Viana do Castelo's city centre was built in 1509 by the Conde da Carreira and successfully extended in the 17th and 19th centuries. It was turned into a first-class inn in the 1990s in a way that fully respected the appearance of the imposing stone building. The furnishings and décor are a subtle blend of traditional styles and a modern preference for sobriety and sleek lines. There's a manageable total of 20 rooms and suites, so personal service is guaranteed.

🔡 210 A4 ✉ Avenida Conde da Carreira 28
☎ 258 808 200; www.meloalvimhouse.com

BARCELOS

Quinta do Convento da Franqueira €€

Perched on a hill overlooking Barcelos and surrounded by gardens and woods of pine and eucalyptus trees, this converted 16th-century Franciscan monastery (with a spring-fed swimming pool) is a charming retreat. Piers and Kate are your welcoming hosts. Centred around an inner courtyard that's dotted with fountains, the spacious rooms are furnished with antiques, paintings and Portuguese fabrics. For romance, choose the Blue Room with its hand-painted four-poster bed. The breakfasts are delicious. Be sure to visit the winery. The guesthouse is open from mid-April to late October. Minimum stay: two nights.

Insider Tip

🔡 212 B3 ✉ Carvalhal, C.C. 301
☎ 253 831 606; www.quintadafranqueira.com

TRÁS-OS-MONTES

Quinta Entre Rios €–€€

Welcoming farmhouse accommodation about 3km (1.5mi) outside of the town of Mirandela, with 10 comfortable rooms and a lovely large drawing room for guests to use. The 18th- century building has good sized bedrooms, attractively furnished although aiming at functionality rather than luxury. There are plenty of opportunities to relax here – a snooker room, cards, chess, a large terrace for reading, and a pool. Enjoy home-cooked breakfasts.

🔡 211 F3
✉ Chelas, Mirandela, Rua das Eiras 4
☎ 278 263 160; www.quintaentrerios.com

Where to...
Eat and Drink

Prices
Expect to pay per person for a three-course meal, excluding drinks and tips.
€ under €20   €€ €21–€30   €€€ €31–€40   €€€€ over €40

PORTO

Café Majestic €

An intellectuals' haunt dating from the 1920s, this is arguably Portugal's most beautiful café. *Insider Tip* Miraculously, it has survived intact, complete with stucco cherubs and mouldings, chandeliers, leather upholstery, marble-top tables, huge art deco mirrors and a grand piano. Ideal for coffee or tea and *pastéis*. Snacks and simple meals at lunchtime, served by liveried waiters.

✚ 210 B2 ✉ Rua de Santa Catarina 112
☎ 222 003 887; www.cafemajestic.com
🕐 Daily 9:30am–midnight

Casa da Música Restaurant €–€€

This fusion restaurant is on the 7th floor of the imposing Casa da Música, and is *Insider Tip* one of the best – and most fashionable – places to eat in Porto. The wonderful terrace affords sweeping views over Porto. Chef Artur Gomes puts his creative stamp on fresh, seasonal dishes. The fixed-price lunch and dinner menus represent excellent value. The wine list is extensive also, with a good selection of reds from the local Douro Valley, and further afield in Portugal.

✚ 210 B2 ✉ Avenue da Boavista 604–610
☎ 220 107 160; www.casadamusica.com/restaurante 🕐 Mon–Wed 12:30–3, 7:30–11; Thu–Sat 12:30–3, 7:30–midnight

O Comercial €€

High ceilings and chandeliers set the scene at this refined restaurant in the 19th–century Palácio da Bolsa (Stock Exchange Palace). The service is polished and the food is prepared with top-quality ingredients.

✚ 210 B2
✉ Palácio da Bolsa, Rua Ferreira Borges
☎ 223 322 019; www.ocomercial.com
🕐 Mon–Fri 12:30–3, 7:30–10:30, Sat 730–11:30

VILA NOVA DE GAIA

Barão de Fladgate €€€–€€€€

Set in Taylor's wine lodge on the hill, this restaurant with attentive service commands peerless views over Porto and the River Douro. Seafood is the main attraction on their classic Portuguese menu. Finish off with a glass of the excellent house port. The wine and tapas bar is also open from May to October.

✚ 210 B2 ✉ Rua do Choupelo 250
☎ 223 772 951; www.baraofladgate.com
🕐 Mon–Sat 12:30–3, 7:30–10; Sun 12:30–3

BRAGA

Arcoense €€

A seriously good local restaurant, serving up traditional Portuguese meals, plenty of local cheeses and a large range of sweet custard-based desserts. The location is excellent, right next to the River Este.

✚ 210 B4
✉ Rua Engenheiro José Justino Amorim 96
☎ 253 278 952; www.arcoense
🕐 Daily noon–3 and Mon–Sat 7:30–10:30

Café Vianna €

This low-key and great value art nouveau coffee-house is a great place for people-watching, either inside or on the *esplanada* (terrace) on warm days. The coffee, cakes and *pregos* (bread rolls filled with a sliver of sizzling steak) are excellent. Some of the delicious local pastries to sample are *rabanadas* (cinnamon-flavoured French toast) and *charutos de chila* (pumpkin-filled pastry rolls).

➕ 210 B4 ✉ Praça da República
☎ 253 262 336
🕐 Mon–Sat 8am–2am, Sun from 9am

GUIMARÃES

Tapas e Manias €€

This little restaurant offers an appealing selection of tasty tapas and excellent Portuguese wines, including some sparkling varieties. Guests can sit out on the beautiful square outside.

➕ 210 C3
✉ Praça de São Tiago 12 ☎ 932 959 888
🕐 Mon, Thu noon–3, 7–10, Wed 7–10, Sat, Sun noon–3, 7–10:30

VIANA DO CASTELO

Os Três Potes €€

With its granite walls and dark-wood furniture, this place may seem a little sombre. Nonetheless, it offers a good range of Minho specialities. Try the wood-oven-roasted kid (*cabrito*) or the char-grilled octopus (*polvo na brasa*) with a glass of house wine.

➕ 210 A4 ✉ Beco dos Fornos 7/9
☎ 258 829 928 🕐 Daily noon–3:30, 7–10:30

BRAGANÇA

Geadas €€–€€€

Good regional produce in attractive surroundings with pretty views. This is just the kind of local restaurant that you hope to stumble across, and has high standards of food and service. Plenty of freshly caught fish and local meats on the menu, and all served up in generous portions.

Insider Tip

➕ 212 B4 ✉ 32 Rua do Loreto 32
☎ 273 326 002; www.geadas.net
🕐 Daily noon–3 and Mon–Sat 7pm–10pm

TRÁS-OS-MONTES

Bagoeira €€

A cavernous place to dine on the Campo da Feira (marketplace). Minho dishes and roasts are served in traditional style with jugs of Vinho Verde. *Bacalhau à Bagoeira* is the house variation on *à minhota* (with onions and potatoes). The restaurant belongs to the 3-star hotel of the same name.

➕ 212 B3
✉ Avenida Sidónio Pais 495, Barcelos
☎ 253 813 088; www.bagoeira.com
🕐 Daily noon–3, 7–10:30

Where to...
Shop

PORTO

A triangle between the Estação São Bento, the University and the City Hall is the main shopping area, with stationers, grocers and clothes and shoe shops along **Rua de Santa Catarina**. **Via Catarina** (Rua de Santa Catarina 312–350, www.viacatarina.pt) is a shopping mall with over 90 shops in which to browse.

Insider Tip

For a more authentic experience, head for the covered **Bolhão Market** (all week), on Rua Sá da Bandeira, by Bolhão station.

For crafts, go to **Prometeu Artesanato** (Rua São João 19; tel: 222 011 510; e.g. *azulejos*), **Galeria de Artesanato O Galo** (Rua de Mouzinho da Silveira 68; tel: 223 325 294) and **Artesanato Clérigos** (Rua da Assunção 33–34; tel: 222 000 257).

For fine wines and ports, visit **Garrafeira do Carmo** (Rua do Carmo 17; tel: 222 003 285; http://garrafeiracarmo.com) or **Garrafeira A Flor de São Tomé** (Rua Antero de Quental 534; tel: 225 022 034).

Azeitoneira do Porto (Cais da Ribeira 36; tel: 222 007 303) sells a wide variety of olives.

If you are stuck for time visiting the various lodges at **Vila Nova de Gaia** (►88), go to **Sandeman's** (►89) or **Taylor's** (►89).

BARCELOS

Every Thursday, the lively **Campo da Feira** takes over. *Insider Tip* Pottery, wicker baskets, fresh fruit and flowers, clucking chickens, coffee, crusty bread – you'll find it all here. The "Barcelos rooster" (►102) and distinctive Barcelos pottery – a rich brown with cream dots – originated here.

Where to… Go Out

FESTIVALS

São Jão (St John's Day), 24 June, is celebrated everywhere. In Porto, it is a huge festival with music, dancing, feasting, and hitting people with squeaky hammers! It ends with a regatta of *barcos rabelos* (►88) and fireworks.

The **Romaria de Sete Paços** – a famous Good Friday procession – starts at the Igreja Matriz in Freixo de Espada à Cinta. Braga celebrates **Holy Week** in impressive style.

Viana do Castelo's famous *romaria* (pilgrimage) carnival takes place around 20 August. It features processions and the blessing of fishing boats.

SPORT & OUTDOOR PURSUITS

Hire **surf** gear at Viana do Castelo; the **Surf Club de Viana** (Rua Manuel Fiúza Júnior 133; tel: 258 826 208; www.surfingviana.com) offers lessons while **Amigos do March** (Parque Empresarial da Praia Norte; tel: 258 827 427; www.amigosdomar.pt) offers diving and sailing.

Hiking is popular in the national parks such as Peneda-Gerês (►99); enjoy watersports on the Caniçada reservoir; hire boats, kayaks, surfboards and gear at **AML** (Lugar de Paredes, Rua 6, Rio Caldo; tel: 253 391 779; www.aguamontanha.com).

For one- or two-day cruises on the Douro, contact **Douro Acima** (tel: 222 006 418; www.douroacima.pt) or **Douro Azul** (Rua Miragaia 103; tel: 223 402 500; www.douroazul.com). The latter also offer multi-day trips.

MUSIC & NIGHTLIFE

For classical music, there's Porto's **Pavilhão Rosa Mota** (Rua D. Manuel II; tel: 225 430 360) or **Casa da Música** at the Rotunda da Boavista (Avenida da Boavista 604–610; tel: 220 120 220; www.casadamusica.com). **Hot Five Jazz Club** (Largo Actor Dias 51; 934 328 583; http://hotfive.pt) is a great little venue for live jazz and blues.

Enjoy sipping fine wines and ports at Ribeira's bars, pubs, lounge bars and open-air cafés. Check out **Plano B** (Rua Cândido dos Reis 30; tel: 222 012 500; http://planobporto.net), for theatre, dance, live music and DJ nights.

The hottest clubs in Porto include **Tendinha** (Rua das Oliveiras 45), **More Club** (Rua Galeria de Paris 80), **Tendinha dos Clérigos** (Rua do Conde de Vizela 80) and **Act** (Rua de Manuel Pinto de Azevedo 15).

Nightlife in smaller towns and cities tends to be focussed around the main square.

Central Portugal

 **Little Treats**

The Estate of Tears

Marvel at the grounds of Coimbra's **Quinta das Lágrimas** estate (▶118, 135, 136) and learn all about its tragic love story.

Hard-to-find *Fado*

If you'd like to hear and experience some *fado* in Coimbra, head to "**À Capella**" (▶121).

Panoramic Pilgrimage

Stride out on a hike along the pilgrimage route (▶123) at the edge of **Fátima** – you'll be rewarded with fantastic views.

Getting Your Bearings

Central Portugal stretches almost from Lisbon to Porto and from the Spanish border to the Atlantic coast – yet apart from the charming university city of Coimbra and the fascinating pilgrimage town of Fátima it receives few visitors and is little known outside the country.

The heart of central Portugal is the Beira (border) region, a group of three provinces between the Douro and the Tagus rivers. This was the historic homeland of the *Lusitani* tribe, Celto-Iberians who resisted the Roman invasion of Portugal, whose leader Viriatus, killed in 139BC, remains a national hero. Coimbra, which takes its name from the Roman settlement at Conímbriga, was the capital of Portugal for more than 100 years. These days it is the capital of Beira Litoral, a seaside province of sandy beaches, pine forests and dunes, which is popular with Portuguese holidaymakers in summer.

Further inland, Beira Alta is a region of solid towns and granite villages, where Dão wines and Serra cheese are made, the latter by the sheep farmers of the highlands of Serra da Estrela, while remote Beira Baixa is the setting for Monsanto, one of Portugal's most spectacular hilltop villages.

The twin provinces of Estremadura and Ribatejo are dotted with castles and monuments recalling the time when the Christian armies marched south through this region, reconquering land from the Moors. This is where you will find the holy trinity of great Portuguese churches, at Alcobaça, Batalha and Tomar, as well as the moving modern shrine at Fátima, attracting pilgrims from across the Catholic world.

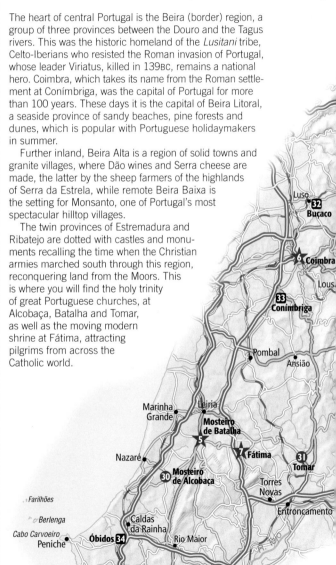

Óbidos is a great place to stroll around and relax in a café

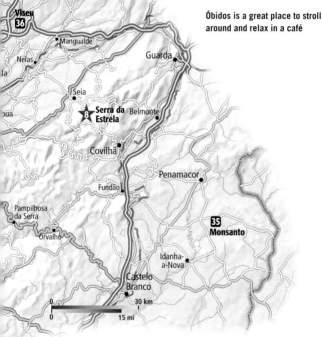

TOP 10

Don't Miss

At Your Leisure

Central Portugal

Four Perfect Days

If you're not quite sure where to begin your travels, this itinerary recommends a practical and enjoyable four days out in central Portugal, taking in some of the best places to see. For more information see the main entries (➤ 114–134).

Day 1

Morning
Start by exploring ⭐**Coimbra** (➤ 118) on foot. Climb the hill to visit one of the oldest universities in the world and see its library, chapel and graduation halls, before dropping down through the Old Town and passing the old cathedral on the way to the church of Santa Cruz. Have lunch in the neighbouring **Café Santa Cruz** (➤ 136).

Afternoon and Evening
Cross the river and drive south on the N1 to see the Roman remains at **㉝ Conímbriga** (above, ➤ 133). Continue as far as Leiria, then pick up the A8/IC1 motorway to pretty **㉞ Óbidos** (➤ 134). Book ahead to stay in the castle, a *pousada*; walk around the hilltop ramparts.

Day 2

Morning
Admire the views and whitewashed houses in Óbidos, then go back along the A8/IC1 north to **㉚ Alcobaça** (➤ 126) to visit the monastery before lunch.

Afternoon and Evening
Take the short drive to visit the no-less impressive ⭐**Mosteiro da Batalha** (➤ 114). Then head east on the N356 to the sanctuary at ⭐**Fátima** (➤ 122). Stay at the *pousada* (➤ 135) in the walled town of Ourém. Climb the hill up to the castle to enjoy some wonderful views across the plain.

Day 3

Morning

Drive to riverside ㉛ **Tomar** (► 128) to check out the mysterious UNESCO church-fortress of the Order of Christ. Then visit the town centre and have a spot of lunch. Bring a hearty appetite to try *leitão* (roast suckling pig, ► 41), a central Portuguese speciality.

Afternoon and Evening

Allow three hours for the drive to rugged ⭐8 **Serra da Estrela** (► 124), the highest mountain range in mainland Portugal. Penhas da Saúde is a great place to set off on a round-trip driving tour of the Zêzere Valley (above). While you're there, stay at the Pousada Serra da Estrela (N339, Covilhã; tel: 210 407 660; www.pestana.com). Otherwise, spend the night at an altitude of 1,500m (4,921ft) in the Casa das Penhas Douradas (tel: 275 981 045, www.casa daspenhasdouradas.pt) on the way to Manteigas. An alternative route leads south of Manteigas to the boulder-strewn village of ㉟ **Monsanto** (► 134) along the N239, N345 and N232, taking in rugged hill country, meadows and postcard-perfect hill villages.

Day 4

Spend a full day exploring the "Star Mountain Range". Visit the Manteigas tourist office for walking maps, then take a picnic to the **Poço do Inferno waterfall** (► 124). If you don't want to walk, drive the circuit from **Penhas da Saúde** (► 124) to **Torre** (► 125) for spectacular views of the high sierra.

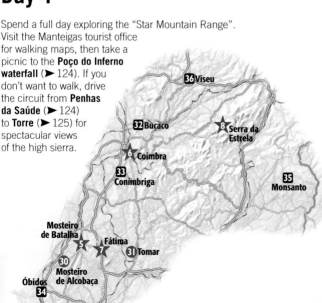

⭐5 Mosteiro da Batalha

As you round a corner on the busy N1, a great church comes into view, with pinnacles, turrets and flying buttresses in honey-coloured limestone. This is the Mosteiro da Batalha, a masterpiece of Gothic architecture that has become a symbol of Portuguese history and of the country's independence from Spain.

The **Mosteiro de Santa Maria da Vitória**, commonly known as the Mosteiro da Batalha (Abbey of the Battle), was built to celebrate the Portuguese victory over the Spanish at the Battle of Aljubarrota in 1385. Three years after King João I's victory work on the abbey began.

Mosteiro de Santa Maria da Vitória

Admire the worn exterior of the abbey and the **statue of Nuno Álvares Pereira** (►above) on horseback on the square in front of the church. The main portal, beneath a Gothic window, features carved statues of Christ and the apostles, with angels, saints and João I's coat of arms. The long, tall nave is beautifully simple, with Gothic pillars and vaulting and stained glass.

THE BATTLE OF ALJUBARROTA

King Fernando I of Portugal died in 1383 without leaving a male heir. King Juan I of Castile claimed the throne from his marriage to King Fernando's daughter, Beatriz, but was opposed by Fernando's illegitimate half-brother, João I. Heavily outnumbered by Spanish troops, João promised to build a magnificent church to the Virgin if he was successful, and with the help of his faithful lieutenant Nuno Álvares Pereira, and 500 English archers supplied by King Richard II, his supporters won the day. João's victory ushered in a new era for Portugal, with 200 years of independence under the rule of the House of Avis.

Mosteiro da Batalha

The Founder's Chapel

Immediately to the right as you enter is the **Capela do Fundador** (Founder's Chapel), where João I and his wife, Philippa of Lancaster (➤ 80), are buried beneath an octagonal lantern, their tombs carved with effigies of the couple lying hand in hand. Also buried here are their four younger sons, including Henry the Navigator (➤ 12, 80).

Batalha Monastery: as big as Notre-Dame Cathedral in Paris

The original **Claustro Real** (Royal Cloister) was embellished with rich Manueline tracery by Diogo de Boytac, architect of the monastery at Belém (➤ 48). All the main symbols of Manueline art are here, including armillary spheres, crosses of Christ, twisted branches and exotic foliage.

On one side of the cloister, the **Sala do Capítulo** (chapter house) contains Portugal's two Unknown Soldiers, one from World War I and the other from Portugal's wars in Africa. A museum dedicated to them is in the former refectory.

A second cloister leads to the **Capelas Imperfeitas** (Unfinished Chapels), begun by Dom Duarte, João I's eldest son, as a royal mausoleum, containing the tombs of Duarte and his queen, Éleonor of Aragón. The chapels, also accessible from behind the main abbey, are perhaps the highlight of the entire complex, with an Indian-inspired Manueline portal and a magnificent roofless octagonal rotunda.

TAKING A BREAK

After visiting the abbey, the **Burro Velho** (Rua Nossa Sra. do Caminho 6A; tel: 244 764 174, www.burrovelho.com; daily noon–3 and Mon–Sat 7–10) is a good place for a glass of wine and a light Portuguese snack.

🔢 213 F2 ☎ 244 765 497
🕐 April–Sep 9–6:30; Oct–March 9–5:30 (last entry 30 mins before closing)
💶 €6; free Sun 9–2

INSIDER INFO

Insider Tip

■ The abbey is best seen on a **day trip** from Nazaré or Fátima, although there are express buses from Lisbon.

■ During the weekends of **13 May and 13 October**, Batalha is packed with people visiting from Fátima (➤ 122).

In more depth Visit the **battlefield of Aljubarrota**, 4km (2.5mi) south of Batalha in the village of São Jorge. There is a small chapel, a military museum, a shop and café (tel: 244 480 060; www.fundacao-aljubarrota.pt, May–Sep Tue–Sun 10–7, Oct–April Tue–Sun 10–5:30; entrance fee: €7).

Batalha Monastery

Dedicated to Saint Mary of the Victory, Batalha Monastery is the symbol of Portugal's independence from Spain. Before his legendary battle (Portuguese = *batalha*) near Aljubarrota in 1385, King João I vowed that he would build a monastery if he emerged victorious from the fight with his Castilian foe.

❶ West Portal: The main entrance. Decorated with 78 figures, including angels, prophets, kings, saints and the 12 Apostles.

❷ Capela do Fundador: A chapel containing the sarcophagus of the royal couple and the graves of their offspring (including Henry the Navigator).

❸ Monastery Church: This structure's impressive interior space measures 88m (289ft) in length, 32m (105ft) across and 32.5m (106ft) in height, making it a similar size to Cologne Cathedral and the Cathedral of Notre-Dame in Paris.

❹ Capelas Imperfeitas: These 8-sided "Unfinished Chapels" were intended to serve as burial chambers. The 8 buttresses pointing into the sky were added to support a domed roof that was never built.

❺ Claustro Dom João I: One of the finest examples of Manueline ornamentation. Two main motifs can be seen in the tracery – the cross of the Order of Christ and the armillary sphere.

The Twelve Apostles can be admired at the main entrance

The polygonal choir forms the eastern end of the monastery church's mighty central nave

Coimbra

Portugal's oldest university sits on the crown of a hill overlooking the River Mondego. With historic buildings and churches, parks and gardens, and a lively student feel, Coimbra is one of the most enjoyable Portuguese cities in which to spend some of your time.

The first king of Portugal, Afonso Henriques (1109–85, ▶ 80), moved the capital here from Guimarães (▶ 93), but it was his successor, Dom Dinis, who founded the university that is today synonymous with Coimbra. Established in 1290 by papal decree to teach medicine, arts and law, the university moved back and forth between Lisbon and Coimbra before settling in João III's royal palace at Coimbra in 1537. Despite clinging to traditions, the students here are known for their liberal outlook. During the 20th century, Coimbra was a focus for radical opposition to the Salazar régime.

Visiting the University

The university is in the upper town, on the summit of Alcáçova hill. Despite the steep gradients, Coimbra is best explored on foot and it is easiest to start by climbing to the top of the hill and working your way back down.

From the river, head for the **Pátio das Escolas**. This handsome quadrangle, with buildings on three sides and a terrace overlooking the Mondego, is at the heart of the old university. A statue of João III stands at the centre and in one corner is a baroque bell-tower.

Entry to some of the buildings is free, although you'll need a ticket to visit the most interesting edifices. Highlights include the frescoed **Biblioteca Joanina** (library) –which boasts a collection of more than

---

Insider Tip

ACROSS THE RIVER

Walk across the Ponte de Santa Clara for the best views of the Old Town and the university. On the south bank, the Gothic convent of **Santa Clara-a-Velha**, once home to Inês de Castro (▶ 126), has been sinking into the sand for centuries. It's now being recovered. The site includes a visitor centre (Rua das Parreiras; tel: 239 801 160; http://culturaacentro.pt; May–Sep Tue–Sun 10–7, Oct–April until 5:30; entrance fee: €5). The convent closed due to flood damage in January 2016, but should be open again soon, as 2016 was also its 700th anniversary. Near here is 🎠 **Portugal dos Pequenitos** (Rossio de Santa Clara; tel: 239 801 170; www.portugaldospequenitos.pt, March–May, mid-Sep to mid-Oct 10–7, June to mid-Sep 9–8; mid-Oct to Feb 10–5; entrance fee: €9.50, kids up to age 13: €5.95, family ticket: €25.95). Aimed mainly at children, the park has a play area and miniature models of houses, monuments and historic buildings from all over Portugal. Heading outside the city, the peaceful gardens of **Quinta das Lágrimas** (Villa of Tears) mark the spot where Inês de Castro was murdered. The palace at the centre of the gardens is now a luxury hotel (▶ 135).

The venerable Coimbra University

30,000 books dating back to the twelfth century – and the ruby-red **Sala dos Capelos** (ceremonial hall). The library, named after its benefactor, João V, is decorated in gilded wood and lacquered in green, red and gold. The Sala dos Capelos, where investitures and degree ceremonies take place, occupies the grand hall of the Manueline (➤ 18) palace, with its panelled ceiling and portraits of Portuguese monarchs. The **Sala do Exame Privado** is also worth checking out.

On the east side of the square, the **Porta Férrea** (Iron Gate), built in 1634, contains carved figures representing the original faculties and statues of Dom Dinis and João III.

Two Cathedrals

From the statue of Dom Dinis, steps lead down to **Praça da República**, with its student cafés. Behind the 21-arch São Sebastião Aqueduct, which was completed by Italian architect Filippo Terzi in the late 16th century, is the vast **Jardim Botânico da Universidade de Coimbra** (Calçada

Martim de Freitas; tel: 239 855 233; www.uc.pt/jardim botanico; April–Sep 9am–8pm, Oct–March 9am–5:30pm; free). It is Portugal's largest botanical garden and the formal gardens were laid out in the late 18th century.

Go back up the steps and turn right to explore the rest of the upper town. The **Sé Nova** (New Cathedral) was built in 1598 and includes the choir stalls and font from the old cathedral. Just down the hill, the **Museu Nacional Machado de Castro** is housed in the 16th-century bishops' palace that's been given some contemporary architectural additions. It includes medieval paintings, sculpture and the *cryptoporticus*, a series of underground galleries containing various archaeological finds, jewellery, textiles, ceramics, etc.

Further downhill, the **Sé Velha** (Old Cathedral) is a Romanesque church-fortress on the site of the first cathedral in Portugal. Of interest here are the 13th-century cloisters and the Hispano-Arab tiles covering the walls.

Mosteiro de Santa Cruz

From here you can walk down to **Arco de Almedina**, the 12th-century gateway to the city. Go through the arch and turn right along a busy pedestrian street to the **Mosteiro de Santa Cruz**. Many of the leading artists of the Coimbra school, such as Jean de Rouen, worked on pieces for the monastery in the 16th century. The Renaissance porch is by Diogo de Castilho and Nicolas Chanterène, who also designed the pulpit and was responsible for the tombs of Portugal's first kings, Afonso Henriques and his son, Sancho I, behind the high altar. Buy a ticket to visit the **Sala do Capítulo** (chapter house) by Diogo de Boytac, with its Manueline ceiling, and the **Claustro do Silêncio** (Cloister of Silence), one of the purest examples of Manueline art. Turn left on coming out of the church to return to the river at Largo da Portagem.

Cross the water for the best views of Coimbra

🎠 **Portugal dos Pequenitos**, a theme park filled with miniature buildings, is a good destination for younger families.

TAKING A BREAK

Try the **trendy student cafés** around Praça da República, or **O Trovador** (➤ 137), by the Sé Velha.

➕ 214 A4
✉ Largo da Portagem ☎ 239 488 120; www.turismodecoimbra.pt

Universidade Velha (Biblioteca Joanina and Sala dos Capelos)
✉ Paço das Escolas ☎ 239 859 900; www.uc.pt
◉ Easter–mid-Oct, daily 9–7:30; mid-Oct–Easter, Mon–Fri 9:30–1, 5–5:30, Sa, Sun 10:30–4:30
💶 €9; tower €2; audio guide €2.50; you can buy tickets in the atrium of the Biblioteca Geral, Largo da Porta Férrea (opposite the Faculdade de Letras).

Sé Velha dates back to the reign of King Afonso Henriques

Museu Nacional Machado de Castro
✉ Largo Dr José Rodrigues
☎ 239 853 070; www.museumachadocastro.pt
◉ April–Sep Wed–Sun 10–6, Tue 2–6;
Oct–March Tue–Sun 10–12:30, 2–6
💶 €6; Criptopórtico €3

Sé Velha
✉ Largo da Sé Velha
☎ 239 825 273; http://sevelha-coimbra.org
◉ Mon–Sat 10–6, Sun 1–6, limited access during services
💶 €2.50

Mosteiro de Santa Cruz
✉ Praça 8 de Maio ☎ 239 822 941
◉ Mon–Fri 9–5, Sat 9–noon, 2–5; Sun 4–5:30 only
💶 Church: free. Further interior spaces: €2.50

INSIDER INFO

- Parking in central Coimbra is difficult – it is generally easier to leave your car on the other side of the river and walk across the Ponte de Santa Clara.
- To avoid the climb to the university, take **tram No 1A** from the city centre.
- In summer, there are river trips from a jetty in the park beside the Santa Clara bridge on the north bank.
- The **Museu da Ciência** actually served as the university's chemistry lab back in the eighteenth century. It's now the University of Coimbra's interactive science museum that also boasts a collection of scientific instruments (www.museudaciencia.com, entry: €4).
- Keep your eyes peeled for the chance to listen to **Coimbra's version of** *fado* (➤ 22) performed by men in long, black capes. It's less melancholy than its Lisbon counterpart. You're mostly likely to hear it sung in bars and restaurants and in the streets during student festivities. Alternatively, check out one of the regular performances at **À Capella** (Rua Corpo de Deus-Largo da Vitória; tel: 239 833 985; www.acapella.com.pt), a small cultural centre.

Insider Tip

Fátima

The so-called "altar of Portugal", Fátima is Portugal's greatest Roman Catholic shrine. The story of what happened to three shepherd children in 1917 has moved millions, and made the town one of the biggest centres of pilgrimage in Europe.

The Vision

It was on 13 May 1917 that the Virgin Mary appeared in an oak tree to 10-year-old Lúcia dos Santos and her cousins Jacinta and Francisco as they were tending their family's sheep in the village of Cova da Iria, near Fátima. The children spoke of a lady "brighter than the sun" who called them to return at the same time each month for six months. Although their story was greeted with much scepticism, the children returned and the visions continued.

On the final occasion, 13 October, a crowd of 70,000 people witnessed the sun dancing in the sky like a ball of fire and countless miracles occurred – the blind could see, the sick were cured and the lame walked.

On the same day, the Virgin revealed to Lúcia the "three secrets of Fátima", which are said to have foretold World War II, Russian communism and the assassination of a pope.

The Children

Jacinta and Francisco died of pneumonia in 1920, but Lúcia entered a Carmelite convent in Coimbra in 1928, where she died in 2005, aged 97. Jacinta and Francisco, who are buried inside the basilica, were beatified in 2000.

The Basilica

A vast, neoclassical basilica was completed in 1953, and accommodates the millions of pilgrims who flock here from

The Basilica of Our Lady of Fátima towers over its steps and the tarmac esplanade

Pilgrims light candles for Our Lady of Fátima

Portugal and all over the world. The esplanade in front of the basilica can hold a million people and is twice the size of St Peter's Square in Rome. In a corner of the square stands the **Capela das Aparicões** (Chapel of the Apparitions), on the site of the original visions, where pilgrims pray, offer gifts and light candles to a statue of the Virgin. The sea of candles and dripping wax is a captivating sight. Inside the basilica are 15 altars symbolizing the 15 mysteries of the Rosary.

Pilgrimages to Fátima take place all year, and particularly on 13 May and 13 October. Many pilgrims complete the journey to the basilica on their knees. A 34m (111ft)-high crucifix and the mighty **Igreja da Santíssima Trindade**, which seats around 9,000 people, add a modern touch to the area around the sanctuary.

TAKING A BREAK

The *pousada* at Ourém (➤ 135), built on a hilltop 10km (6mi) northeast of Fátima, makes a good overnight stop. *Ginja*, a Portuguese liqueur, is served in the local bars.

➕ 213 F2
🛈 Avenida Dom José Alves Correia da Silva
☎ 249 531 139; www.turismodocentro.pt/pt/

Shrine of Our Lady of the Rosary of Fátima
✉ Apartado 31
☎ 249 539 600; www.santuario-fatima.pt

INSIDER INFO

- From Easter to October, there are **candlelit processions** in front of the basilica at 9:30 each night. The largest procession is on 12th of the month.
- A short way outside the city, the **Via Sacra** (pilgrimage route) climbs up through natural surroundings to a hill which bears a chapel and a group of sculptures surrounding a crucifix. Go there to enjoy some great views of Fátima.
- Two little museums in the **Aljustrel** district tell of the three child seers.

⑧ Serra da Estrela

Rocky hillsides are carved up by glacial valleys in the Serra da Estrela, the highest mountain range in mainland Portugal. In summer you can walk across carpets of scented grasses and wild flowers, and in winter the peaks are covered in snow. Much of the area is a designated natural park.

The Serra da Estrela mountain range spreads out over an area of 100km by 30km (62mi by 19mi), and boasts a summit that rises to an altitude of 1,993m (6,537ft). Although a wonderful nature reserve, it's not entirely free of civilization. This is a land of shepherds, long-horned sheep, cheese-making and wool. The mainstays of the economy are farming and forestry, though outdoor tourism is becoming increasingly important. Visitors can enjoy skiing and hunting in winter, while trout fishing in the rivers and walking in the hills are popular pastimes in summer.

Getting into the Mountains

There is good access to the mountains from Covilha, a busy textile town with views over the mountains, where you can buy gloves, jackets and woollen goodies. From here, the N339 climbs through **Penhas da Saúde**, Portugal's only ski resort, on its way to the high sierra. In winter, you can try dog sledging and sleigh rides as well as skiing. This is a good starting point for a circular tour, allowing at least half a day. Soon after Penhas da Saúde, turn right on the N338 for a beautiful drive along the Zêzere Valley, a deep glacial gorge.

All along the valley you'll get distant views of **Manteigas**, the small town that sits at the centre of the park. Go there to pick up information on walking and hiking in the mountains, *Insider Tip* including the half-day circular walk from Manteigas to the **Poço do Inferno** (Hell's Well) waterfall that's also an option for 👪 families with kids.

Magnificent views of the High Sierra near Torre

The glacial scenery of the Zêzere Valley

From Manteigas, you can follow the twisting N232 towards Gouveia. You pass a *pousada* and the source of the River Mondego, which empties into the sea near Coimbra. The scenery is stunning, with rock formations of wind-sculpted granite such as the Cabeça do Velho (Old Man's Head).

A minor road leads to **Sabugueiro**, Portugal's highest village, where cheese, ham, sausages and woollen blankets are on sale. Turn left on the N339 for the slow climb to **Torre**. The highest mountain in Portugal (1,993m/6,537ft) takes its name from the stone tower built there in the 19th century so that the peak would top 2,000m (6,560ft). Families flock here to go sledging at the weekend in winter. On the way down to Penhas da Saúde, look out for the statue of **Nossa Senhora da Boa Estrela**, carved into a niche in the rock. The 🐑 sheep farms in the mountains are also worth a visit.

Two places that make good bases for visiting the park are **Guarda** – the loftiest town in Portugal (1,056m/3,464ft) and home to a 14th-century Gothic cathedral – and **Belmonte**, the birthplace of Pedro Álvares Cabral (► 17) who "discovered" Brazil. Belmonte was once home to a large population of *marranos* (Jews who fled here after their expulsion from Portugal in 1497). A new synagogue shows there's still a large Jewish community in the town today.

TAKING A BREAK

There are **cafés** in all the main villages offering sandwiches made with the local cheese, *queijo da serra* (see below).

✚ 215 D5

Park Tourist Information Office
✉ 2 Rua Doutor Esteves Carvalho, Manteigas
☎ 275 981 129; http://cm-manteigas.pt

INSIDER INFO

- Try **queijo da serra** (► 31), a strong cheese made from sheep's milk and curdled with thistle flowers. The runny, ripe cheese, usually scooped out with a spoon, is at its best in winter.
- The mountains need to be **treated with respect**. The weather can change quickly, and it may be sunny in Manteigas while Torre is obscured in mist. Be prepared for anything, even in summer, and allow yourselves plenty of time. Check out www.manteigastrilhosverdes.com, a good website that provides free downloads of various helpful maps and brochures in Portuguese and English.

㉚ Mosteiro de Alcobaça

This mighty, UNESCO World Heritage monastery complex is a supreme example of Gothic architecture. It would be worth visiting Alcobaça just to see this building alone. What makes it even more special is that the church has become a shrine to one of the most tragic love stories in Portuguese history.

The tomb of
Dom Pedro I
and Inês
de Castro

The **Mosteiro de Alcobaça** (sometimes referred to as the Mosteiro Santa Maria) was founded by Afonso Henriques (►90) in 1153 to give thanks for his victory over the Moors at Santarém. The baroque façade dates from the 18th century, but everything is pure Gothic once you head inside.

DOM PEDRO I AND INÊS DE CASTRO

Visitors crowd the transept to see the tombs of Dom Pedro I and his lover, Inês de Castro. Inês was lady-in-waiting to Pedro's wife, Constanza of Castile, but Pedro's father, Afonso IV, had her banished from court to end the affair. After Constanza died, Inês lived with Pedro at Coimbra, where she was murdered in 1355 on the orders of Afonso IV who feared Spanish influence over the Portuguese throne. Two years later, when Pedro assumed the throne, he wrought revenge on the killers by having their hearts torn out and eating them. He also revealed that he and Inês had been secretly married at Bragança; her corpse was exhumed and he ordered the court to pay homage to their dead queen by kissing her decomposed hand.

Clean Lines and Soaring Columns

Unlike many Portuguese churches, the central nave is simplicity itself. The only exception to the almost complete absence of decoration is the richly sculpted sacristy portal behind the high altar, designed by João de Castilho in a highly floral, 16th-century Manueline style (► 52).

Tombs and Cloisters

The limestone **tombs of Dom Pedro I and Inês de Castro**, carved with scenes from the Bible, face each other across the aisle. The reclining figure of Inês is held by six angels, while her assassins are thrown into Hell at her feet. On Pedro's orders, the lovers were buried foot to foot, so that they could see one another when they rose on Judgement Day. The tombs are inscribed with *Até ao fim do mundo* ("Until the end of the world").

The entrance to the cloisters is through the **Sala dos Reis**, with statues of Portuguese kings and tiled walls telling the story of the monastery. The **Claustro de Silêncio**, added in the 14th century, is considered one of the finest Gothic cloisters in Portugal, with its orange trees and a Renaissance *lavabo* for the monks to wash their hands before entering the refectory.

Along here are the rather grand 18th-century **kitchens**, once famed for their extravagant banquets, with huge conical chimneys, and a stream that flowed straight from the River Alcôa, providing a plentiful supply of fish. Next to the kitchens is the rib-vaulted **refectory**. Note the pulpit on the western flank where the monks once read holy scriptures. A staircase from the cloister leads to the 13th-century dormitory.

TAKING A BREAK

You'll find little cafés and restaurants on the large square in front of the monastery and in the surrounding streets.

➕ 213 E2
☎ 262 505 120; www.mosteiroalcobaca.pt
🕐 April–Sep daily 9–7; Oct–March 9–5 (last entry 30 mins before closing)
💶 €6

㉛ Tomar

The third in the trio of medieval monasteries, the Convento de Cristo, stands in the grounds of a castle on a wooded slope overlooking Tomar. Once a powerful military and religious capital, Tomar is now a peaceful town on the banks of the River Nabão and makes a pleasant base to stay for exploring the surrounding area.

The Monastery

The town is dominated by the 🏰 castle of the Knights of the Order of Christ who succeeded the Knights Templar in the Middle Ages. It's home to the **Convento de Cristo** (➤ 130, one of Portugal's UNESCO World Heritage Sites. Begun in 1160, it boasts Gothic and Manueline (➤ 18) additions. Younger visitors will also enjoy exploring the stronghold.

The 12th-century Convento de Cristo (Convent of Christ)

The tour of the monastery begins in a pair of cloisters, **Claustro da Lavagem** and **Claustro do Cemitério**, both added by Henry the Navigator (1394–1460, ➤ 12, 80), whose ruined palace can be seen through the arches.

Next you come to the **Charola** (Rotunda), the spiritual heart of the complex, a curious 12th-century round church that was modelled on the Holy Sepulchre in Jerusalem. It has an octagonal chapel where the knights are reputed to have held services on horseback. The columns are richly painted with 16th-century frescoes. The Charola now forms the eastern end of a Manueline church, built during the reign of Manuel I.

From here you move into the **Claustro Principal** (Great Cloister), added in 1557 in neoclassical and Renaissance style. Climb onto the roof for the best views of the **great western window** by Diogo de Arruda and the **south portal** by João de Castilho, two of the most sumptuous examples of Manueline art in Portugal. The window in particular contains all the familiar symbols of the Manueline era, including anchors, cables, twisted ropes, an armillary sphere and the Cross of the Knights of Christ. From here you can wander along corridors of monks' cells and step onto the rooftop terrace before finishing with the walkway around the castle walls.

The Town

The Old Town, to the west of the river, is centred around the elegant **Praça da República**, where a statue of Gualdim Pais stands in front of the town hall. On one side of the square, the church of **São João Baptista** has an elegant Manueline portal and a pulpit carved with the Templar cross and the royal coat of arms.

Just south is the oldest surviving **synagogue** in Portugal. Built around 1430, and abandoned after the expulsion of the Jews in 1497, it has been used as a prison, chapel, hayloft and cellar, but is now a museum containing 13th- and 14th-century Jewish tombstones as well as sacred items donated by members of Jewish communities across the world.

Tomar's other museum, **Museu dos Fósforos** (Matchbox Museum) is housed in a wing of a 17th-century convent. An eccentric display features more than 40,000 matchboxes, the largest collection in Europe, beginning with Queen Elizabeth II's coronation in 1953 and continuing with Portuguese politicians, Spanish bullfighters and Japanese topless models.

Praça da República, with the statue of Gualdim Pais

Convento da Ordem de Cristo

Tomar's castle of the Knights of the Order of Christ is one of the nation's preeminent monuments. The 12th-century church of the Knights Templar and the Manueline façade topped with the famous "window of Tomar" are of particular interest to art historians.

❶ Church of the Knights Templar: Built in the 12th century in the style of Jerusalem's Church of the Holy Sepulchre, the Church of the Knights Templar sits at the heart of the castle complex. Its sixteen-sided exterior walls enclose a hexagonal interior space known as the *Charola*.

❷ Church of the Order of Christ: Work on the church of the Order of Christ began in the 16th century following plans by João de Castilho. This fresh structure was added onto the old Knights Templar church, which formed the choir of the new building. The former monks' prayer room became the high choir that fills nearly two thirds of the new edifice today. The chapter house lies underneath.

❸ South Portal: The entrance to the church of the Knights of the Order of Christ is embellished with rich ornamentation by João de Castilho.

❹ Manueline Window: This window – possibly the most famous in Portugal – can best be seen from the Claustro Santa Bárbara. It's a magnificent example of Manueline decoration, adorned with stone ropes, flowers, shells and coral, the Portuguese coat of arms, the crown and cross of the Knights of Christ, and two armillary spheres.

❺ Claustro Principal: This Italian-inspired main cloister is an example of late Renaissance architecture.

❻ Claustro de Santa Bárbara: Come here to see the very best view of the Manueline window in all its splendour.

❼ Claustro da Hospedaria: Guests staying at the monastery were accommodated in this part of the complex.

❽ Claustro do Cemitério: The graves here include that of Diogo da Gama, brother of the famous Vasco da Gama.

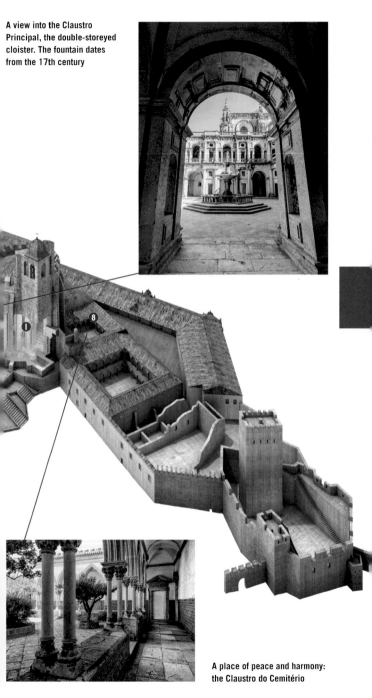

A view into the Claustro Principal, the double-storeyed cloister. The fountain dates from the 17th century

A place of peace and harmony: the Claustro do Cemitério

Central Portugal

Insider Tip

INSIDER INFO

- Come here on Friday when the riverbanks are taken over by the **Feira Semanal**, the large weekly market.
- Try a *Fatias de Tomar* (a slice of Tomar), a sweet treat made with a mixture of egg yolks, sugar and water, purchased in many shops and restaurants around the town.
- Cross the Ponte Velha (Old Bridge) to the chapel of Tomar's patron saint, **Santa Iria**, a young nun who was murdered. Built in the 16th century, the structure features a stone-carved calvary, a coffered painted ceiling and a wealth of 17th-century *azulejos* (➤ 32). Ask about current opening times at the tourist office in advance.
- The **Feira de Santa Iria**, Tomar's well-known saint's festival, is held in October each year.

Insider Tip

- A short drive away from Tomar is **Constância**, one of the most attractive villages in the area. The Festival of the Tabuleiros (heavy baskets stacked with bread and flowers) takes place here once every four years (the next one will be held in July 2019).

A warren of narrow streets leads down to the River Nabão, where the shady **Parque do Mouchão** – located on an island in the middle of the river – is an inviting spot for a stroll. The park is a cool, calm place planted with willow trees.

TAKING A BREAK

The **Restaurante Infante** (Av. Cândido Madureira 106; tel: 249 314 513; www.restauranteinfante.com) serves typical regional cooking for lunch and dinner every day. You'll also find places for refreshments in the area around the main square.

A Manueline carving in Tomar

🞤 214 A2
🛈 Avenida Dr Cândido Madureira
☎ 249 329 823; www.cm-tomar.pt

Convento de Cristo
✉ 15-minute walk above the town
☎ 249 315 089; www.conventocristo.pt
🕐 June–Sep daily 9–6:30; Oct–May 9–5:30
💶 €6, free 1st Sun of the month

**Sinagoga/
Museu Hebraico Abraão Zacuto**
✉ Rua Dr Joaquim Jacinto 73
☎ 249 322 427
🕐 May–Sep Tue–Sun 10–1 3–7;
Oct–April Tue–Sun 10–1, 2–5
💶 Free

Museu dos Fósforos
✉ Avenida General Bernardo Faria,
Convento de S. Francisco
🕐 May–Sep Tue–Sun 10–1, 3–7;
Oct–April Tue–Sun 10–1, 2–5
💶 Free

At Your Leisure

Gardens at Palace Hotel do Bussaco

32 🏃 Buçaco

Buçaco is a place where you can still believe in fairies. Once a monastic retreat from which women were banned by papal decree, the walled **Mata Nacional** (National Forest) is a landscape of sylvan glades and cedar-scented woods dotted with fountains, hermitages, shaded walks and even its own vineyard. At the centre is the bizarre neo-Manueline **Buçaco Palace**, designed as a royal hunting lodge and now one of Portugal's top hotels (► 135). The Carmelite convent (Convento Santa Cruz do Bussaco; closed at the time of writing) has cork-lined cells and mosaic walls. Walk through the Buçaco forest up to Cruz Alta (High Cross), which offers impressive views over the ocean.
Insider Tip

✚ 214 B5

Mata do Buçaco
☎ 231 937 000; www.fmb.pt
🕐 June–Sep 15 8:30–7, Sat, Sun until 8; 3–6 rest of year
💳 free for pedestrians; regular car with passengers €5

33 Conímbriga

The best-preserved Roman remains in Portugal are situated 15km (9mi) south of Coimbra. Some of the houses have detailed mosaics, with images of birds, fish, horses and dragons. Note the **Casa das Fontes**, a second-century villa with ornamental gardens and baths. The excavations here have uncovered evidence of a forum, aqueduct, shops, taverns and public baths. A museum contains archaeological finds, some of which date from a Celto-Iberian settlement before the arrival of the Romans in the first century BC.
Insider Tip

✚ 214 A4 ✉ Condeixa-a-Velha
☎ 239 941 177; www.conimbriga.pt
🕐 10–7
💳 €4.50

🏃 A COOLING DIP

If you've had enough of sightseeing, take a cooling dip at some of the beaches along the **Costa da Prata** in Central Portugal.
Insider Tip

Central Portugal

34 Óbidos

This walled town of whitewashed houses and maze-like lanes is one of the most beautiful in all of Portugal. You'll be itching to explore as soon as you arrive, so leave your car on the edge of the settlement and get stuck in. The **Porta de Vila**, the town's gateway, is lined with 18th-century *azulejos* and leads to **Rua Direita**, the main thoroughfare with its souvenir shops and *ginja* (cherry brandy) bars. Halfway up the street, the church of **Santa Maria** boasts *azulejo* walls. There's a striking Manueline pillory in the church square. The castle at the top of town was converted into a royal palace in the 16th century and is now one of Portugal's finest *pousadas* (▶ 136). From here, climb onto the ramparts to make a circuit of the walls, which should take around 45 minutes. The castle is illuminated atmospherically by night.

✚ 213 E1

35 Monsanto

Inhabited in pre-Roman times, Monsanto is one of Portugal's oldest settlements. It is perched on the side of Monte Santo (Sacred Mountain), its houses built into the mountainside between huge granite boulders. This village has the odd claim to

fame of having been once voted "Most Portuguese village in Portugal". Climb to the ruined 12th-century **castle**, for magnificent views stretching as far as the Serra da Estrela (▶ 124).

During the Festa das Cruzes on 3 May (or the following Sunday), the younger women of the village toss flowers from the ramparts in memory of a famous siege in which the starving inhabitants threw their last calf from the castle walls in a successful attempt to fool their attackers into thinking they were able to hold out for a long time.

There are a few signs of tourist development – a couple of restaurants and craft shops – but life mostly goes on as it always has in this remote, quintessential hilltop village.

✚ 215 E3

36 Viseu

The capital of the Beira Alta and the Dão wine region, Viseu is an attractive town. At the heart of the Old Town is **Largo da Sé**, with two churches facing one another across the square. The larger and more imposing façade is that of the baroque church of Misericórdia; the Sé (cathedral) has Renaissance cloisters and a Manueline ceiling.

The main attraction is the **Museu de Grão Vasco**, named after Vasco Fernandes (1475–1542), a leading figure in the Viseu school of painting. It includes his painting, *St Peter Enthroned*.

✚ 211 D1

🛈 Casa do Adro, Adro da Sé

☎ 232 420 950; www.cm-viseu.pt; www.visitcentro.com

Museu de Grão Vasco

✉ Paço dos Três Escalões, Adro da Sé

☎ 232 422 049; www.patrimoniocultural.pt

🕐 Tue 2–6 Wed–Sun 10–6

💶 €4; free 1st Sun of the month

The roofless Church São Miguel in the ruins of the castle in Monsanto

Where to…
Stay

Prices
Expect to pay for a double room per night in high season
€ under €80   €€ €80–€110   €€€ €110–€150   €€€€ over €150

COIMBRA

Casa Pombal €
By the university and command-ing views across the rooftops to the river, this pleasant guesthouse is a delightful place to stay. You feel as though you are staying at one of the famous *repúblicas* or student houses. A steep staircase leads to a number of antiquated but com-fortable rooms, some with bath-rooms. A hearty breakfast is served.
🔁 214 A4 ☒ Rua das Flores 18
☎ 239 835 175; http://casapombal.com

Quinta das Lágrimas €€€–€€€€
Famous for receiving the Duke of Wellington in 1808, this luxurious hotel is set in 12ha (29.5 acres) of wooded parkland, with a pool, a spa and a golf academy (featuring a 9-hole pitch-and-putt and a driving range). Inside the main house, the décor is elegant and the bedrooms huge. Rooms in the modern spa wing are minimalist-chic. There's also a restaurant and a cellar with more than 600 vintages. The tragic legend of Inês and Pedro (➤ 118, 126) played out behind the hotel.
🔁 214 A4 ☒ Rua António Augusto Gonçalves
☎ 239 802 380; www.quintadaslagrimas.pt

OURÉM

Pousada Ourém €€–€€€
This charming, renovated *pousada*, (➤ 19, 39) is a good base from which to visit Fátima and Tomar. An historic walking route leads around the town. The rooms are spacious and comfortable, and the pool is

open in summer. The *pousada*'s restaurant offers local specialities.
🔁 214 A2 ☒ Largo João Manso, Castelos
☎ 249 540 930; www.pestana.com

TOMAR

Estalagem de Santa Iria €–€€
This is the best choice, especially if tranquillity are your criteria. The unpretentious inn, with 14 bright, spacious rooms, is idyllically located on a wooded island in the middle of the town. The dining room serves delicious, well-cooked dishes.
🔁 214 A2 ☒ Avenida Marquês de Tomar
☎ 249 313 326; www.estalagemsantairia.com

SERRA DA ESTRELA

Hotel Casa das Penhas Douradas €€€–€€€€
This fancy, 3-star designer hotel sits at a lofty altitude of 1,500m (4,921ft) in the "Star Mountain Range". It's furnished with numerous chic pieces from Scandinavia. The restaurant uses seasonal and regional produce to create some equally stylish cui-sine. The indoor pool, the sauna and the massage treatments are tempting on cooler days.
🔁 215 D5 ☒ Penhas Douradas
☎ 275 981 045; www.casadaspenhasdouradas.pt

BUÇACO

Hotel Palace do Bussaco €€€€
The Buçaco Forest (➤ 133), where Napoleon suffered a major defeat in the Peninsular Wars, benefits from a microclimate and has been under papal protection since the

1800s. The hotel was built as a royal hunting lodge just before the monarchy was abolished in 1910, but it's still fit for a sovereign. The mock-Manueline palace houses 60 luxurious rooms and suites, a fabulous dining room and some impressive *azulejos*. The cellar is one of Portugal's best.

🕂 214 A5 ✉ Mata do Buçaco, Luso
☎ 231 937 970; www.themahotels.pt

ÓBIDOS

Casa das Senhoras Rainhas €€€

The whitewashed walls make this hotel feel like a haven of peace and relaxation. The building itself, right next to the old city walls, has been perfectly renovated and preserved. The interior is a luxurious space with good sized, well-appointed bedrooms, a large terrace for al fresco dining and a cosy drawing room

with a fireplace. Look out for deals on their homepage!

🕂 213 E1 ✉ Rua do Padre Nunes Tavares 6
☎ 262 955 360;
www.hotelcasasenhorasrainhas.pt

Pousada Castelo Óbidos €€€€

The fantastic views from this magnificent site justify the price of staying here alone. With a selection of just 17 rooms, it's one of the most prestigious *pousadas* to be found in Portugal. The D. Dinis suite stretches out over two storeys in the eyrie tower. Exuberant tapestries enhance the romantic atmosphere in the medieval interior. The rooms are comfortable and well appointed. Traditional meals are served in the charming refectory. The ambience is tasteful throughout.

🕂 213 E1 ✉ Paço Real
☎ 210 407 630; www.pestana.com

Where to...
Eat and Drink

Prices
Expect to pay per person for a three-course meal, excluding drinks and tips.
€ under €20   €€ €21–€30   €€€ €31–€40   €€€€ over €40

COIMBRA

Arcadas €€€€

The atmosphere is never anything but elegant in this gourmet restaurant at the Quinta das Lágrimas Hotel (► 135). Local, seasonal ingredients make up the major components of the refined dishes on offer. The waiters are happy to suggest suitable wines. Tables can be reserved online via their website.

 Insider Tip

🕂 214 A4
✉ Rua António Augusto Gonçalves
☎ 239 802 380; www.quintadaslagrimas.pt
🕐 Daily 7:30pm–10:30pm

Café Santa Cruz €

University students keep this wonderfully atmospheric café-bar buzzing, especially in the evening. It is housed in the former sacristy of the 16th-century Igreja Santa Cruz. Coffee, wine, beer and snacks are served in a fabulous vaulted room – stone walls and leather benches. The superb *esplanada* (terrace) is packed out in summer.

🕂 214 A4
✉ Praça 8 de Maio
☎ 239 833 617;
www.cafesantacruz.com
🕐 Daily 7am–midnight

Fangas Mercearia Bar €

This is just the place for an informal dinner. Occupying an old grocery, with bistro-style tables, it's an atmospheric spot to snack on *tapas,* such as tangy salami, cured ham, cheese, and tuna in tomato sauce, which you can pair with top-notch regional wines.

🕂 214 A4 ⊠ Rua Fernandes Tomás 45–49
☎ 934 093 636; http://fangas.pt
🕔 Tue–Thu 12:30–3:30, Fri, Sat 12:30–4 and 7:30–1am, Sun 12:30–4, 7:30–midnight

A Taberna €€

This eatery has been a reliable source of traditional food for more than three decades. The tables are spaced out at comfortable intervals. Try such house specialities as grilled cod or kid goat from the oven.

🕂 214 A4
⊠ Rua dos Combatentes da Grande Guerra 86
☎ 239 716 265; www.restauranteataberna.com
🕔 Tue–Sun 12:30am–3pm and Mon–Sat 7:30pm–10:30pm

O Trovador €€–€€€

All kinds of regional specialities are available here, including *chanfana* (goat in a wine sauce) and a selection of fish (gilthead seabream is a favourite choice). The wine list is top notch, with local Bairradas alongside vintages from all over Portugal. The mix of delightful décor (think wood panelling and crisp white linen), charming service and great food make this restaurant the best in the Old Town.

🕂 214 A4 ⊠ Largo da Sé Velha 17
☎ 239 825 475 🕔 Mon–Sat noon–3, 5:30–10

ALCOBAÇA

Restaurante Antonio Padeiro €€–€€€

Going strong since 1938, this inviting restaurant is just steps from the monastery. Sit on the terrace or in the contemporary cellar restaurant for well-prepared regional cuisine. The generous *couvert* (appetiser plate, ▶ 42) of cured meats, cheese and garlicky dips is followed by specialities such as *cabrito no forno,* (oven-baked goat) and *frango na púcara,* a hearty chicken stew flavoured with garlic, pepper and Port wine. Round out with *trouxos de ovos,* a rich, sticky convent dessert made from eggs and sugar.

🕂 213 E2 ⊠ Rua Dom Maur Cocheril 27
☎ 262 582 295; www.antoniopadeiro.com
🕔 Daily noon–3:30, 7–10:30

O Cantinho €€–€€€

This is a favoured local, with friendly owners and a good range of hearty meals that are based on traditional, regional ingredients. Try the chicken casserole, a speciality of the house. There are some lighter snacks and *tapas*-style meals available, too.

🕂 213 E2
⊠ Rua Engenheiro Bernardo Vila Nova 2
☎ 262 583 471 🕔 Mon–Sat 9am–11pm

TOMAR

O Tabuleiro €

For simple Portuguese fare and a warm welcome, head to this unassuming family-run place close to the main square. It's a laid-back spot for grilled fish and other regional dishes, such as bean casserole with pork and roast lamb. If you aren't feeling very hungry, opt for a "*meia dose,*" or small portion.

🕂 214 A2 ⊠ Rua Serpa Pinto 140–148
☎ 249 312 771 🕔 July–Sep Mon–Sat noon–11; Oct–June Mon–Sat noon–2, 7–11

FÁTIMA

Palatus €€

This good, dependable restaurant at the four-star Lux Fatima Hotel is located just a few minutes' walk from the area round the famous sanctuary itself.

🕂 213 F2 ⊠ Avenida D. José Alves Correia da Silva, Lt. 2, Urb. das Azinheiras
☎ 249 530 690; www.luxhotels.pt
🕔 Daily 12:30–3, 7:30–10

Where to…
Shop

MARKETS

Viseu holds a market (*feira*) on Avenida dos Capitães every Tuesday, and there's a *feira* in **Tomar** on Fridays. Some smaller towns also have a *feira* once a week or every fortnight; head to the nearest local tourist office to find out more. You can stock up on marinated olives, cheese, sausages, etc., in the small market building in Rua 13 de Maio in **Fátima**, and buy organic produce on Saturdays at the Mercadinho do Botânico (Botanical Garden) in **Coimbra**.

CRAFTS

Óbidos has ceramic and craft shops along Rua Direita – try the **Centro de Artesanato**.

Ruas Ferreira Borges and **Visconde da Luz** are Coimbra's main shopping streets, lined with boutiques and shops.

Various artisans are still hard at work in the region around the city. **Armando Moita Domingues** in Ameal (Rua da Fonte 109; tel: 239 981 442, http://amdomingues.no.sapo. pt) specializes in ceramics, while **Mário Ferreira** in Eiras (Rua do Santo Cristo 50; tel: 239 439 355) weaves baskets.

FOOD & DRINK

Garrafeira de Celas (R. Bernardo de Albuquerque 64; www.garra-feiradecelas.pt) in **Coimbra** has has an excellent range of wines.

The **Pastelaria Arco Iris** deserves its reputation for superb pastries (Av. Fernão Magalhães 22; http://pastelariaarcoiris.co).

Buy bottles of Dão wine from Viseu's grocers.

You can get your hands on *queijos da serra* (mountain cheeses, ▶ 31) in such places as Sabugueiro in the Serra da Estrela.

Where to…
Go Out

SPORT & OUTDOOR PURSUITS

Surfing is first class at **Buarcos** near Figueira da Foz.

In **Aveiro**, rent bikes from **BUGA** (Praça do Mercado Manuel Firminho; free, leave a form of ID as a deposit).

Hiking in the **Serra da Estrela** (▶ 119–120) is great, and trails well marked.

There are several **spas** in the region, such as the **Termas de Monfortinho** (www.termasde portugal.pt).

FESTIVALS

Coimbra's Queima das Fitas (Ribbon Burning) occurs in May.

Don't miss **Aveiro's Festa da Ria**, in July, when the distinctive *moliceiro* boats are decorated.

"Holy Bathing" can be witnessed at **Figueira da Foz** on and around **St John's Day** (24 June).

MUSIC & NIGHTLIFE

Nightlife is focused around **Coimbra** and **Figueira da Foz**. If you're looking for a good night-club, head to **Revive Fig. Foz** (Rua Cândido dos Reis 49).

Coimbra's **Ocean's Bar** (Avenida Calouste Gulbenkian 22 b) is a popular destination that sometimes features live music.

The Alentejo

 **Little Treats**

Rattle My Bones
The walls and ceilings of the **Capela dos Ossos** (Chapel of Bones) in Évora (► 146) are decorated with human remains!

Prehistoric Premises
The **Cromeleque dos Almendres** (► 146) is a unique megalithic site in an isolated location in the Alentejo.

Cheers!
Enjoy some Alentejo wines and visit the cellars that produce them (near Estremoz (► 152) and Beja (► 154), for example).

Getting Your Bearings

The Alentejo ("Beyond the Tagus") is a sun-baked plain that stretches across southern Portugal, occupying land between the River Tagus and the Algarve. This is both the largest and the most sparsely inhabited region of Portugal, where just 12 per cent of the population are scattered across a third of the country in isolated hamlets and small market towns. It is a region whose proud people share a strong sense of identity, expressed through their music, rural traditions and hearty country cooking.

The landscape of the Alentejo is almost entirely man-made and agricultural. The Romans established vast feudal estates (*latifúndios*) here to grow olives, vines and wheat, many of which survived right up to the 1974 revolution. Even today, when many of these estates have become co-operatives, whitewashed farmhouses surrounded by vineyards are still a familiar sight. Wine and wheat remain important products, but the region is now best known for its cork oaks and the cork industry. Cork isn't just used to seal wine bottles – it serves as fantastic insulation and can be transformed into handbags, purses, belts, hats and a great deal more besides.

Alongside the wide open spaces and strong elemental colours of the landscape, the region has also made some important gourmet contributions to Portugal. The most famous of these is the Alentejo black pig.

Upper Alentejo in particular has several interesting sights, from the Renaissance city of Évora to the marble towns of Estremoz and Vila Viçosa, and the hilltop villages of Monsaraz and Marvão. The Moorish history of the region is more evident in Lower Alentejo, in towns like Mértola and Serpa, with their low, whitewashed, blue-trimmed houses.

Looking down on the walled hilltop village of Monsaraz

Don't Miss

At Your Leisure

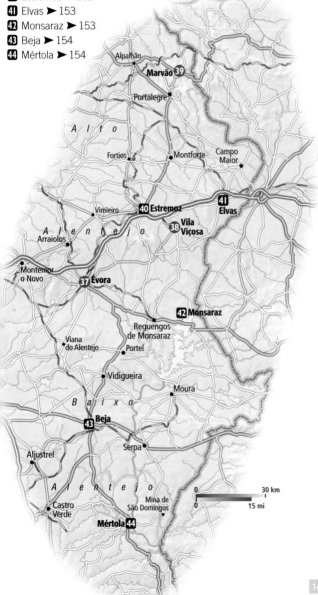

Perfect Days in ...

Two Perfect Days

Experience a different side of the Alentejo by taking a drive around the region. If time isn't on your side, try our two-day itinerary for size. We'll make sure you don't miss any of the highlights. For more information see the main entries (➤ 144–154).

Day 1

Morning
Walk around the walled city of **37 Évora** (➤ 144). Climb to the Roman temple, then visit the cathedral, museum and Capela dos Ossos (Chapel of Bones) before lunch at one of the cafés on Praça do Giraldo.

Afternoon
Leave Évora on the N18 in the direction of **43 Beja** (➤ 154). When the road to Beja turns right, keep ahead on the N256 to Reguengos de Monsaraz. Turn left here, following signs to Monsaraz across a landscape of vineyards and olive groves. Just beyond the pottery-producing village of São Pedro de Corval, look out for Rocha dos Namorados (Lovers' Rock), a prehistoric *menhir* (stone) standing beside the road. Continue to **42 Monsaraz** (➤ 143), visible on its hill across the plain.

Evening
Spend the night in quiet Monsaraz. Admire superb views from its 13th-century castle walls over the plains and the new **Alqueva Dam** (➤ 153). Book ahead for a room at **Casa Rural Santo Condestável** (➤ 156).

Day 2

Morning
Retrace your route back to Reguengos de Monsaraz and follow signs north to Alandroal and the regal town of Vila Viçosa on the N255. Arriving in **38 Vila Viçosa** (left, ➤ 148), park outside the old royal palace, once home to the Dukes of Bragança, and go exploring. Then wander up to

the castle and down to the town centre. Have lunch beside the orange trees and the marble fountain on Praça da República.

Afternoon

The road from Vila Viçosa to Borba leads past the quarries that are the source of the local marble. Turn right in Borba to reach the N4, passing more quarries on your way to **40 Estremoz** (➤ 152). Drive up to the castle at the top of the town for a drink at the **Pousada da Rainha Santa Isabel** (➤ 156) and visit the municipal museum to admire the pottery. Leave Estremoz on the IP2, go north to Portalegre, bypass Portalegre and turn right towards **39 Marvão** (➤ 150), whose hilltop castle (below) dominates the view as you approach. Leave your car outside the village and walk up to the castle in time to enjoy the sunset walk around its walls.

Evening

Stay the night at the **Pousada Marvão** (➤ 155), or ask at the tourist office (➤ 151) about rooms in private houses in Marvão and celebrate your arrival with a hearty Alentejan meal of roast lamb or goat.

③⑦ Évora

With its idyllic alleyways, shady squares, fountains and Renaissance mansions, the largest city in the Alentejo makes a good place for a stroll. Founded by the Romans, strengthened by the Moors and wrested back from them by Geraldo Sempavor (Gerald the Fearless) for Afonso Henriques (➤ 80), Évora rose to prominence in the 15th and 16th centuries as a centre of the arts and learning – a reputation that survives to this day.

The Romans built their walled city of *Ebora Cerealis* high on a hill above the Alentejo plain. At the summit of the town, they erected the temple of Diana, now the **Templo Romano** and the best-preserved Roman monument in Portugal.

Used as a slaughterhouse during the nineteenth century, the granite columns and marble capitals of this second-century temple have been restored today. There's a small park directly opposite.

Convento dos Lóios

All the main sights are within the walled town, a UNESCO World Heritage Site. Directly behind the temple, the **Convento dos Lóios** is a 15th-century monastery that has been converted into an appealing *pousada* (➤ 155), where you dine in the cloisters and sleep in the remodelled monks' cells. Even if you're not staying, it's worth going in to admire the Gothic cloisters and the Manueline (➤ 18) chapter-house door.

The attached church, the **Igreja dos Lóios**, was the private chapel of the dukes of Cadaval, who are buried

The Templo Romano illuminated at night

Carved apostles on the door of the cathedral

beneath marble tombstones. The nave is lined with floor-to-ceiling *azulejos* (➤ 32) depicting the life of a former patriarch of Venice. You can peek through a pair of grilles in the floor to see a medieval cistern and an ossuary of human bones.

The Cathedral

Completed in around 1250, the **Sé** (cathedral) has a fortress-like Romanesque appearance similar to the one in Coimbra (➤ 119). A Gothic portal decorated with carved figures of the Apostles stands between two strangely mismatched towers. Once inside, you'll see marble every-where – in the lectern, the pulpit and the high altar. You can't fail to miss the 16th-century organ and the marble-clad chancel. A separate entrance leads into the **Museu de Arte Sacra**, whose treasures include a carved ivory Madonna in the form of a mini triptych and what's believed to be a relic of the True Cross. You also shouldn't leave without seeing the **Gothic cloister** and walking out onto the 🔢 **roof of the cathedral** for views over Évora and a close-up look at the building's lantern and towers.

Insider Tip

Museu de Évora

The **Museu de Évora** is housed in the former archbishop's palace. It contains Roman bronzes and funerary inscriptions, medieval and Renaissance sculpture and 17th-century *azulejos* from Lisbon.

Among the paintings on the first floor, look for *Holy Virgin with Child* by Álvaro Pires de Évora, painted around 1410. Pires is the earliest identified Portuguese artist, and although a number of his paintings are on show in Pisa and Florence, this is the first to be permanently exhibited in Portugal.

Also here is a 16th-century Flemish polyptych of 13 panels depicting the *Life of the Virgin*, which was previously the cathedral altarpiece.

The Alentejo

The Town

A staircase by the cathedral leads down towards **Largo da Porta de Moura**, one of Évora's most attractive squares. It's home to a Renaissance fountain and 16th-century houses with Manueline-Moorish arcades. Alternatively, take Rua 5 de Outubro (lined with souvenir and craft shops) opposite the cathedral to reach **Praça do Giraldo**, a handsome square with arcades, a marble fountain and café terraces. Despite serving as an execution ground during the Inquisition, it's now a lively square that's sometimes used to stage book fairs, music concerts and open-air theatre today.

A short distance away, the Gothic-Manueline **Igreja de São Francisco** is home to one the most macabre sights to be found anywhere in Portugal. To the right of the façade, with its unusual portico of pointed, rounded and horseshoe arches, a separate entrance leads to a cloister and the **Capela dos Ossos** (Chapel of Bones), whose walls and columns are liberally covered with the skulls, femurs, tibias and other bones of approximately five thousand people. A rather gruesome inscription over the entrance sends a sobering message to visitors: *Nós ossos, que aqui estamos, pelos vossos esperamos* ("Our bones are waiting here for your bones to arrive").

For something completely different, take a walk across the square to the **Jardim Público**, and the remains of a 16th-century Moorish-style palace.

About 20km (12.5mi) west of Évora is the enigmatic ⚄ **Cromeleque dos Almendres**, a megalithic complex with some of the oldest prehistoric remains in Europe. The elliptical site consists of 95 menhirs (standing stones), and is said to date back to 3,000 or 4,000BC. This striking remnant of the distant past will also interest historically-minded kids.

The drive there runs via the village of Guadalupe (where the road becomes a track). You'll also see the 4m (13ft)-tall

Praça do Giraldo, the heart of the Old Town

Menir dos Almendres signposted along the last stretch of the route (down a short footpath leading from the track).

TAKING A BREAK

There are **outdoor cafés** on Praça do Giraldo, in the Jardim Público and the gardens by the Templo Romano.

✚ 217 F4 ℹ️ Praça do Giraldo
☎ 266 777 071; www.cm-evora.pt/guiaturistico, www.visitalentejo.pt

Igreja dos Lóios
✉ Rua Augusto Filipe Simões ☎ 967 979 763
🕐 Tue–Sun 10–1, 2–5:30
💶 €4, combined ticket with Palácio dos Duques de Cadaval: €7

Sé
✉ Largo Marquês de Marialva ☎ 266 759 330
🕐 Daily 9–noon, 2–4:30 (sometimes open without a lunch break in summer)
💶 Cathedrale: €1.50; cathedral & cloisters: €2.50

Museu de Arte Sacra
✉ Entrance inside the cathedral itself
🕐 Tue–Sun 9–11:30, 2–4 💶 €4

Museu de Évora
✉ Largo do Conde de Vila Flor ☎ 266 73 04 80; http://museudevora.imc-ip.pt
🕐 Tue 2:30–6, Wed–Sun 10–6 💶 €3; free 1st Sun of the month

Igreja da São Francisco/Capela dos Ossos
✉ Praça 1 de Maio ☎ 266 704 521
🕐 Mon–Sat 9–12:45, 2:30–5:45, Sun 10–12:45, 2:30–17:30
💶 €2, photo permit €1

INSIDER INFO

- If you're driving, it is best to **park on the outskirts** and walk in.
- Head to Évora's **Fórum Eugénio de Almeida** to see some exhibitions of contemporary art in an Old Town setting (Largo do Conde da Vila Flor; tel: 266 748 350; www. fundacaoeugeniodealmeida.pt; Tue–Sun 10–7).
- Visit the small **Alentejo Wine Route visitor centre** to learn all about the region's wines, cellars and wine routes. You can also taste some wines, usually free of charge (Praça Joaquim António de Aguiar 20–21; Mon 2–7, Tue–Fri 11–7, Sat 10–1; tel: 266 746 489; www.vinhosdoalentejo.pt).

Insider Tip

- A steep hill behind the cathedral and the Museu de Évora leads to the **old Jesuit university**, founded by Cardinal Henrique, the future king, in 1559. The university was closed down in 1759 by the Marquês de Pombal, but is now open, so you can wander around its beautiful tiled courtyard.

In more depth Take a walk through the old Moorish quarter, **Mouraria**, with its whitewashed houses and lamplit, cobbled streets. From beneath the gardens in front of the temple, Rua dos Fontes drops steeply to Largo do Avis, beside the only remaining medieval gateway to the walled town.

㊳ Vila Viçosa

The power and wealth of the Portuguese kings is on display in Vila Viçosa, the seat of Portugal's last ruling dynasty, the dukes of Bragança. Built of marble, this is a prosperous town whose shining "white gold" can be seen everywhere.

Begin at **Terreiro do Paço**, the vast square in front of the Paço Ducal. A statue of João IV on horseback stands at the centre. The palace, fronted with marble, dominates the square. To one side is the royal chapel; to the other, Convento das Chagas, the mausoleum of the duchesses of Bragança, now a *pousada* (▶ 15–16). Across the square is the Mosterio dos Agostinhos, where the dukes are buried.

The **Paço Ducal** can only be visited on a guided tour, with further charges to see the armoury, treasury, Chinese porcelain and Colecção de Carruagens (Coach Museum). Most interesting are the private apartments of Dom Carlos (Portugal's penultimate king) and Dona Amelia, abandoned on the day of Carlos' assassination in 1908, with the table still set for dinner, family portraits and Dona Amelia's sketches on the walls. A large park outside the palace is home to deer and wild boar.

The **Colecção de Carruagens**, in the Royal Stables, contains beautifully maintained coaches, landaus and state carriages from the 18th–20th centuries. This is an annex to the popular Museu Nacional dos Coches in Lisbon, and exhibitions are sometimes exchanged between the two sites.

From the Terreiro do Paço, the **Avenida dos Duques de Bragança** leads towards the old walled town, dominated by a 13th-century *castelo*. This castle was the original residence of the dukes of Bragança and has a small archaeological museum, with a stash of Roman finds. It's well worth visiting to get a peek behind the scenes of the castle's chambers and tunnels.

A statue of Dom João IV, the first of Bragança's kings, stands before the Paço Ducal

THE DUKES OF BRAGANÇA

The dukes of Bragança were the first to put Vila Viçosa on the map: the title of Bragança was created in 1442 for an illegitimate son of João I of Avis; the second duke, Dom Fernando, moved his court to Vila Viçosa; and the fourth duke, Dom Jaime, began building the Paço Ducal (Ducal Palace) in 1501. Vila Viçosa became the finest address in Portugal, with banquets, balls and bullfights held in the palace. All that changed in 1640 when the eighth duke, João IV, reluctantly accepted the throne, ending 60 years of Spanish rule. The Braganças ruled Portugal until the fall of the monarchy in 1910 and continued to live in the palace, though many of its treasures were taken to other locations.

TAKING A BREAK

O Framar (Praça da República) serves regional dishes.

➕ 218 B4
ℹ️ Praça da República
☎ 268 889 317; www.cm-vilavicosa.pt

Paço Ducal

✉️ Terreiro do Paço
☎ 268 980 659; www.fcbraganca.pt
◉ Mon afternoon only; July/Aug: Tue–Fri 10–1, 2:30–6, Sat, Sun 9:30–1, 2:30–6; April–June, Sep: Tue–Fri 10–1, 2:30–5:30, Sat, Sun until 6; Oct–March: Tue–Fri 10–1, 2–5, Sat, Sun from 9:30. Last entry one hour before closing.
💶 Paço Ducal: €6; with additional charges for the armoury (Armaria): €3, porcelain collection (Colecção de Porcelana Chinesa): €2.50, treasury (Tesouro): €2.50, coach museum (Colecção de Carruagens): €3

The main street is overlooked by the 13th-century castle

INSIDER INFO

■ **Accommodation** in Vila Viçosa is not plentiful, although the tourist office should be able to help you find somewhere.

■ What looks like a pair of red garage doors at the end of a row of houses on Avenida dos Duques de Bragança opens up to reveal a **Passo**, one of a series of 16th-century Stations of the Cross remodelled in the 18th century with a marble portal and *azulejo* (► 18) tiles depicting scenes from the life of Christ.

㊴ Marvão

The most spectacular of all Portugal's hilltop villages perches like an eagle's nest on a rocky ridge 862m (2,827ft) up in the Serra de São Mamede. The castle and medieval walls seem to grow out of the rock, and it is clear that this must have been a near-impregnable fortress. During the 16th century, Marvão had a population of more than 1,400, but today fewer than 500 people live here.

The Romans and then the Moors came here – the village takes its name from Ibn Maruán, the 9th-century Islamic Lord of Coimbra (Marvão comes from Maruán). After the Christian conquest, Dom Dinis, King of Portugal (1279–1325), fortified the castle here. It was to become one of a long chain of defensive outposts protecting the border with Spain.

Marvão sits surrounded by fortified walls on the top of a hill

Unless you are staying the night, it is best to park outside the village and enter on foot through the main gate, **Porta de Rodão**. From Praça do Pelourinho, with its 16th-century pillory, Rua do Espírito Santo, known for its whitewashed houses with wrought-iron balconies, leads into Rua do Castelo, which leads to the castle.

Rua do Castelo – a Living Museum

The Gothic and Renaissance architecture of Rua do Castelo has been preserved untouched during the centuries of Marvão's decline with just a little restoration work here and there. You can climb onto the walls and make a complete circuit of the battlements, turrets and towers, but it's easier to walk up to the castle along the village streets. Originally dating from the 13th century but rebuilt almost from scratch in the 17th century, the 🏰 **castle** is truly magnificent – younger explorers will think so, too! Held high on a rocky crag, the town's most visible icon was constructed to withstand assaults from Spanish invaders. Two fortified gates lead to a courtyard where you can climb onto the parapet for **views over the village**.

Marvão was one of a chain of fortified towns and villages along the Portuguese border with Spain

Breaching a second line of defence, you come to another courtyard, which contains the castle keep. The view from here are impressive: to the north are the snow-capped peaks of the Serra da Estrela (➤ 124); to the south, the mountains of the Serra de São Mamede; to the west, the Alentejo countryside; to the east, Spain.

Outside the castle walls, the **Museu Municipal** in the 13th-century **church of Santa Maria** displays folk costumes, archaeological finds and religious art from the Middle Ages.

TAKING A BREAK

Casa do Povo in Travessa do Chabouco, has a pretty terrace and offers well-prepared, filling Alentejan cuisine (tel: 245 993 160; 9am–10pm, Thu until 2pm).

➕ 215 E1   ℹ️ Largo da Silveirinha   ☎ 245 993 456; www.cm-marvao.pt

Museu Municipal
✉ Largo de Santa Maria   ☎ 245 909 132
🕐 Tue–Sun 9–12:30, 2–5:30   💶 €1.30

INSIDER INFO

- Try to stay overnight to watch the **sunset** from the castle walls and enjoy the evening peace of the village after the day-trippers have left.   *Insider Tip*
- As well as the **Pousada Marvão** (➤ 155), there are several **private houses** with rooms to let – ask at the tourist office.
- **Chestnut trees** thrive in this area, and a festival (*Feira da Castanha*) is held in November that sees the village come alive with music, wine and chestnut roasting.
- Walk down the steps inside the castle entrance to see a **monumental cistern** that is capable of storing six months' water.
- The surrounding **Serra de São Mamede** is a natural park with Roman and Neolithic remains and wildlife including griffon vultures, red deer and Europe's largest colony of bats. Also here is **Castelo de Vide**, with an attractive old Jewish quarter, a golf course and its own spring.

At Your Leisure

The picturesque medieval village of Monsaraz with its former Knights Templar castle offers sweeping views out over the Alentejo

40 Estremoz

The largest of the Alentejo "marble" towns seems to have an extra sheen of white as marble from the local quarries is used as an everyday building material. Life here centres on the Rossio Marquês de Pombal, a huge square where one of Portugal's biggest markets is held on Saturdays, selling local goodies like ewe's cheese, olive oil and *chouriço* (salami).

Insider Tip

Although now famous Pousada Castelo Estremoz (► 156), you can

THREE OF THE BEST... ALENTEJAN CUISINE

- **Ensopado de borrego** – lamb stew served on slices of bread.
- **Porco à alentejana** – Alentejo pork stewed with clams.
- **Sopa alentejana** – soup with bread, garlic, coriander and poached egg.

also visit parts of the 13th-century **castle** built by Dom Dinis for his future wife, Isabel of Aragón. As queen, Isabel became known for her devotion to the poor and she was sainted after her death. Her story is told in *azulejos* (► 32) in the Capela da Rainha Santa Isabel, including that of the Miracle of the Roses. Her husband disapproved of her giving alms, so she hid bread in the folds of her skirt where he would not see it. When he became suspicious and challenged her, she opened her skirt and the bread had miraculously turned into roses. A marble statue of the saint stands on the castle terrace, from where there are views to Évoramonte.

The **Museu Municipal** opposite features folk art in marble, cork and oak, and *bonecos* (terracotta figurines for which Estremoz is famous).

Head to the tourist office to find out which wine cellars are currently open to visitors in the surrounding area. There are plenty to choose from, including Bacalôa, Adega do Monte Branco and Encostas de Estremoz.

➕ 218 A4 ℹ️ Rossio Marquês de Pombal 88A
☎ 268 339 227; www.cm-estremoz.pt

Museu Municipal
✉️ Largo Dom Dinis ☎ 268 339 200 🕐 Tue–Sun 9–6 💶 €2

41 Elvas

Elvas is a heavily fortified frontier town, which sits just 12km (7.4mi) from Portugal's border with Spain and 15km (9.3mi) from the Spanish citadel at Badajoz. Captured by Afonso Henriques in 1166, retaken by the Moors, and finally seized by Christian forces in 1226, Elvas has been besieged many times but only once been taken by Spanish troops.

Designed by Vaubun, a French military engineer, the star-shaped fortifications surrounding the town largely date from the 1600s. They're supplemented by two fortresses, one of which, the **Forte de Santa Luzia** (home to the Museu Militar) is open to visitors.

The streets of the Old Town radiate from Praça da República. At one end stands the **Igreja de Nossa Senhora da Assunção**, which had cathedral status until 1882, when the town lost its bishopric. The fortified church dates back to the 16th century and ornate Manueline touches (➤ 18) can be seen on the south portal, though much of its design is a potpourri of 17th- and 18th-century styles.

Behind the church, Largo de Santa Clara is an attractive triangular "square" with a Manueline marble pillory, still with its original iron hooks to which prisoners were tied.

On one side, the **Igreja de Nossa Senhora da Consolação** looks plain

🚣 MESSING ABOUT IN BOATS

Europe's largest manmade reservoir at **Alqueva** in the southern Alentejo has become a popular day trip destination, particularly for families with kids (www.alqueva.com, www.roteirodo alqueva.com). During the warmer months, Alquevaline (tel: 285 254 099; www.alquevaline.com) run boat tours starting from the south side of the water next to the big dam. You can also rent boats to take out yourself.

but the interior is extraordinary, an octagonal chapel with painted marble columns and blue-and-yellow *azulejos* lining the walls. Its layout was inspired by a Knights Templar church that once stood close by.

Just outside of the town, there is a large reservoir, Barragem da Caia, where you can enjoy fishing and swimming in attractive surroundings.

➕ 218 C5 ℹ️ Praça da República
☎ 268 622 236; www.cm-elvas.pt

Museu Militar/Forte de Santa Luzia
☎ 268 628 357
🕐 Tue 1–5, Wed–Sun 10–5 💶 €3

42 Monsaraz

Monsaraz would be just another attractive hilltop village were it not for the famously fantastic views enjoyed by the day trippers who flock here in their droves. The picturesque little settlement can be seen for miles around.

There are two parallel streets – **Rua Direita**, with the parish church, the Igreja Matriz, and 16th-century houses, and **Rua de Santiago**, which has a more lived-in feel, with shops and restaurants. Rua Direita leads to the 13th-century **castle**, once a Knights Templar fortress. The ramparts have unparalleled views over the village and the Alentejo countryside.

➕ 218 B3 ℹ️ Rua Direita ☎ 927 597 316

You can climb the 40m (131ft) high walls of the castle keep at Beja

43 Beja

The capital of Lower Alentejo is a pleasing place with around 24,000 inhabitants. It was founded by Julius Caesar as *Pax Julia* to commemorate a peace (*pax*) treaty between the Romans and the Lusitani tribe. Beja Airport has finally put this beautiful Portuguese city on the tourist map. The settlement's rather sober fringes stand in contrast to the Old Town with its whitewashed houses and Praça da República.

The most striking monument is the 13th-century **castelo** (castle); you can climb the keep for views over the Alentejo wheatlands.

Beja is best known as the home of Mariana Alcoforado, the nun whose (possibly fictional) love letters to a French cavalry officer were published as *Lettres Portugaises* in France in 1669. The convent where she lived, Nossa Senhora da Conceição, is now the **Museu Regional**, with many interesting prehistoric and Roman finds.

Of more interest are the convent buildings, especially the baroque chapel, tiled cloisters and 16th-century Hispano-Arab

azulejos (► 32) in the chapter house.

Another convent is now the Pousada de São Francisco (► 156).

You'll find lots of wine cellars in the surrounding area that gladly welcome visitors. Head to a tourist office to find out which ones are currently open.

🗺 218 A2
ℹ️ Largo Dr Lima Faleiro (in the castle courtyard)
☎ 284 311 913; www.cm-beja.pt

Castelo
✉ Largo Dr Lima Faleiro ☎ 284 311 912
🕐 Tower (Torre): daily, April–Oct 9:30–noon, 2–5:30; Nov–March 9:30–noon, 2–4:30
💶 €2.50; free 1st Sun of the month

Museu Regional
✉ Largo da Conceição
☎ 284 323 351; www.museuregionaldebeja.pt
🕐 Tue–Sun 9:30–12:30, 2–5:15
💶 €2; free Sun

44 Mértola

This pretty little walled town at the confluence of the Guadiana and Oeiras rivers has a long history as a trading port at the highest navigable point on the Guadiana.

Several small museums dotted around Mértola are devoted to its Roman, Islamic and Portuguese past. You can visit all of them on one ticket (also valid for the castle keep with its views over the rooftops). Don't miss the parish church, converted from a mosque at the end of the 12th century, whose *mihrab* (niche facing east to Mecca) is visible behind the altar. The arches and columns retain a strong Islamic feel.

🗺 219 E1
ℹ️ Rua da Igreja 31
☎ 286 610 109; www.cm-mertola.pt

Museums
☎ http://museus.cm-mertola.pt
🕐 Tue–Sun 9:45–1, 2–6:15 (summer), 9:15–1, 2–5:45 rest of year
💶 single ticket: €2, combined ticket: €5

Where to…
Stay

Prices
Expect to pay per person for a three-course meal, excluding drinks and tips.

€ under €20   €€ €21–€30   €€€ €31–€40   €€€€ over €40

ÉVORA

Monte da Serralheira €
So near and yet so far from the city, this country estate on 130ha (320ac) of land approximately 3km (2mi) outside town is a great place to recharge. The selection of nicely furnished rooms and apartments are good value for money. The accommodation is ably run by Lucia and George, your friendly Dutch hosts. Print out the instructions on how to get there from the website in advance.
✚ 217 F3
☎ 266 741 286; www.monteserralheira.com

Pousada dos Lóios €€€–€€€€
The fabulous 15th-century monastery of the Lóios has an excellent restaurant in the ornate cloisters, and is one of the country's leading *pousadas* (► 19, 39). The majestic rooms are furnished with antiques, in particular the "presidential" suite, which has Indo-Portuguese furniture. There is also a good-sized swimming pool. This is the perfect choice if you want to experience staying in an authentic *pousada* while enjoying plenty of modern comforts.
✚ 217 F4
✉ Largo Conde de Vila-Flor
☎ 266 730 070; www.pousadas.pt

Residencial Riviera €–€€
Well located in the centre of town, near to the cathedral square, this modern and well-priced hotel is a good base for exploring the town. The interior and public areas are functional rather than luxurious, but the 21 bedrooms are all a good size and well appointed to ensure a comfortable stay. There is an attractive dining room where a large Alentejo breakfast is served by the friendly staff.
✚ 217 F4
✉ Rua 5 de Outubro 49
☎ 266 737 210; www.riviera-evora.com

VILA VIÇOSA

Casa do Colégio Velho €€–€€€
Tucked down a cobbled lane, this wonderful B&B occupies a 16th-century mansion, commanding terrific views over landscaped gardens and the Old Town. The light, high-ceilinged rooms are scattered with art and antiques, some have wrought-iron bedsteads. All rooms boast flat-screen TVs and marble bathrooms. Take time to relax by the pool and on the *azulejo*-tiled benches in the garden. The generous breakfasts are prepared with regional produce.
✚ 218 B4
✉ Rua Dr Couto Jardim 34
☎ 268 889 430;
www.casadocolegiovelho.com

MARVÃO

Pousada Marvão €€–€€€
Cool in summer and warm in the winter, like the other whitewashed houses in this pretty hilltop village,

The Alentejo

this well-appointed *pousada* is a delight inside and out. The large spacious rooms and simple dining room look across the beautiful olive trees and cork oaks of the Alentejo. Enjoy the views while sampling local specialities, including excellent cheeses and well-chosen wines.

➕ 215 E1
✉ Rua 24 de Janeiro 7
☎ 245 993 201; www.pestana.com

ESTREMOZ

Pousada Castelo Estremoz €€€

Generally regarded as the most prestigious *pousada*, this is housed in an austere-looking medieval castle (► 152). Four-poster beds, tapestries fit for a museum, entire walls of *azulejos* (► 32) and the long vaulted refectory earn it the epithet of "grandiose". When you are not exploring the local sights, you can relax by the swimming pool and dine on Alentejo specialities accompanied by fine wines from the extensive cellar.

➕ 218 A4
✉ Castelo de Estremoz, Largo Dom Diniz
☎ 268 332 075; www.pestana.com

MONSARAZ

Casa Rural Santo Condestável €

This small country house hotel in the middle of the village is simple but stylishly furnished. Guests get to enjoy the settlement after the day's visitors have gone. The prices are very reasonable, and some of the rooms have great views.

➕ 218 B3 ✉ Rua Direita 4 ☎ 919 970 831;
www.cm-reguengos-monsaraz.pt

BEJA

Pousada Convento Beja €€–€€€

The cells of this ancient Franciscan monastery have been turned into comfortable rooms. Don't be put off by the huge entrance hall – the guest areas are intimate and the pool is popular. The restaurant serves local specialities.

➕ 218 A2 ✉ Largo Dom Nuno Álvares Pereira
☎ 284 313 580; www.pestana.com

Where to...
Eat and Drink

Prices
Expect to pay for a three-course set menu without drinks:
£ under £8   ££ £8–£12   £££ over £12

ÉVORA

Cozinha de Santo Humberto €€–€€€

Évora probably has more reliably excellent restaurants than any other city outside Lisbon. This is one of them. As soon as you head down into the pristine wine cellar you'll be itching to try out the seasonal specialities on offer. The menu includes oven roast lamb (*borrego*

assado no forno), a selection of game (in season – the wild boar ragout is exceptional), and *chispe assado* (roast pork).

➕ 217 F4 ✉ Rua da Moeda 39
☎ 266 704 251 🕐 Fri–Wed noon–3, 7–10

O Cruz €

O Cruz is a simple, down-to-earth eatery with no-nonsense, typical cooking. Depending on the time of year, they might serve lamb and pork dishes, grilled sardines, and traditional bread soup from the Alentejo (*açorda à alentejana*). Sit out on the inviting terrace to dine with a view over the square in front of the Igreja de São Francisco.

➕ 217 F4 ✉ Praça 1 de Maio 20
☎ 266 747 228 ⏰ Fri–Wed 10–10

O Fialho €€€

Justly famous O Fialho is surprisingly simple to look at. What sets the food apart is the use of herbs and spices. *Lombinhos de javali* (medallions of wild boar) are complemented with a hint of rosemary. The roast lamb and – during the hunting season towards the end of the year – the wild rabbit and partridge have an excellent reputation. Attentive service and outstanding wines round off the experience.

Insider Tip

➕ 217 F4 ✉ Travessa das Mascarenhas 14
☎ 266 703 079; www.restaurantefialho.com
⏰ Tue–Sun 1–4, 7–11

VILA VIÇOSA

Taverna dos Conjurados €€–€€€

Classic interior with exposed stone wall and whitewashed walls, this is a deceptively simple restaurant, which serves well-cooked, authentic cuisine. All the food is very fresh and local, and is well regarded by local residents. Expect to sit at the classic wooden tables and enjoy excellent food and hearty portions.

➕ 218 B4 ✉ Largo 25 de Abril
☎ 268 989 530 ⏰ Daily noon–2:30, 7:30–10

ESTREMOZ

Adega do Isaías €€

Huge, age-old amphorae tell you this has long been a wine cellar, and jugs of red are plonked onto every table. This wonderfully down-to-earth place attracts locals from every walk of life interested only in the delicious food, from *pimentos assados* (roast red peppers) to *bolo de mel* (honey cake), via *borrego no forno* (roast lamb) or *estufado de lebre*

(hare stew). Meat and fish are barbecued out on the street.

➕ 218 A4 ✉ Rua do Almeida 21
☎ 268 322 318 ⏰ Mon–Sat noon–3, 7–10:30

ELVAS

A Coluna €

This is a discreet but popular restaurant with a whitewashed interior and white table linen. The menu is simple, and everyone swears by the *cabrito* (goat) and *bacalhau* (salt cod, ▶ 31, 41) dishes and the *cataplana* (▶ 30). It's slightly hidden away from the central square, but soon fills up with locals, so get there early.

➕ 218 C5 ✉ Rua do Cabrito 11
☎ 268 623 728 ⏰ Wed–Mon noon–3, 7–10

MONSARAZ

Lumumba €–€€

Lumumba is located on one of the two main thoroughfares running through this village that looks like an open-air museum. The cooking and décor are both simple and typical of the region. Specialities include lamb (*borrego*) prepared in a variety of different ways.

➕ 218 B3 ✉ Rua Direita 12
☎ 266 557 121 ⏰ Tue–Sun noon–3, 7–9

BEJA

Luiz da Rocha €–€€

If you linger long enough over your coffee, you'll see an interesting cross section of the city as people pop in for a coffee or a beer and a chat. The *queijadas* (cheese-filled cakes) are excellent. Luiz da Rocha isn't just a cafeteria and bakery, however – it's also a restaurant serving lamb and a variety of omelettes. Boasts fair prices and a good location in the main shopping district.

➕ 218 A2
✉ Rua Capitão João Francisco de Sousa 63
☎ 284 323 179; www.luizdarocha.com
⏰ Restaurant: Mon–Sat noon–3:30, 7–10, Sun noon–3:30; Café: Mon–Sat 8–11, Sun 8–8

Where to...
Shop

MARKETS

You'll find **Évora's** small market hall on Praça 1 de Maio below the Igreja de São Francisco. It's a good place to stock up on cheese and fresh vegetables, etc. Praça 1 Maio also hosts a *feira* on Saturdays and Sundays that sells a selection of wares ranging from second-hand books and antiques to bric-à-brac and art.

The **Mercado Municipal** in **Beja** (Mon–Sat 6:30–1) is located on Rua Afonso de Albuquerque.

The **Mercado 25 de Abril** (7–1) is held on Largo do Santo Amaro on Saturdays.

CRAFTS

For carpets, visit **Arraiolos**, 20km (12.5mi) northwest of Évora, where fine, local hand-knotted rugs are sold at workshops at Ilhas; or at several shops, where prices are far lower than in Lisbon.

Rua 5 de Outobro in **Évora** might be touristy, but it's home to a concentrated selection of ceramics and original craft items fashioned from cork, including a variety of bags and hats.

Flôr da Rosa, west of **Portalegre**, is renowned for its pottery.

FOOD & DRINK

This is bread country; the grain is often used as a key ingredient in soups, too. Also buy some Alentejo charcuterie. Look for the *Denominação de Origem Protegida* DOP status to be sure of quality.

Picnic provisions can be bought at Évora's or Beja's markets.

Where to...
Go Out

FESTIVALS

The last third of June is Évora's **Feira de São João**, which combines music and crafts with food. There is also a **film festival** FIKE (www.fikeonline.net) in late October.

In **Elvas**, the Festa de São Mateus features a large procession. It takes place in mid/late September.

Ovibeja – **Beja**'s livestock and agricultural show – is held in April or May.

The Festa da Vinha e do Vinho, a big Alentejo wine festival, comes to **Borba** in November.

SPORT & OUTDOOR PURSUITS

The Atlantic beaches on the west coast are the most dramatic – head for **Zambujeira** and **Odeceixe**.

Skydive Europe offer tandem parachute jumps for daredevils (tel: 210 190 952; www.skydiveeurope.com). The school and the airfield lie 40km (25mi) west of Beja near **Figueira dos Cavaleiros**.

Passeios e Companhia in **Grândola** (Rua 22 de Janeiro 2 A; tel: 269 476 702; www.passeiosecompanhia.com) specialize in bicycle rentals and guided mountain bike tours (through the Serra de Grândola, for example).

NIGHTLIFE

The towns and cities of the Alentejo are known for their peace and quiet rather than their exuberant nightlife. Your best bet is to head to **Évora**; concerts are sometimes held there at the Sociedade Harmonia Eborense (Praça do Giraldo 72).

The Algarve

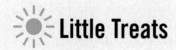 **Little Treats**

Island Living

Head over to the **Ilha de Tavira** (➤ 171), a flat, elongated island blessed with some lengthy expanses of sand.

A Sublime Spot for a Stroll

Take a walk among the typical houses of **Cacela Velha** (➤ 171) for an extremely memorable experience.

Wild Coasts

If raw, natural vistas are your thing, check out the **Costa Vicentina** (➤ 165), a paradise for surfing and coastal walks.

Getting Your Bearings

Sandy beaches and sunny skies. Whitewashed villas with geraniums around the door. Fishing boats and the scent of freshly grilled sardines. These are the classic images of Portugal, and they are also the images of the Algarve.

For many people, the Algarve *is* Portugal, yet this small region at the southwest corner of Europe is, in fact, the least typical of all. The climate is more Mediterranean than Atlantic, the landscape more North African than Portuguese. This was *al-gharb*, the western outpost of Moorish Spain, which held off the Christian Reconquest for a century after the fall of Lisbon. Reminders of the Arab presence are everywhere, from latticed chimneys to the almond trees that carpet the ground with a "snowfall" of white blossom in January.

The Algarve shoreline is neatly divided in two by the provincial capital, Faro. East of here is the *sotavento* (leeward) coast, sheltered by the barrier islands and lagoons of the Ria Formosa. To the west, the *barlavento* (windward) coast is battered by the Atlantic, producing the Algarve's typical rock formations of sandstacks, grottoes, cliffs and coves.

Although the region was levelled by the 1755 earthquake with its epicentre near Lagos, the greatest influence here has been mass tourism, which brings in up to 8 million visitors a year. High-rise resorts, golf courses and waterparks have mushroomed from Faro to Lagos, and some areas have become swamped in concrete. To escape it, head inland to the villages of the Barrocal and the cool mountains of Monchique, or visit the charming towns of Tavira, Silves and Lagos.

Left: Praia dos Pescadores, Albufeira

Right: the Ria Formosa Natural Park seen from the Castelo de Cacela

Getting Your Bearings

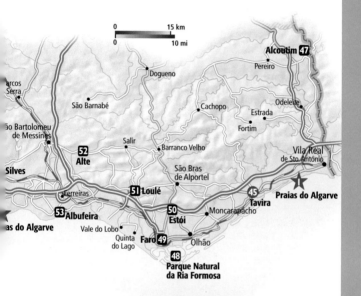

The Algarve

Three Perfect Days

The Algarve is home to a diverse array of landscapes, a wealth of pretty towns and such attractive hinterland regions as the Serra de Monchique. Follow our three-day itinerary and you won't miss any of the highlights. For more information see the main entries (► 164–177).

Day 1

Morning
Explore the elegant Old Town of **45 Tavira** (► 170) with its 18th- and 19th-century town houses. Head up to the castle ruins for some fantastic views before walking down to eat a picnic in the park by the river.

Afternoon and Evening
Catch the ferry to **Ilha de Tavira** (► 164, 171) from Quatro Águas – 2km (1.2mi) east of Tavira – and make your way to the beach. Sample some seafood at a restaurant on the banks Gilão River in the evening.

Day 2

Morning
Leave Tavira on the N125 towards Faro. Stop in Luz da Tavira to see its 16th-century church and *platibanda* houses decorated with floral and geometric motifs. At Quinta de Marim, visit the bird-rich wetlands of the **48 Parque Natural da Ria Formosa** (► 174) before heading to **40 Faro** (► 162) with its beautiful Old Town. Have lunch by the harbour.

Afternoon and Evening
Continue northwest on the N125. Just before Almancil, pull off the road to see the astonishing church of São Lourenço, whose interior is completely covered in blue-and-white *azulejos* (► 32). Arrive at **53 Albufeira** (► 164, 176) in time for a quick sea dip or a bracing walk along the cliff-flanked

beach (left). Albufeira has restaurants to suit every taste and budget, but the traditional food here is salt-baked fish. If you want to splash out, book a table at **Vila Joya** (➤ 180).

Day 3

Morning
Make an early start and head inland through olive and citrus groves towards Paderne and Portela in the foothills of the Barrocal region. Take a brief diversion east on the N124 to see the pretty village of **52 Alte** (➤ 176), renowned for its natural springs, before returning on the same road to **54 Silves** (above, ➤ 176). Walk up to the castle and visit the Gothic cathedral before enjoying a lunch break at Café Inglês (➤ 182).

Afternoon and Evening
Head west on the N124 and right on the N266 to climb to the lush mountains of the **46 Serra de Monchique** (➤ 172). Drive up to the summit of Fóia for great views, then explore the spa village of Caldas de Monchique. Next take a scenic drive through eucalyptus and pinewoods to Aljezur, and follow the N268 south along the wild west coast. You should arrive in ★ **Sagres** (➤ 167) in time to visit the fortress before watching the sun set from ★ **Cabo de São Vicente** (➤ 168).

★ Praias do Algarve

Stretching for 200km (124mi), the Algarve has some of the finest beaches in Europe. You could spend your entire holiday searching for your favourite: from crescents of soft golden sand to tiny coves hidden beneath grottoes and ochre cliffs. There are beaches for families, watersports or for an away-from-it-all feeling – just take your pick.

👪 Family Beaches

Aptly named **Praia Verde** (Green Beach) is reached by crossing a valley of pine trees and walking down through the dunes. The sea here is calm and warm – perfect for small children. This is one of a chain of beaches that stretches from Cacela Velha to Monte Gordo, 2km (1.2mi) east.

In Tavira, take the ferry to reach **Ilha de Tavira** (➤ 171), a popular island beach. The main beach is suitable for families, but be warned that there are some nudist sections further along. Praia do Barril, 4km (2.5mi) away at the island's western end, is usually less crowded.

Albufeira is another classic beach. Walk through the rock tunnel or take the elevator to reach the beach, with sandstacks beneath the cliffs. West of Albufeira is a series of attractive cove beaches, such as Praia de São Rafael and Praia da Galé.

The biggest and possibly most famous beach in the Algarve is **Armação de Pêra.** This superb beach has sand-stacks at one end and flat sands stretching towards Albufeira. The resort is popular with Portuguese families.

Praia da Rocha was the first tourist town in the Algarve, giving it a certain time-worn appeal, although a new paved beachside walk has smartened up the resort. From the old fortress, there are views over the wide beach of sand, with eroded rocks sheltering beneath 70m (230ft) cliffs.

Praia da Dona Ana near Lagos

Sheltered Coves

Praia da Marinha is the largest of the cove beaches around Carvoeiro, a place that's rapidly turning into an extremely popular holiday resort. In summer, you can take boat trips from Carvoeiro to other nearby cove beaches, including Praia do Benagil and Praia Senhora da Rocha. Another perfect cove beach is **Praia da Dona Ana** – it's located just outside Lagos, so can get crowded on summer weekends. You can also take a boat trip to see the grottoes and caves of Ponte da Piedade (➤ 197).

Insider Tip

Perfect for Watersports

Many beaches are popular for watersports. One of the best is 🏨 **Meia Praia,** on the east side of Lagos, which has a long crescent-shaped beach stretching for 4km (2.5mi). Popular with windsurfers, children like this beach too, as there are lots of shells washed up on the sand. Watch the strong currents!

The largest resort to the west is **Praia da Luz**. This beach has windsurfing and diving schools and a splendid beach backed by cliffs at its eastern end. A clifftop path leads past Ponte da Piedade to Lagos (➤ 197). The sheltered, dark sandy cove of **Praia de Odeceixe** on the borders of the Alentejo and the Algarve is also popular with surfers. It sits at the mouth of the Seixe estuary 4km (2.5mi) from the nearest village.

Off the Beaten Track

If you have your own transport, then it is worthwhile heading to some of the more remote beaches, such as **Boca do Rio**, located halfway between Burgau and Salema on the edge of the Budens wetland reserve. This small beach is situated at a river mouth inside the **Costa Vicentina** natural park. You can walk along the cliffs to the beach at Cabanas Velhas.

Alternatively, boats depart from the fishing port of Olhão for the attractive holiday island of **Ilha da Armona**. There are sand dunes on the sheltered, landward side, or you can escape the crowds by walking across to the other side of the island to a fine white-sand beach. You can also camp on the island.

Insider Tip

A boat tour near Lagos

The wave-thrashed west coast known as the Costa Vicentina boasts a string of spectacular beaches, including the remote **Praia da Cordoama**, which can be reached by following a dirt track beneath grey slate cliffs. Popular with surfers, the nearby golden-red beach of **Praia do Castelejo** is slightly more accessible and surrounded by black schist rocks. Alternatively, head for the huge, curving beach of **Praia da Bordeira**,

backed by sand dunes and situated around a lagoon at the mouth of the Bordeira River near Carrapateira. It's a fantastic place to take a walk along the sand. Huge Atlantic rollers attract surfers to the dune-flanked **Praia do Amado**, 4km (2.5mi) to the south on the other side of the headland – it's a real hotspot for wild wave riders!

Insider Tip

Praia da Arrifana is another beautiful crescent of sand, 10km (6mi) outside Aljezur. There are sweeping views along the coastline from the ruined fortress above the beach. The long, sheltered sandy beach of ⚽**Praia de Monte Clérigo**, 8km (5mi) from Aljezur, is a great choice for families.

Insider Tip

The magnificent beach near Boca do Rio between Burgau and Salema

TAKING A BREAK

Most of these beaches have **summer restaurants and bars**. If you are visiting remote beaches like Cordoama and Odeceixe out of season, take a **picnic**.

Praia Verde ✚ 219 E3	Praia de Odeceixe ✚ 219 B2
Ilha da Armona ✚ 219 D3	Boca do Rio ✚ 219 B3
Ilha de Tavira ✚ 219 E3	Praia da Rocha ✚ 219 B3
Albufeira ✚ 219 C3	Praia do Castelejo ✚ 219 B3
Armação de Pêra ✚ 219 C3	Praia da Bordeira ✚ 219 B3
Praia da Marinha ✚ 219 C3	Praia do Amado ✚ 219 B3
Praia de Dona Ana ✚ 219 B3	Praia da Arrifana ✚ 219 B3
Meia Praia ✚ 219 B3	Praia de Monte Clérigo ✚ 219 B3
Praia da Luz ✚ 219 B3	Praia da Cordoama ✚ 219 A3

INSIDER INFO

■ Beware of **dangerous currents** on the west coast beaches (Arrifana, Amado, Bordeira, Castelejo, Cordoama and Odeceixe). On calm days the sea can seem almost benevolent, but only experienced swimmers should go in.

■ The easiest **access** to the west coast beaches is from Lagos to Arrifana/Aljezur or Sagres to Bordeira.

⭐2 Sagres & Cabo de São Vicente

This wild and windswept cape at the southwest tip of Europe was once known as *O Fim do Mundo* (The End of the World). Standing on the headland and gazing out into the ocean as the waves crash against the cliffs, it is difficult not to feel the excitement of the medieval explorers who set off from Sagres into the great unknown, wondering what perils lay ahead and whether they would ever return.

School of Navigation

It was here that Prince Henry the Navigator founded his School of Navigation in the 15th century, gathering together the greatest cartographers, astronomers, mariners and ship-builders in Europe. Huge advances were made, including a new design for a ship, the *caravel*, a lateen-rigged sailing vessel that was later used by Christopher Columbus for his Atlantic crossings. It was the invention of the *caravel* that paved the way for Portugal's era of maritime discovery (▶ 16). Among the explorers who studied at Sagres were Vasco da Gama, Pedro Álvares Cabral and Ferdinand Magellan.

Henry's school was pillaged in 1587 by the British buccaneer Sir Francis Drake, and his precious library was burned to the ground. It probably stood on the site of the **Fortaleza de Sagres**, a late 18th-century fortress on a windy

Fishermen near Sagres

The Algarve

promontory on the edge of town. All that remains from an earlier age are the simple chapel of **Nossa Senhora da Graça** and the huge **Rosa dos Ventos** (Wind Compass), 43m (47 yards) in diameter, possibly dating from Henry's time. Today, there is a visitor centre, shop and café.

The Town
Sagres is an end-of-the-road sort of town, attracting surfers and backpackers in summer. Wealthier visitors prefer to stay a short way away at the beautiful Martinhal Beach Resort & Hotel.

The town's real attraction is its **beaches**, which are some of the best in the Algarve, despite the coldness of the water and the strength of the waves and ocean winds. You'll find more sheltered stretches of sand east of the fortress.

Praia da Mareta is the most accessible, just below the main square. From **Praia da Baleeira**, by the harbour, it is a short walk to the windsurfing beach of **Praia da Martinhal**.

The rugged cliffs at Cabo de São Vicente

Cabo de São Vicente
From the *fortaleza*, the road continues for 6km (3.7mi) across the headland to Cabo de São Vicente, named *Promontorium Sacrum* (Sacred Promontory) by the Romans, who thought the sun sank into the water here every night. Later, it became a Christian shrine, based on the legend that the body of St Vincent had been washed ashore here in the fourth century AD. Later still, in the 12th century, the relics were said to have been transferred to Lisbon in a boat piloted by ravens, and St Vincent is now the patron saint of the capital.

Henry the Navigator is thought to have built his palace on the headland, roughly where the lighthouse now stands. This is one of the most powerful lighthouses in Europe, its 3,000-watt bulb visible up to 100km (62mi) out at sea. The waters around the cape have been the site of numerous naval battles, but these days there is not much to disturb the peace, although it is still one of the world's busiest shipping routes.. The gusts up on the 60m (197ft) cliffs can be fierce, and fishermen risk their lives by dangling oversize rods into the sea from the edge of the rock face. Come up here at sunset for magical views.

TAKING A BREAK
The best places to eat are the **Pousada Sagres** (Ponta da Atalaia; tel: 282 620 240; www.pestana.com) which serves tasty, typical regional food, or anywhere on Praça

INSIDER INFO

■ Take a **sweater** to the cape, even in summer. If you forget, stalls by the light-house sell cardigans and rugs. A cult takeaway stand there also serves the "last bratwurst before America" (www.letztebratwurst.com; N.B. the website's written entirely in German).

■ Concentrate more on the views and the pathways when you're in the **Fortaleza de Sagres**; the rather diminutive historic site itself is a little disappointing.

■ There's a small **museum** next to the Cabo de São Vicente's lighthouse.

■ **Praia do Beliche** is a secluded, sheltered cove beneath the cliffs on the way from Sagres to Cabo de São Vicente.

In more depth If Sagres has given you a taste for wild Atlantic beaches, continue up the west coast on the **Costa Vicentina** (➤ 165).

Insider Tip

da República in Sagres. Alternatively, head to the terrace restaurant at the **Martinhal Beach Resort & Hotel** (tel: 282 240 200; www.martinhal.com). Located a short way behind Praia da Martinhal, it's stylish but not exactly cheap.

✚ 219 A3 ✉ Rua Comandante Matoso, Sagres
☎ 282 624 873; www.cm-viladobispo.pt

The huge wind compass at Sagres is thought to date from the 15th century

Fortaleza de Sagres
✉ Ponta de Sagres ☎ 282 620 140; www.monumentosdoalgarve.pt
🕐 Daily, July, Aug 9:30–8:30; May, June, Sep 9:30–8; April, Oct 9:30–6:30; Nov–March 9:30–5:30
💷 €3

🄸 Tavira

This elegant riverside town has somehow managed to escape the tourist tide sweeping the Algarve. It straddles the River Gilão and is close to some of the area's best beaches. A seven-arched historic bridge joins one side of the town to the other, and its noble houses are adorned with wrought-iron balconies and latticework doors.

Tavira is the most beautiful town on the Algarve's *sotavento* (leeward) coast. It boasts palm-lined gardens, handsome eighteenth-century mansions overlooking the river and a handful of churches that are worth a visit. One of the most enjoyable ways to sample Tavira's many places of worship is through the *Música nas Igrejas* – a series of concerts held in different churches throughout the year.

Praça da República, Tavira's central square

During the Islamic era, this was one of the three biggest towns in *al-gharb* (► 160) and it continued to flourish up to the 16th century as a port. Tuna fishing became a major industry until it was ended by the 1755 earthquake and tsunami, which caused destruction and silted up the harbour. Today, the town thrives as a low-key, low-rise resort.

The best place to start is **Praça da República**, the arcaded square on the west bank of the River Gilão. Climb the steps to the **Igreja da Misericórdia**. Its ornate 16th-century portal features carvings of Our Lady of Mercy flanked by saints Peter and Paul and the coats of arms of Tavira and Portugal. The high altar and the *azulejos* are the highlights of the building's interior.

A short climb to the left ends at **Castelo dos Mouros**, a ruined Moorish castle fortified by Dom Dinis, where you can walk around the ramparts for great views over Tavira and its distinctive *telhadas de tesouro* (treasure roofs), hip-gabled, pyramid shaped rooftops, which each cover a single room.

Behind the castle, the **Igreja de Santa Maria do Castelo**, built on the site of an old mosque, contains the tombs of

Out and about in Tavira's Old Town

Dom Paio Peres Correia, who captured the city in 1242.

Centro Ciência Viva de Tavira, an interactive science and technology museum offers more modern diversion, with exhibits on everything from the solar system to the internet.

Shady **waterfront gardens** with an iron bandstand at the centre lead from Praça da República to the **old fish market**. Several benches and cafés are ideally placed for a relaxing break.

Ilha de Tavira

From the jetty at Quatro Águas, 2km (1.2mi) east of town, ferries depart (regularly in summer and occasionally in winter; time tables: www.silnido.com; inexpensive) for Ilha de Tavira, an offshore island that forms part of the **Parque Natural da Ria Formosa** (➤ 174).

Walk across the mudflats to reach the magnificent 11km (6.8-mile) **beach**, backed by sand dunes and lapped by the warmest waters in the Algarve. With beach bars and a campsite, this is a world away from the big resorts to the west. You can also reach the island by boat from Santa Luzia. Boat shuttles arrive here from the centre of Tavira in summer, too. 🎎Younger visitors will have a great time shell hunting on the island.

TAKING A BREAK

Veneza, on Praça da República, has a popular pavement terrace for watching the world go by over sweets and strong coffee. **Praça Velha** (➤ 167–168), a fish restaurant in the old market building, is also excellent.

✚ 219 E3

ℹ Praça da República 5 ☎ 281 322 511; www.cm-tavira.pt

Centro Ciência Viva de Tavira

✉ Convento do Carmo 9 ☎ 281 326 231; www.cvtavira.pt
🕐 Tue–Sat 10–6; mid-July–mid-Sep until 7:30 💰 €4

INSIDER INFO

- Try the local speciality, *bife de atum em cebolada* (tuna steak with onions) at one of the riverside restaurants. **Insider Tip**

- It's free to visit **Tavira Castle**, a little fort whose walls shelter a wealth of lush vegetation. It's open from 8–7 on Mon–Fri and 10–8 on Saturdays and Sundays in summer, and from 9–5 every day at other times of the year.

- **Cacela Velha**, 10km (6mi) northeast of Tavira, is a tiny village with a fort, church and houses perched on a cliff overlooking the Ria Formosa. It is one of the few unspoiled Algarve coastal spots. **Insider Tip**

㊶ Serra de Monchique

The green hills of the volcanic Monchique mountain range provide a welcome respite from the summer heat of the Algarve coast. A trip into the mountains offers the chance to experience a different Algarve, far removed from the overcrowded beaches and busy resorts of the south.

The mountains provide a natural barrier between the Alentejo and the Algarve, sheltering the coastal region and helping to ensure its famous mild climate. Cork oaks, chestnut and eucalyptus trees grow on wooded hillsides, and the meadows are alive with wild flowers in spring.

A Spa Village and a Monastery

The easiest approach to the mountains is to drive north from **Portimão**, one of the Algarve's largest towns. After 20km (12.5mi), you'll reach **Caldas de Monchique**. A spa resort since Roman times, the village boasts a range of accommodation today. Climb up to the vantage point for views of the spa nestling in the valley. It's a delightful place that's been made even more attractive by the renovation of the 19th-century spa buildings and the neo-Moorish casino.

You can taste the water at **Fonte dos Amores** (Lovers' Spring), then walk up through the woods to a picnic area. Bear in mind that the most famous visitor to the spa, King João II, died after taking the waters in 1495.

The vast view out over the Algarve countryside from the vantage point on the summit of Mount Foia

The road continues for 6km (3.7mi) to **Monchique**, the region's main town. Climb steps in the Old Town to reach the 16th-century parish church, Igreja Matriz, with Manueline portal columns carved into knotted ropes.

Keep going to eventually reach the **Nossa Senhora do Desterro**, a Franciscan monastery, destroyed in the 1771 earthquake, with gardens of lemon and magnolia trees and views to the peak of Picota (773m/2,535ft).

The small spa resort of Caldas de Monchique

A short drive from Monchique is the highest summit in the Algarve, **Pico da Fóia** (902m/2,960ft), topped by a radio transmitter, café and gift shop. Often shrouded in mist, on clear days the views stretch to Portimão, Lagos (► 177) and Cabo de São Vicente (► 168). A few hours' hike away, the Algarve's second-highest peak, **Picota** (773m/2,536ft) offers less crowded views. Return to Portimão, the same way you came, or follow the N267 on a scenic mountain road to Aljezur and the **beaches of the west coast** (► 164).

TAKING A BREAK

If you want a break, spend some time at the **O Tasco** wine bar in the thermal resort of Caldas de Monchique. Alternatively, try **Restaurante 1692**, where you can sit down for a meal.

➕ 219 B2
ℹ️ Largo de São Sebastião, Monchique
☎ 282 911 189; www.cm-monchique.pt

Villa Termal das Caldas de Monchique – Spa Resort
✉ Caldas de Monchique ☎ 282 910 910; www.monchiquetermas.com
(The pools are for guests only)

INSIDER INFO

- Look out for *medronho*, a local firewater spirit made from the fruit of the arbutus (wild strawberry) tree.
- If you'd like to sample the Serra de Monchique's typical hearty mountain cuisine, it's worth paying a visit to the **Restaurante Jardim das Oliveiras** (Sítio do Porto Escuro; tel: 916 249 070; www.jardimdasoliveiras.com). The turnoff to the restaurant is signposted on the right-hand side as you drive up to Fóia from Monchique.

  Insider Tip

- Ask at the tourist information office in Monchique for information about **walking in the mountains**. A popular walk is the climb to the summit of Picota, the second highest in the range, which takes around 1.5 hours from Monchique.

At Your Leisure

Alcoutim – a place of peace and tranquillity

47 Alcoutim

A giant 14th-century castle rises up at the top of the village of Alcoutim and looks out across the River Guadiana to the Spanish village of Sanlúcar de Guadiana. It's close enough to Spain to hear dogs barking, children playing and the church clock chiming the hour on the opposite bank. Climb to the castle for the best views and take the time to explore the little archaeological museum inside. It's also worth enjoying a walk down the river bank. Later, follow the beautiful drive along the valley on the twisting road to Foz de Odeleite.

⊞ 219 E1
🛈 Rua 1º de Maio
☎ 281 546 179; www.cm-alcoutim.pt

Castelo/Núcleo de Arqueologia
🕓 Daily April–Sep 9:30–7;
Oct–March until 5
💶 €2.50

48 Parque Natural da Ria Formosa

The Ria Formosa nature reserve covers 60km (37mi) of coastline, sheltered from the ocean by sand dunes and a network of salt marshes and lagoons.

This extremely complex ecosystem begins in the east near Manta Rota and stretches right across to Faro via Tavira and Olhão. Its watery lagoon landscape makes for great birdwatching. Bring binoculars and you might spot herons, storks, purple gallinule and migratory flamingoes taking advantage of the rich pickings on the marshes. Fiddler crabs also live here. You can explore the natural park on foot, by bike, or on a boat tour (of Tavira Island (▶ 171), for example). The bike routes running between the salt marshes and the south east of Quinta do Lago are particularly beautiful. Piles of salt shine blindingly white in the sun, and the pools are used as a refuge for flamingoes and other water birds. Head to the local tourist offices for more information.

⊞ 219 D3 ✉ 3km (2mi) east of Olhão, signposted off the N125
☎ 289 700 210; www.icnf.pt/portal/ap/p-nat/pnrf
🕓 Daily from 9am

49 Faro

The capital of the Algarve is one of the most underrated cities in Portugal, known mainly for its airport through which millions pass on their way to the beaches on the south coast.

Starting at the marina, you enter the Old Town through Arco da Vila, a handsome gateway. An 11th-century horseshoe arch just inside this entrance is all that remains of the Moorish walls. Climb up to the cathedral square, cobbled and lined with orange trees, then make your way to the **Museu Municipal**, housed in a former convent. Besides the Renaissance cloisters, the chief attraction here is a third-century Roman mosaic depicting the head of Neptune surrounded by the four winds. Kids will also love seeing the 🐦 storks that have become a favourite fixture of the Old Town.

It's worth making the short stroll through the new town to the Igreja do Carmo, best known for its chilling **Capela dos Ossos** (Chapel of Bones), whose walls are covered with more than 1,200 skulls and body parts.

✚ 219 D3

ℹ Rua da Misericórdia 8–12

☎ 289 803 604; www.cm-faro.pt

Museu Municipal

✉ Largo Dom Afonso III

☎ 289 897 400

🕐 June–Sep Tue–Fri 10–7, Sat, Sun 11:30–6; Oct–May Tue–Fri 10–6, Sat, Sun 10:30–5 (last entry 30 mins before closing) 💶 €2

Capela dos Ossos (Igreja do Carmo)

✉ Largo do Carmo ☎ 289 824 490

🕐 April–Oct Mon–Fri 10–1, 3–6, Sat 10–1; Nov–March Mon–Fri 10–1, 3–5, Sat 10–1 💶 €2

🔟 Estói

The pink, neo-rococo palace that dominates the village was begun in 1840 for the Conde de Cavalhal. It has been restored and opened as a glamorous *pousada* (you can visit the gardens and some rooms) with a very good restaurant. Just down the hill from the village are the Roman ruins at **Milreu**, which

The handsome Arco da Villa, which marks the entrance to Faro's Old Town

include some well-preserved mosaics depicting leaping dolphins and fish.

✚ 219 D3

Milreu

☎ 289 997 823; www.monumentosdoalgarve.pt

🕐 May–Sep Tue–Sun 9:30–1, 2–6:30; Oct–April Tue–Sun 9–1, 2–5:30 (last entry 30 mins before closing)

💶 €2; free 1st Sun of the month

🔟 Loulé

The Algarve's second city is also a thriving craft centre and market town. Saturday is the best time to come, when the busy market sells local produce and pottery in and around the neo-Moorish market hall. Loulé is known across Portugal for its Carnival celebrations, which take place just before Lent and are the biggest in the country. Look out for two contrasting churches – the parish church of **São Clemente**, its bell tower housed in a 12th-century minaret, and the space-age **Nossa Senhora da Piedade** next

Insider Tip

The Algarve

The Castle of Silves

to an 18th-century chapel on a hill overlooking the town. A small archaeology museum has been integrated into the remains of the castle.

➕ 219 D3

ℹ️ Avenida 25 de Abril 9

☎ 289 463 900; www.cm-loule.pt

52 Alte

This charming village of white-washed houses is in the foothills of the Barrocal, a fertile region north of Loulé, which produces figs, almonds, and oranges. You could easily spend an hour or two in the village, admiring the parish church with its Manueline (➤ 18) portal and 16th-century *azulejos* (➤ 32) and walking up to the Fonte Pequena and Fonte Grande to cool down by the springs at this well-known beauty spot by the River Alte. While you're there, *don't miss the stunning Queda do Vigario waterfall.*

Insider Tip

➕ 219 C2

53 Albufeira

This formerly quiet fishing village has been transformed over the last 50 years into Portugal's biggest seaside resort. Nonetheless, its Old Town – a maze of medieval streets on a cliff overlooking the beach – has survived intact. Look for the Moorish archway and whitewashed houses lit by lanterns at night. A tunnel carved through the cliff face and a new elevator lead to the main beach. For nightlife, try the raucous pedestrian zone around Largo Duarte Pacheco known as "the Strip" – it's packed with British-focused pubs, karaoke bars, restaurants and clubs. Alternatively, head to the marina outside town (also the starting point for boat tours).

➕ 219 C3 ℹ️ Rua 5 de Outubro

☎ 289 585 279; www.cm-albufeira.pt

54 Silves

The Moorish capital of *al-gharb* (➤ 160) was once a magnificent city, a place of poets, princes and splendid bazaars described in Islamic chronicles as a place of "shining brightness" that was several times greater than Lisbon. Rising dramatically above the town is the crenellated Moorish

castle, once the centrepiece of the *medina* (Old Town), which affords far-reaching views across to the River Arade and the surrounding countryside dotted with citrus groves, cork oaks and carob trees. Nearby is the 13th-century **cathedral** (Sé), the pink granite columns of its Gothic nave uncluttered by the baroque decoration of so many Portuguese churches. The tombstones are those of medieval crusaders who helped capture the town in 1242.

History buffs should take a look in at the **Museu Municipal de Arqueologia**, which showcases the ebb and flow of local history during the Moorish, Roman and Phoenician eras.

🕂 219 C2   🚹 Rua 25 de Abril
☎ 282 416 556; www.cm-silves.pt

Castelo
☎ 282 445 624
🕐 Daily 9–7 (summer); 9–5:30 (rest of year). Last entry 30 mins before closing
💶 €2.80, combined ticket (Castelo & Museu Municipal de Arqueologia): €3.90

Sé
☎ 282 442 472
🕐 Mon–Fri 9–1, 2–6, Sat 9–1   💶 €1

The heart of Lagos is the place to party after dark

55 Lagos

Partly enclosed by medieval walls and bordered by cliff-backed beaches, Lagos is a town of great visual and historical interest. Ships sailed to Africa from here during the Age of Discovery, and a statue of Henry the Navigator (➤ 16) stands facing the harbour on Praça Infante Dom Henrique. More ominously, on a corner of the same square you'll see the site of the first European *mercado de esclavos* (slave market). The building serves as an art gallery today. In the backstreets, the **Museu Municipal** boasts a wide-ranging collection of Bronze Age menhirs (standing stones), Roman mosaics, African artefacts, fishing nets, weapons and coins. The museum is also connected to the baroque church known as the Igreja de Santo António, a cultural-historical highlight that's adorned with decorative *azulejos* and paintings depicting various episodes from the life of Saint Anthony.

🕂 219 B3   🚹 Praça Gil Eanes
☎ 282 763 031; www.cm-lagos.pt

Museu Municipal/Igreja de Santo António
✉ Rua General Alberto da Silveira
☎ 282 762 301
🕐 Tue–Sun 10–12:30, 2–5:30
💶 €3, combined ticket (Museu Municipal, Castelo and Mercado dos Escravos): €5

Where to…
Stay

Prices

Expect to pay for a double room per night in high season

€ under €80　　€€ €80–€110　　€€€ €110–€150　　€€€€ over €150

TAVIRA AND AROUND

Herdade da Corte €–€€

If you want to get away from the main tourist areas, you'll love this country estate around 8km (5mi) northwest of Tavira that's surrounded by the green landscape of the Serra do Caldeirão. The rustically furnished rooms are split between two complexes: Monte do Lavrador and Monte da Beleza. The little pool is a great place for a cooling dip. Their homepage often features special deals. Print off the route description on the site – the estate isn't easy to find!

✚ 219 E3 ⊠ Sítio da Corte, Hortas, Catarina da Fonte do Bispo
☎ 281 971 625; www.herdadedacorte.com

Hotel Vila Galé Tavira €€–€€€

This large, well-kept, four-star hotel is a good choice if you want to stay in central Tavira. Lots of the rooms have balconies facing the open-air pool. It's a great base for exploring the town on foot.

✚ 219 E3 ⊠ Rua 4 de Outubro
☎ 281 329 900; www.vilagale.pt

Pousada Convento Tavira €€€–€€€€

This romantic and blissfully peaceful *pousada* (➤ 35) is housed in a converted convent, founded in the 16th century by Augustinian nuns. The centrepiece is a beautiful Renaissance cloister, which lends the place an air of grandeur. High-ceilinged spaces lead to rooms that are decorated in warm hues with Moorish elements. All have cable TV, air conditioning and WiFi, and the best have private balconies. The swimming pool is great for cooling off on hot days. Activities, including golf, can be arranged.

✚ 219 E3 ⊠ Rua Dom Paio Peres Correia
☎ 201 407 680; www.pestana.com

FARO AND AROUND

Hotel Eva €€–€€€

Attractively positioned on the edge of the marina, this hotel boasts a rooftop pool with superb views over the Ria Formosa and the harbour. Some of the more expensive rooms share this stunning panorama. Sleek and contemporary in feel throughout, the main areas are light and airy. The hotel block's exterior isn't exactly beautiful, but the service is excellent and all the rooms have WiFi. The Old Town is just a stone's throw away, and everything's within easy walking distance. They'll even arrange boat trips for you out to sea.

✚ 219 D3 ⊠ Avenida da República 1
☎ 289 001 000; www.tdhotels.com/eva

Hotel Quinta do Lago €€€€

The Quinta do Lago – a 30-minute drive from Faro – sits in verdant luxury with views of the lagoon and the sea. Its first-rate facilities include a spa with a gym and a jacuzzi overlooking the Ria Formosa. There's also a private beach club, a kids' club, golf courses and a variety of sports (➤ 182). Guests can dine on Italian cuisine in the intimate Cá d'Oro restaurant or opt for Portuguese gourmet fare.

The stylish rooms have spacious terraces.

✚ 219 D3 ✉ Quinta do Lago, Almancil
☎ 289 350 350; www.hotelquintadolago.com

SERRA DE MONCHIQUE

Villa Termal das Caldas de Monchique Spa Resort €€–€€€

This resort is the only thermal spa in the Algarve. It's made up of a collection of little hotels. The Hotel Central retains its historic air, while the Hotel Termal is a rather more modest affair.

The open-air pool sits in the middle of the leafy complex, and the spa is found in the Hotel Central. Although not overly luxurious, the resort in the lush, green hills is a good base for discovering another side to the Algarve. What's more, the beaches aren't far away.

✚ 219 B2 ✉ Caldas de Monchique
☎ 282 910 910; www.monchiquetermas.com

PORCHES

Casa Bela Moura €€–€€€

A modern house decorated in Moorish style, this is a family-run guesthouse with rooms divided between the main house and a nearby annexe. The bar, breakfast room and reception are welcoming, and the 13 rooms are very clean. It has its own pool and is only 1.5km (1mi) from the pretty cove of Nossa Senhora da Rocha.

✚ 219 C3
✉ Estrada de Porches 530, Alporchinhos
☎ 282 313 422; www.casabelamoura.com

SILVES

Casa das Oliveiras €

Peace and quiet reign at this comfortable guest house, which is not far outside of Silves and surrounded by orange groves and olive trees. There's no restaurant, but the breakfast is substantial and the friendly owners will point you in the direction of a number of good local places to eat. It makes a very good base for exploring the beautiful inland towns and villages and heading off on trips to the nearby coast. The reasonable prices are even more attractive in the low season.

✚ 219 C2 ✉ Montes da Vala
☎ 282 342 115; www.casa-das-oliveiras.com

LAGOS AND AROUND

Casa Grande €–€€

Located around 13km (8mi) from Lagos, the Casa Grande is a delightful, rambling guesthouse furnished with antiques and curiosities. The attractively furnished rooms, all with en-suite bathrooms, are large, comfortable and good value for money. Upstairs rooms have their own balconies. There's also a restaurant.

✚ 219 B3 ✉ Burgau
☎ 282 697 416; www.casagrandeportugal.com

Marina Club Lagos Resort €€€

This excellent four-star resort enjoys a great location right next to the marina. The studios, apartments and suites are modern, generous and comfortably furnished. The inviting pool sparkles in the centre of the complex.

✚ 219 B3 ✉ Marina de Lagos
☎ 282 790 600; www.marinaclub.pt

ALBUFEIRA

Sheraton €€€€

One of the Algarve's most beautiful hotel complexes. It stretches out over the cliffs to the east of Albufeira. The rooms are generous. 👪 Families with kids are also welcome (there's even a large play area). Everyone loves the indoor and outdoor pools, the O Pescador fish restaurant and the Piri Piri Steak House. You can get to Falésia beach in the hotel's elevator or via the stairs.

✚ 219 C3 ✉ Praia da Falésia
☎ 289 500 100; www.sheratonalgarve.com

Where to...
Eat and Drink

Prices
Expect to pay per person for a three-course meal, excluding drinks and tips.
€ under €20   €€ €21–€30   €€€ €31–€40   €€€€ over €40

TAVIRA

Ponto de Encontro €€
This restaurant in the city centre has been a successful fixture in Tavira for more than three decades. Locals enjoy coming here to meet friends and enjoy the fresh fish and meat dishes on offer. There's also a small selection of fare for vegetarians. Guests can choose to sit outside during the warmer months of the year.
➕ 219 E3
✉ Praça Doutor António Padinha 39
☎ 281 323 730; www.rest-pontoencontro.com
🕐 Wed–Sun 12:30pm–3:30pm and Tue–Sun 6:30pm–10:30pm

Praça Velha €€-€€€
This restaurant's main attraction is its seating on the terrace at the old market building near the river. The menu majors in fish and shellfish, and they serve a range of dishes for two people to share.
➕ 219 E3 ✉ Mercado da Ribeira,
Rua José Pires Padinha ☎ 281 325 866
🕐 Mon–Sat 12:30–3:30, 6:30–10:30

SERRA DE MONCHIQUE

A Rampa €–€€
Perched high above Monchique on the road to Foia, this rustic restaurant is famous for chicken piri-piri. It doesn't disappoint. Portions are generous, the chicken is tender and the piri-piri is spicy. The views are just as good, reaching over forested hills and fields to the glittering Atlantic.
➕ 219 B2 ✉ Caminho Foia ☎ 282 912 620
🕐 Wed–Mon noon–2:30, 7–10

FARO

Adega Nova €
The prices are modest, the welcome warm and the food second to none at this unpretentious restaurant near the station. Try some of their Portuguese delicacies from the Algarve. Fish steals the show, but they usually also serve a different speciality on each day of the week. Enjoy it all with a glass of crisp house white. The *tarta de alfarroba* (carob cake) is the star of the dessert menu.
➕ 219 D3
✉ Rua Francisco Barreto 24 ☎ 289 813 433;
www.restauranteadeganova.com
🕐 Daily 11:30–11

ALBUFEIRA

Cabana Fresca €€
Cabana Fresca on the seafront promenade fringing Praia do Pescador (Fisherman's Beach), ticks all the boxes with its buzzy ambiance, friendly service and excellent fresh fish. Dishes like king prawns in garlic and seafood risotto are matched with reasonably priced Portuguese wines. Be sure to save room for dessert. It's worth booking ahead in summer.
➕ 219 C3 ✉ Largo Cais Herculano 9
☎ 289 585 456; www.cabanafresca.pt
🕐 Daily 8:30am–midnight

Vila Joya €€€€
Considered by many people to be one of the very best restaurants in the Algarve. Originally from Austria, the talented chef, Dieter Koschina, whips up some fantastic treats

with the very best international ingredients, ranging from Wagyu beef to Italian white truffles. Make sure to book well in advance. The opening times are subject to change. Holds two Michelin stars.

✚ 219 C3 ✉ Praia da Galé ☎ 289 591 795; www.vilajoya.com 🕓 Thu–Tue 1–3, 7:30–9:30

LAGOS

Don Sebastião €€

This eatery's warm welcome and central location on the main pedestrian street ensure a steady stream of visitors. It's not the cheapest place in town, but there are some great appetisers, the fish and seafood are excellent and the desserts are home-made. Choose from prawns, crayfish and lobster, or the fish risotto. There's also an extensive wine list. You'll find other Old Town restaurants on the same street.

✚ 219 B3 ✉ Rua 25 de Abril 20 ☎ 282 762 795; www.restaurantedonsebastiao.com 🕓 Daily noon–10:30

Where to...
Shop

MARKETS

The market halls in **Olhão** are an absolute treat. They're home to a fruit and vegetable market and the very best fish market in the Algarve. The market in **Loulé** is particularly lively on Saturday mornings, when various stalls spill out into the side streets. The food market at **Lagos** (indoors, Av. dos Descobrimentos, Mo–Sa) bustles until midday. The Feira de Velharias, an antiques market, takes place every fourth Sunday of the month (Barão de São João, Polidesportivo). The municipal market (Mercado Municipal) in **Tavira** is held on

Insider Tip

Avenida D. Manuel I. It's also worth looking in at the fish market near the harbour in **Quarteira**.

CLOTHING & CRAFTS

You'll find lots of artisans at work around **São Brás de Alportel**. They sell a variety of wares, including cork picture frames and purses and spectacle cases made of "cork leather". The artists usually set up stalls at the town and village markets that take place once a month. Find out dates from your nearest tourist office. **Pelcor** sells posh cork leather bags on the main square in São Brás de Alportel (Mon–Fri 10–1 and 2–7; www.pelcor.pt).

Rua de Santo António is **Faro's** main shopping street. You can watch craftsmen hard at work in **Loulé**. You'll also find shops selling ceramics and braided rag rugs near the little castle.

There are lots of places to shop in the eastern Algarve town of **Vila Real de Santo António**. The stores there sell a gigantic selection of clothing and homeware.

FOOD & DRINK

Head to Sítio do Tesoureiro, a district of **São Brás de Alportel**, to visit Fátima Galego's Tesouros da Serra (tel: 289 843 581, www.fatima galego.com). They sell a selection of delicious baked goods alongside bottles filled with carob tree and herb liqueurs.

You can buy wine straight from the cellar at the elite **Quinta dos Vales** wine producers in the countryside inland from Carvoeiro (Sítio dos Vales; tel: 282 431 036, www. quintadosvales.eu).

The **Adega Cooperativa** between Portimão and Lagoa offers guided tasting tours (tel: 282 342 181).

The **Serra de Monchique** is famous for its high-percentage *medronho* made from the fruit of the strawberry tree.

Where to...
Go Out

WATERSPORTS

The Algarve's watersports are excellent. There are several surf schools at **Praia da Rocha**, e.g. the **Future Surfing School** (tel: 918 755 823, www.future-surf.com/en). The likes of the **Amado Surf Camp** (tel: 927 831 568, www.amadosurf camp.com) teach at the superb **Praia do Amado** near Carrapateira.

WATERPARKS

In Lagoa, **Slide & Splash** (N125, Vale de Deus, Estômbar; tel: 282 340 800; www.slidesplash.com) is a huge complex.

GOLF

There are about 50 excellent golf courses in the region (www.portugal golf.pt). The luxury resorts of **Quinta do Lago** (tel: 289 390 705; www. quintadolago.com) and **Vale do Lobo** (tel: 289 353 465, http://valedolobo. com) have several scenic courses between them. One of Vilamoura's top ranking courses is the **Oceanico** (tel: 289 310 333; www.oceanico golf.com); the **Sir Henry Cotton Championship Course** (outside Portimão on the N125; tel: 282 420 200; www.penina.com) is an 18-hole course.

HIKING

Head west to discover some great stretches of the **Rota Vicentina** long-distance hiking trail. Check out the routes between Arrifana–Carrapateira (24km/15mi), Carrapateira–Vila do Bispo (22km/13.5mi) and Vila do Bispo–Cabo de São Vicente (14km/ 8.5mi), for example. You'll have to be fit to tackle a whole section! Visit the official website (www.rotavicen-tina.com) for route descriptions, tips and downloads.

BIRDWATCHING

The **Ria de Formosa** nature park (► 174) is an ideal place for birdwatching. You can also see flamingoes at the Lagoa dos Salgados near Armação de Pêra.

MUSIC & NIGHTLIFE

The best clubs in **Albufeira** are out of town. Recommended is **Kadoc** (www.kadoc.pt) on the Albufeira–Vilamoura road where top DJs such as David Guetta play to up to 7,000 clubbers. Various events are also held in **Kiss Club** (Rua Vasco da Gama, Areias de São João, www. kissclubalgarve.com).

In Silves, the **Café Inglês** (Rua do Castelo 11; www.cafeingles.com.pt) is a relaxed venue for jazz concerts and jam sessions. In Lagos, **Stevie Ray's** (Rua da Senhora da Graça 9; tel: 914 923 883; www.stevie-rays. com) hosts live jazz, soul, blues and funk. Other venues for live music are **Harry's Bar** and **Central Station** on Largo Duarte Pacheco, Albufeira. **Faro**'s nightlife is concentrated on **Rua do Prior** and **Rua Conselheiro Bivar**.

BOAT TRIPS

Riosul Travel (tel: 281 510 200; www.riosultravel.com) and **Trans-guadiana** (Rua Diogo Cão 8; tel: 281 512 997; http://transguadiana.co) arrange boat trips along the River Guadiana, some of the Algarve's least spoiled scenery. Most of the boats leave from the promenade in Vila Real de Santo António.

Algarve Charters (tel: 289 314 867; www.algarvecharters.com) operate day trips on board a catamaran from the marina in Albufeira.

Lots of boats also set sail from Vilamoura marina.

Walks & Tours

Walks & Tours

1 LISBON
Walk

DISTANCE 4km (2.5mi) walking plus tram and funicular rides
TIME 2–2.5 hours
START/END POINT Praça do Comércio ✚ 209 D2

This walk introduces you to four very different districts – Alfama, Baixa, Chiado and Bairro Alto – which together make up the rich and diverse historic core of Lisbon. The journey includes a tram ride and a climb on a funicular, which are not only enjoyable in themselves, but also a convenient way of getting up the hills. Although the walk can be done in as little as two hours, it is best to allow at least half a day, giving some time

for window shopping, cafés and visits to churches and museums along the way.

1–2

Start in **Praça do Comércio**, the large open square on the waterfront, with your back to the river. The square is still known as Terreiro do Paço after the royal palace that once stood on this site. At the centre is a statue of Dom José I, who was

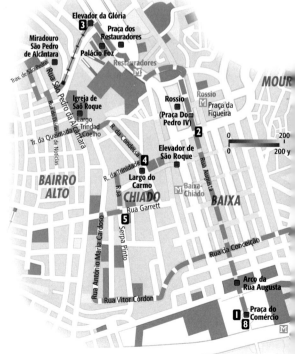

king of Portugal during the 1755 earthquake and the subsequent rebuilding of Lisbon. Walk straight ahead through the triumphal arch, the symbolic gateway to the city from the river. This brings you into **Rua Augusta**, the principal shopping street of the Baixa (lower town). On sunny days, the promenade comes alive with buskers, street traders, busy news stands and café terraces. The shops along here are an eclectic mix of high street fashion chains and quirky local stores such as **Casa Macário** (No 272–274), an old-fashioned coffee shop founded in 1913 where bottles of vintage port gather dust on the shelves. Approaching the top of the street, glance to your left to see the **Elevador de Santa Justa**, a much-loved iron lift designed by a pupil of Gustave Eiffel; it opened in 1902 to connect Baixa with Chiado. Although the escalators inside the Baixa-Chiado metro station now do a more efficient job, the ride on the *elevador* is still an exhilarating experience. The views across Lisbon from the top are breathtaking.

The grand Arco da Rua Augusta, Praça do Comércio, in the Baixa area

2–3

Rua Augusta ends in the **Rossio**, the nearest thing in Lisbon to a central square, with its fountains, flower stalls and wavy mosaic pavement. The square is officially named Praça Dom Pedro IV after the statue of the king at its centre – though the statue was initially designed as a likeness of Emperor Maximilian of Mexico, who was executed before it could be completed. Café Nicola and Pastelaria Suiça, facing each other across the Rossio, offer a choice of terraces for people watching, and there are good views of the ruined **Igreja do Carmo** on the hill above the western side of the square. Leave

The statue of Dom Pedro IV in front of the Dona Maria National Theatre in Rossio Square

the square by the far left corner and you'll find yourself in front of Rossio station, with its imposing neo-Manueline façade. Built as Lisbon's central station in 1892, it is the departure point for trains to Sintra (➤ 56).

Continue onwards into **Praça dos Restauradores**, a large square with an obelisk at the centre commemorating Portugal's independence from Spain. On your left is **Palácio Foz**, a former nightclub and Ministry of Propaganda building now housing the city tourist office.

3–4

Just beyond the palace, the **Elevador da Glória** funicular trundles up to the Bairro Alto on what must be one of the world's steepest, and most enjoyable, public transport rides, emerging opposite the **Solar do Vinho do Porto** (➤ 80). Turn right at the

upper terminus to reach the garden and **Miradouro of São Pedro de Alcântara**, with magnificent views of the cathedral, castle and Tagus estuary. Now you can head into the intriguing warren of medieval streets that make up the **Bairro Alto** (➤ 71).

The Bairro Alto rewards random exploration, but one possible route is to follow Travessa de São Pedro from opposite the fountain, take the second left along Rua dos Mouros (Street of the Moors), then turn left and immediately right along Rua do Diário de Notícias. As you reach Travessa da Queimada, turn left, passing Café Luso, one of Lisbon's famous *fado* (➤ 22) houses, which has *fado* and folk dancing on most nights.

This brings you out opposite Largo Trinidade Coelho, known as Largo da Misericórdia, dominated by the Jesuit **Igreja de São Roque**.

This is the headquarters of the Misericórdia charity, beneficiaries of Portugal's national lottery – hence the bronze statue of a ticket seller in front of the church. Leave this square by the Calçada do Duque steps and take the second right along Rua da Condessa to reach **Largo do Carmo**, a pretty square located at the heart of the Chiado district. The ruined convent here, an empty shell following the 1755 earthquake, is now an interesting archaeological museum.

4–5

Leave the square by Rua da Trinidade. When you see a house with an *azulejo*-tiled façade on your right, turn left along Rua Serpa Pinto. This brings you out onto Rua Garrett, Chiado's most fashionable shopping street, restored after a disastrous fire in 1988.

Treat yourself to a *bica* (espresso) and something to eat on the lovely terrace or in the magnificently old-fashioned interior of **A Brasileira** (►78), an historic café. The Portuguese poet Fernando Pessoa used to meet his friends here – his statue on the pavement acts as a magnet for tourists.

5–6

Cross Rua Garrett to reach Rua António Maria Cardoso, where you can get tram 28, dropping back down to Baixa. Get off the tram opposite the **Museu de Artes Decorativas** (►56).

From the *miradouro* (viewpoint), there are fantastic views over the Alfama rooftops to the churches of São Vicente de Fora and Santa Engrácia. From here you descend to explore **Alfama** (►65).

6–7

Take the staircase beside **Santa Luzia church** to a secret world of cobbled lanes, washing hanging from balconies, fountains, patios and hidden courtyards of orange trees. Turn left down more steps to Largo de São Miguel, where a palm tree stands guarding the church. Turn left along Rua de São Miguel. At the end of this street, turn right and right again to reach Largo do Chafariz de Dentro, an open square facing the **Museu do Fado** (►67).

7–8

Leave this square by the far corner along Rua de São Pedro, where women sell sardines from their doorways on weekday mornings. Continue along Rua de São Pedro, passing a rare surviving section of Moorish wall. The road widens and becomes Rua de São João da Praça, where several of the apartment blocks and shopfronts are decorated with *azulejo* tiles. Continue on this street, passing the Sé, then follow the tramlines down to Rua da Conceição and turn left along Rua Augusta to return to Praça do Comércio.

2 PORT COUNTRY
Drive

DISTANCE 130km (80.5mi)
TIME 4 hours
START/END POINT Vila Real 🕂 211 D3

This spectacular drive takes you through the steeply terraced vineyards of the Douro Valley, where the grapes in port wine are grown. The scenery is magnificent at any time of year but at its best in summer when the grapes are ripening on the vines, or in September and October when the harvest is taking place. Some of the roads are twisting and narrow, so allow plenty of time.

1–2

Start in **Vila Real** (►95) and follow signs for the IP4 in the direction of Porto and Amarante. Take care as this motorway climbs steeply and it is a notorious spot for accidents.

After 24km (15mi), turn off at the sign for "pousada" and cross the bridge to reach the **Pousada do Marão in São Gonçalo**. Turn right, follow the minor N15 for around 12km (7.4mi) as it snakes down

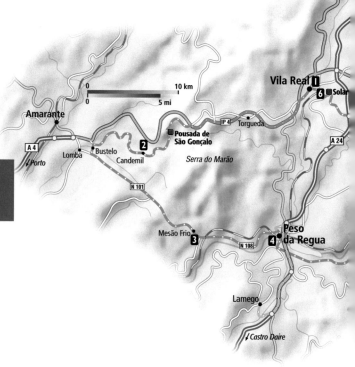

One of several *quintas* (wine estates) in Pinhão

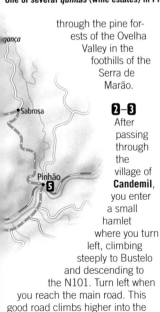

through the pine forests of the Ovelha Valley in the foothills of the Serra de Marão.

2–**3**

After passing through the village of **Candemil**, you enter a small hamlet where you turn left, climbing steeply to Bustelo and descending to the N101. Turn left when you reach the main road. This good road climbs higher into the sierra, offering fine views of the mountains and their strange granite boulders, then reaches

a plateau and drops down through the vineyards to **Mesão Frio**. Cross the stone bridge across the River Teixeira to enter the town and soon you have your first view of the great sweep of the River Douro down below.

3–**4**

Now you are in the heart of port wine country, surrounded by the steep slopes of the vineyards, carved into terraces by generations of farmers. As a local saying has it: "God created Earth, but man created the Douro."

The road narrows, twisting and turning as it drops to the river. Follow the river along its north bank (N108) through the spa town of **Caldas de Moledo** as far as **Peso da Régua.**

This busy town, usually known as Régua, was built to serve the port trade and is a centre for transporting wine to Porto. Ships known as *barcos rabelos* (►88) are

Walks & Tours

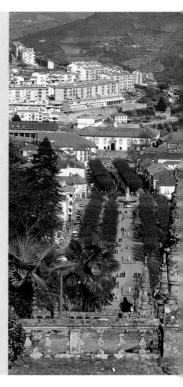

LAMEGO

A short detour south from Peso da Régua on the IP3 motorway leads to Lamego, an attractive town of Renaissance and baroque mansions overlooked by two hills. On one hill stands a ruined 12th-century castle; on the other is the sanctuary of Nossa Senhora dos Remédios, reached by a magnificent baroque stairway similar to that at Bom Jesus near Braga (➤ 89). The chapel is the focus for a major pilgrimage that takes place on 8 September each year. Lamego was the setting for the first Cortes (National Assembly), a meeting of the nobility, clergy and townspeople, which proclaimed Afonso Henriques the first king of Portugal in 1143. These days it's better known as the centre of production for Raposeira, Portuguese sparkling wine. Take a tour at the Quinta da Pacheca to see how port and still wine are made. The trip finishes with a tasting session (tel: 254 313 228, www.quintadapacheca. com; usually daily 10:30–5:30; booking recommended; tour: €7).

The town of Lamego, set in hilly, fertile countryside

Insider Tip

moored on the riverbank – you can cruise on them to the nearby *quintas* (wine estates) in summer. *Rabelos* is also the name for local baked goods shaped like little ships. The Igreja Matriz and the Capela do Cruzeiro (both 18th-century) are the town's most significant buildings.

Quinta de São Domingos in the town centre (Peso da Régua; tel: 254 320 260; www.quintadesao domingos.com, e-mail: geral@ quintadesaodomingos.com; daily 9–6), offers tours and tastings throughout the year. It's worth checking their availability by sending them an e-mail in advance. You'll find cafés and eateries along the waterfront. The Cacho d'Oiro restaurant specializes in local cuisine.

An optional extra: make a detour to **Lamego** (➤ box above) from Peso da Régua.

4–5

Take the lower of the two bridges across the River Douro and keep right to swing back under the bridge and emerge beside the river. Now follow the N222 along the south bank of the Douro to Pinhão. This is a lovely drive, clinging close to the river with views of vineyards, olive groves, dry-stone walls and white-painted *quintas* with the names of the famous port houses emblazoned on the hillsides. Several of the *quintas* are open to visitors – Fonseca Porto's **Quinta do Panascal** (tel: 223 742 800, www.fonseca.pt/en/

visitors-centre; Mon–Fri 10–6, also weekends Easter to Oct) boasts audio tours in nine languages, vineyard walks and a stone *lagar* where the grapes are still crushed by foot in the traditional way.

About 23km (14mi) from Peso da Régua, turn left to enter **Pinhão**, crossing an iron bridge over the Douro to return to the north bank. Drive along the main street; don't miss the station building with its *azulejo* tiles depicting vineyards and rural scenes. This small town is one of the main centres of quality port production, and several of the leading houses have *quintas* here. For a glass of port, drop into the five-star **CS Vintage House Hotel** (Rua António Manuel Saraiva, Pinhão; tel: 254 730 230; www.csvintagehouse.com). It's located in a beautiful setting on the riverbank.

The fountain at Nossa Senhora dos Remédios, Lamego

5–6

Leaving Pinhão, fork left where the road divides, following signs for Sabrosa and Vila Real. The road climbs through terraced vineyards. At **Sabrosa**, birthplace of the great navigator Ferdinand Magellan (1480–1521), turn left towards Vila Real. You pass the Roman site of **Panóias** on your way to **Casa de Mateus** (➤ 94), the impressive Portuguese manor house that you can see from a bend in the road as you approach. Turn right immediately after Mateus to return to Vila Real.

LEAVING THE CAR BEHIND

The dramatic landscapes of the Douro Valley can also be explored on **scenic train and boat journeys** from Porto. River trips run from Porto and Vila Nova de Gaia between March and October, typically travelling upstream as far as Peso da Régua and returning to Porto by train. Several trains a day leave Porto's São Bento station on the Douro Valley train line, which joins the river about 60km (37mi) from Porto and follows its banks as far as Peso da Régua (2.5 hours), Pinhão (3 hours), Tua and Pocinho. Tickets are inexpensive and can be bought in advance or at the time of travel from São Bento station in Porto, or from the stations at Peso da Régua or Pinhão. Such operators as **Barcadouro** offer organized tours on the Douro (tel: 223 722 415, www.barcadouro.pt), and **Douroazul** run river cruises that last for three, five or even eight days (tel: 223 402 500, www.douroazul.pt).

3 LOWER ALENTEJO
Drive

DISTANCE 222km (138mi)
TIME 4 hours
START/END POINT Beja ✚217 F2

This enjoyable drive takes you into Lower Alentejo, a region ignored by most visitors in the dash from Lisbon to the Algarve. Few people live here and there are few must-see sights – the pleasures of this region are to be found driving along empty roads and pottering around small towns. Despite, or perhaps because of, the absence of other visitors, it is in places like Serpa and Moura that you can really feel the soul of southern Portugal and the influence of its Moorish past.

❶–❷

Start in **Beja** (➤ 154) and leave the city by following the IP2 in the direction of Faro. The road crosses a wide open landscape of wheat fields and cork oak trees, many with numbers painted on the stripped bark to indicate the date of the harvest. After 15km (9.3mi), turn left on the N122 towards Mértola, on a quiet road with more cork oaks and the occasional isolated farmhouse or roadside hamlet. Enter **Mértola** (➤ 154) and park beneath the castle in the centre of town.

❷–❸

Once you've explored Mértola, leave by the same way you entered and take the bridge across the River Guadiana, following signs to Serpa –

A little local museum is housed in Beja's former convent

be sure to glance back as you cross the bridge for a lovely view of the town. The road climbs steeply at first, then levels out. After 17km (10.5mi), you'll reach **Mina de São Domingos**, an old copper-mining town that was first discovered by the Romans and still mined until the 1960s. Visitors to the town today can check out the 'Documentation Centre' (Centro de Documentação) and the 'House of Mine Workers' (Casa do Mineiro) (Mon–Fri 9–12:30, 2–5:30). There is also a large reservoir here with a picnic area and a small beach.

3–4

Continue driving across the typical Alentejo countryside with its cork oaks, wheat fields and sheep. The road is long and straight and the absence of traffic is remarkable – it's one of the most sparsely populated regions in Portugal. Shortly after passing through the olive- and orange-growing village of **Santa Iria**, you'll reach a main road. Turn left and immediately left again to **Serpa**. Before entering the town, you can make a short detour to the small, whitewashed, Moorish-style chapel of **Nossa Senhora da Guadalupe**, which enjoys sweeping views out over the plain.

4–5

Serpa is known as *Vila Branca* (white town) because of the typically Portuguese whitewashed houses lining its narrow cobbled streets. Like the other towns on this route, it makes a pleasant place to while away a couple of hours, even if only to take a few photos of the striking castle walls. The tourist office in Rua do Cavalos can give you some helpful tips on things to do. From the town's square, Praça da República, you can climb the steps to reach the parish church. Its separate bell-tower stands opposite. If you'd like to stock up on provisions, buy some *queijão de*

THE STORY OF SALÚQUIA

Look at the coat of arms on the town hall in **Moura** (► 194) and you will see a young girl lying dead at the foot of a tower. This is Salúquia, a Moorish princess, who lived in Moura at the time of the Christian conquest of the town in 1233. The story goes that on her wedding day her fiancé and his entourage were murdered by Christian knights on their way to the wedding ceremony. The Christians put on their victims' clothes and masqueraded as the wedding party in order to gain access to Moura. In this way they were able to capture the castle, and Salúquia threw herself from the tower in despair. There are many similar folk legends in Portugal, but this one is interesting as it casts Christians in the role of villains and Moors as their unfortunate victims.

Serpa, the strong local sheep's cheese. For a fuller meal of hearty Alentejano specialities, walk up the street to Molhó Bico that sits beside the old town walls.

From here it is a short stroll to the castle, where you can walk around the ramparts for views over the town and its surroundings. The castle walls, which incorporate an earlier aqueduct, were built by Dom Dinis (► 150) following the expulsion of the Moors in the 13th century, but were heavily damaged 500 years later during a raid by Spanish troops. Notice the boulder that forms a porch above the castle entrance, precariously balancing in the very spot where it was left after the attack.

Return to the N255 main road (signposted "Espanha" – Spain) and turn left, then take the next right towards Moura. Soon you reach the village of **Pias**, known for its strong red wines and the frescoes in the Santa Luzia church. Turn left to pass through the centre of the village then continue on this

Serpa's whitewashed Ermida Nossa Senhora de Guadalupe

road through the vineyards and olive groves to the spa town of **Moura**.

🄻–🄼

Moura means "Moorish Maiden" and the town takes its name from the legend of Princess Salúquia (▶ 193). This is another town with a ruined castle, cobbled streets and a long history. The Moorish quarter, called Mouraria, has whitewashed houses, ornamental chimneys and is particularly atmospheric.

Follow signs to the castle and park your car near the parish church of São João Baptista, with

PULO DO LOBO

The Pulo do Lobo (Wolf's Leap) waterfall is a place of rapids and weird rock formations in a deep gorge carved out by the River Guadiana between Mértola and Serpa. Although it is signposted from the Mértola to Serpa road, the easier approach is from a minor road 3km (2mi) out of Mértola on the way to Beja.

Insider Tip

its rich Manueline (▶ 18) portal. There are also some fine Sevillian *azulejo* (▶ 32) tiles adorning the high altar, the side chapels and the niche in the façade of the bell-tower. Across the street, storks can be seen nesting in the castle tower. Nearby are the public gardens of the old spa, where people come for an evening stroll and to enjoy sunset views over the hills.

Drive out of Moura with the castle on your right-hand side and stay close to the town walls, following signs to Amareleja as the road swings round to the right beneath the gardens.

After traversing the picturesque River Ardila, you'll reach a fork in the road – keep left for Portel. You'll soon come to **Barragem de Alqueva**, where a dam spans the River Guadiana, creating a large artificial lake that's over 80km (50mi) long. It's crisscrossed by a variety of boats and little day-trip cruisers.

Continue on this road, crossing through rolling countryside on the way to **Portel**, whose castle is visible from afar. Follow signs to Beja and return on the IP2.

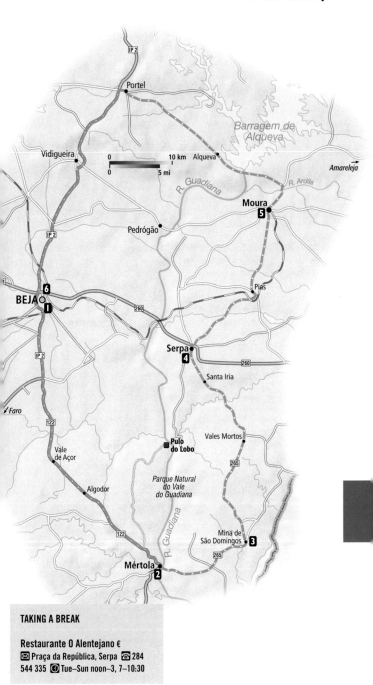

TAKING A BREAK

Restaurante O Alentejano €
✉ Praça da República, Serpa ☎ 284
544 335 ⏱ Tue–Sun noon–3, 7–10:30

4 LAGOS TO PRAIA DA LUZ
Walk

DISTANCE 6km (3.7mi)
TIME 3.5–4 hours
START POINT Lagos ✚ 219 B3 **END POINT** Praia da Luz ✚ 219 B3

The cliffs of western Algarve offer some superb walking, with sweeping views over the Atlantic and the bizarre rock formations that characterize this stretch of coast. Although you are hardly likely to find yourself alone, walking on the cliffs can be a good way of escaping the crowded beaches in summer. This walk is best done in the late afternoon or early evening, when the heat of the day has relented and the sunlight casts a softer glow of ever-changing colours on the ocean. If you are lucky, you might catch one of the famous Atlantic sunsets from the cliffs above Praia da Luz.

❶–❷
Begin on the riverfront at **Lagos** (► 177) opposite the **marina**, and follow **Avenida dos Descobrimentos** towards the sea. Across the road is the municipal market, which opened in 1924. Fresh fish is sold downstairs, and there's a produce market above selling fruit, flowers and much, much more.

As well as the market, **Praça Gil Eanes** contains an extraordinary statue of the boy-king Sebastião, a national hero who died in 1578 during a disastrous naval expedition from Lagos to Morocco. Have a coffee or snack at a pavement café here, as there will be few other opportunities for refreshments on this walk.

Continue strolling down the riverside promenade that's lined with palm trees. This place has a powerful feel of the great Age of Discovery, when Henry the Navigator's (► 16, 167) caravels sailed from here. There's a statue of him across the road in **Praça Infante Dom Henrique** and a statue of the explorer Gil Eanes in front of the remains of the city walls. Beyond the harbour walls to your left, ocean waves wash the shore of Meia Praia, Lagos' long and windswept **town beach**. Walk past the **Ponte da Bandeira fortress**, which contains a small museum devoted to the discoveries. The pretty cove beach of Praia da Batata lies alongside the fort. Climb the main road out of town, passing a *miradouro* (viewpoint) with a monument to São Gonçalo – a local fisherman's son who became a monk and is now the patron saint of Lagos.

Lagos To Praia Da Luz

2–3

At the top of the hill, leave the road and take the path to the left, signposted to Praia do Pinhão, following it as it leads along the cliffs to **Praia de Dona Ana**, one of the Algarve's most attractive beaches, with typical rock formations and sandstacks. Cross the car park above the beach and climb back on to the cliffs, taking care on the partly eroded track. From here, just keep the sea to your left as you continue across the cliffs towards **Ponte da Piedade** (Bridge of Piety), a well-known beauty spot where the red rock has been sculpted by the wind and sea into a series of dramatic boulders, arches and caves. Walk out past the **lighthouse** on to a spit for the best views along the coast. Fishermen offer boat trips into the grottoes from a small landing stage at the foot of the cliffs.

Praça Gil Eanes, with the statue of King Sebastião in the centre of Lagos

3–4

Leaving the lighthouse, hike west along the clifftop path. You need to stay close to the sea to avoid being forced into the resort development at Porto de Mós. Instead, drop straight down to the **beach**,

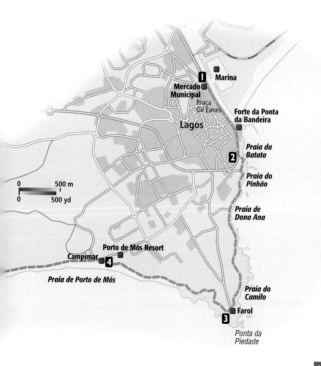

Stop to admire the stunning views over the coves and grottoes of Ponte da Piedade

where you'll find a couple of decent restaurants. If you feel you've done enough walking by now, there are occasional buses from here back to Lagos. If you still fancy carrying on, however, marshal your energy reserves and keep heading out west!

4–5

The next stretch of the walk is the hardest as it involves a long (but steady) climb to the highest point of the cliffs. The path is clear and offers spectacular views over the Atlantic, as far as **Cabo de São Vicente** (➤ 168) on a clear day.

After about 45 minutes you reach an **obelisk** marking the summit (109m/358ft). Just beyond the obelisk, look for a gap in the bushes to your left and scramble down towards **Praia da Luz**, emerging on a cobbled path that leads to the beach. Praia da Luz is a low-key but growing resort of whitewashed apartments and villas above a splendid stretch of sand. Stroll

along the beachfront promenade with its mosaic pavement to reach the balcony at the end. You'll find various places for refreshments near here. Regular buses to Lagos stop beside the church.

TAKING A BREAK

Bora Café €
✚ 219 B3 ✉ Rua Conselheiro Joaquim Machado 17, Lagos
☎ 282 083 438
🕐 June–Sep Mon–Fri 8:30am–midnight, Sat 9am–midnight, Sun 10am–midnight, July–Aug daily until 2am; shorter hours in winter; closed Sun Nov–Feb

Restaurante Atlântico €€€
✚ 219 B3
✉ Ave. dos Pescadores, Praia da Luz
☎ 282 788 799
🕐 Tue–Sun 6pm–10:30pm in winter; usually open daily in summer, when they also serve lunch

Practicalities

Practicalities

WHAT YOU NEED

		UK	USA	Canada	Australia	Ireland	Netherlands
● Required ○ Suggested ▲ Not required	Some countries require a passport to remain valid for a minimum period (usually at least six months) beyond the date of entry – check beforehand.						
Passport/National Identity Card		●	●	●	●	●	●
Visa (regulations can change – check before booking)		▲	▲	▲	▲	▲	▲
Onward or Return Ticket		▲	▲	▲	▲	▲	▲
Health Inoculations (tetanus and polio)		▲	▲	▲	▲	▲	▲
Health Documentation (▶ 204, Health)		○	○	○	○	○	○
Travel Insurance		○	○	○	○	○	○
Driving Licence (national) for car hire		●	●	●	●	●	●
Car Insurance Certificate		●	●	●	●	●	●
Car Registration Document		●	●	●	●	●	●

WHEN TO GO

High season   Low season

JAN	FEB	MAR	APR	MAY	JUN	JUL	AUG	SEP	OCT	NOV	DEC
15°C	16°C	18°C	21°C	24°C	30°C	35°C	37°C	33°C	28°C	19°C	17°C
59°F	61°F	64°F	70°F	75°F	86°F	95°F	99°F	91°F	82°F	66°F	63°F

☀ Sun   ⛅ Sunshine and showers

The temperatures shown are the **average daily maximums** for each month in the Algarve. Spring (April–June) and autumn (September, October) are the best times to visit Portugal as the summer months can be unbearably hot and crowded (depending on the region and the weather). Added attractions include wild flowers in spring and the Douro Valley grape harvest in autumn. Summer is hot and dry inland and mild on the coast, where sea temperatures vary from 16°C (61°F) on the west coast to 23°C (73°F) in the Algarve. Winters are cool and wet in the north, but pleasantly mild in the Algarve, where walking and golf are year-round activities. Swimming is also possible there from March to November, although you'll probably need a wetsuit as the sea can be quite chilly. Hotel rates tend to be much lower in January and February, making it a good time to visit Lisbon.

GETTING ADVANCE INFORMATION

Websites
- www.portugalinsite.pt
- www.algarvenet.com
- www.visitalgarve.pt
- www.justportugal.org
- www.pousadas.pt
- www.solaresdeportugal.pt
- www.portugalglobal.pt
- www.visitalentejo.pt

Practicalities

GETTING THERE

By Air There are international airports at Lisbon, Porto and Faro. **British Airways**, the Portuguese national airline **TAP Portugal** and discount airline **easyJet** operate scheduled flights from London to all three cities (flights take around 2.5 hours). **Ryanair** flies to Porto and Faro from several UK and European cities. There's also a wide selection of charter flights, especially to Faro in summer, from British, Irish and European airports. Most seats on charter flights are sold by tour operators as part of package holidays, but it's usually possible to buy flight-only deals through travel agents or on the internet. The disadvantage of charter flights is that you're sometimes restricted to periods of 7 or 14 days. **From the USA** TAP has scheduled flights to Lisbon from New York (6.5 hours), with connections to other North American cities. Flights are most expensive during the summer and holiday periods. Portuguese school holidays usually run from the end of June to the middle of September. You should also take note of the Easter and Christmas breaks.

By Car There are several entry points along the border with Spain, with few or no border controls. The main roads into Portugal are from Vigo to Porto, Zamora to Bragança, Salamanca to Guarda, Badajoz to Elvas and the motorway from Seville to the Algarve. From Britain, take a car ferry to Bilbao or Santander in northern Spain, from where it is a drive of about 800km (500mi) to Porto and 1,000km (620mi) to Lisbon.

By Rail There are regular trains to Lisbon from Madrid (10 hours) and Paris (24 hours). A train line from Vigo in Spain crosses the border at Valença do Minho to Porto and Lisbon.

TIME

Portugal is on **Greenwich Mean Time** (GMT), and one hour behind most of continental Europe. But between the last Sundays in March and October, it is GMT plus one hour (GMT+1).

CURRENCY & FOREIGN EXCHANGE

Currency The euro (€) is the official currency of Portugal. Euro coins are issued in denominations of 1, 2, 5, 10, 20 and 50 euro cents and €1 and €2. Notes are issued in denominations of €5, €10, €20, €50, €100, €200 and €500.

Foreign Currency and Traveller's Cheques can be changed at banks and exchange bureaux, as well as in many hotels. Exchange bureaux generally offer the best deal, but it pays to shop around and compare commission charges. You will need to show your passport when cashing traveller's cheques. You'll find **ATMs** (*caixa automático*) in all larger settlements. They let you withdraw money with the usual selection of bank/debit and credit cards. The machines in extremely touristy areas often function in several languages.

Major Credit Cards, including Visa, Cirrus and Maestro, are accepted in all major resorts and cities. That said, Portugal is not always plastic-friendly and some shops, restaurants and even hotels only accept cash. In the countryside, keep small denomination notes to hand. It is easier and no more expensive (depending on your credit card charges) to rely solely on plastic, rather than taking travellers' cheques or buying cash in advance.

PORTUGUESE NATIONAL TOURIST OFFICES: www.visitportugal.com

In the UK: 11 Belgrave Square, London SW1X 8PP ☎ 020/7201-6666
In Ireland: 54 Dawson Street, Dublin 2 ☎ 01-670-9133
In the US: 590 Fifth Avenue, 4th Floor, New York, NY 10036 ☎ 1-646/723-0200
In Canada: 60 Bloor Street West, Suite 1005, Toronto, Ontario M4W 3B8 ☎ 1-416/921 7376

Practicalities

NATIONAL HOLIDAYS

1 Jan: New Year's Day; **Mar/Apr:** Good Friday;
25 Apr: Day of the Revolution; **1 May:** Labour Day;
May/Jun: Corpus Christi; **10 Jun:** National Day;
15 Aug: Feast of the Assumption; **5 Oct:** Republic
Day; **1 Nov:** All Saints' Day; **1 Dec:** Independence
Day; **8 Dec:** Feast of the Immaculate Conception;
25 Dec: Christmas Day

Most shops are closed on public holidays

ELECTRICITY

The power supply
is 220 volts AC.
Sockets take
two-pronged round conti-
nental plugs. Visitors from
the UK will need an adap-
tor, and visitors from the
USA will need a transformer
for 100–120 volt devices.

OPENING HOURS

○ Shops
● Offices
● Banks
● Main Post Offices
● Museums/Monuments
○ Pharmacies

8am 9am 10am 12noon 1pm 2pm 4pm 5pm 7pm

☐ Day   ☐ Midday   ☐ Evening

Shops Usually 9–1, 3–7.
Large stores and super-
markets open 9–7 or 10
(5 on Sun).
Banks are open 8:30–3.
Post Offices Mon–Fri 9–6,
Sat 9–noon in cities, shorter
hours in provincial areas.
Museums and Churches
Usually 10–12:30, 2–5,
some museums/monuments
close Mon.
Pharmacies Usually 9–12:30,
2–7, but duty chemists will
be open longer (► 204).

TIPS/GRATUITIES

Tipping is not expected for all services and rates are
lower than elsewhere in Europe. As a general guide:
Restaurant bill
(service not included)   10%
Taxis   round up
Porters   €1 per bag
Chambermaids   €2 per night
Toilet attendants   small change
Tour Guides   half day €3, full day €5

DRINKING LAWS

Drinking and driving laws,
however, are very strict,
and the alcohol limit is
0.5g per litre of blood,
with hefty fines imposed
if found in breach of this
limit (up to €2,000).

TIME DIFFERENCES

Lisbon
12 noon

London (GMT)
12 noon

◄►

New York (EST)
7am

◄

Los Angeles (PST)
4am

◄

Sydney (AEST)
10pm

►

STAYING IN TOUCH

Postal Services Stamps (*selos*) can be bought at post offices, kiosks and tobacconists. Letters to European Union (EU) countries should arrive within three to four days, and to the USA within 10 days. Send urgent deliveries by *correio azul* and anything valuable by registered mail (*correio registado*).

Public Telephones There are public telephones on almost every street corner. They take coins, credit cards or phone cards (*cartaõ para telefonar*), available from post offices, kiosks and shops displaying the PT (Portugal Telecom) logo. International calls are cheaper between 9pm and 9am and at weekends. Calls from hotel rooms will invariably attract a heavy premium.

International Dialling Codes
Dial 00 followed by

UK:	44	Irish Republic:	353
USA / Canada:	1	Australia:	61

Mobile Providers & Services The coverage for mobile phones is fairly extensive, and your mobile should pick up the local network automatically – although US cell phones may have more difficulty. Call charges will vary according to your contract. Check with your service provider before travelling.

WiFi and Internet There's high-speed internet access across Portugal, and WiFi is becoming more and more widely available. You'll find WiFi in most good hotels, restaurants, service areas, shopping malls, and in some cafés and libraries. Whether hotels, etc., provide guests with free internet access varies from place to place, however. Most WiFi is offered through the mobile phone networks, and you pay for usage by the minute or the hour. There are internet cafés in most beach resorts on the Algarve, in Lisbon, and in other larger towns.

PERSONAL SAFETY

Violence against tourists is unusual in Portugal. Theft from cars is the most common form of crime.
- Do not leave valuables on the beach or poolside.
- Always lock valuables in hotel safety deposit boxes
- Never leave anything inside your car. If you have to, lock valuables in the boot.
- Beware of pickpockets in crowded markets, around train stations and on crowded buses in Lisbon and Porto.
- Do not leave bags unattended while standing at a car hire desk or loading suitcases onto a bus.

Police Assistance:
☎ 112 from any phone

There are police stations (*esquadra da policia*) in all towns and villages across Portugal. If your lose your passport, credit cards or any personal items, you will need to fill out a crime report at a police station for insurance or replacement purposes.

The *polícia de trânsito* are responsible for vehicle theft and accidents.

Note that some drugs have been legalized for personal use in Portugal.

POLICE	112
FIRE	112
AMBULANCE	112

Practicalities

HEALTH

Insurance Citizens of EU countries receive reduced-cost emergency health care with relevant documentation (European Health Insurance Card), but private medical insurance is still advised and essential for all other visitors.

Dental Services The standard of dental care is generally excellent. Dental practices advertise in the free English-language magazines and newspapers at hotels. You have to pay for treatment, but your insurance should cover the costs.

Sun Advice The sun is intense at all times of year. Cover up with high-factor sunscreen, wear a hat and drink plenty of water, especially if walking in the hills or along the coast.

Drugs Chemists (*farmâcia*) are open Mon–Fri 9–1, 2:30–7, and Sat 9–12:30. The late-night duty chemist is posted in pharmacy windows. Pharmacists are highly trained and can sell some drugs that require prescriptions in other countries. However, take adequate supplies of any drugs you take regularly as they may not be available.

Safe Water Tap water is safe but its mineral content may make it taste unpleasant. Ask for sparkling (*água com gás*) or still (*água sem gás*) bottled water.

CONCESSIONS

Young People Most museums have lower admission rates for **students** (and entry is generally free for children) on production of a passport or valid student identity card. **Senior Citizens** Senior citizens from many European countries come to the Algarve for its year-round warmth and long-stay low-season rates. Travellers over 65 are usually entitled to discounted admission at museums and reduced fares on public transport (proof of age needed). If mobility is a problem getting around can be a bit of a trial (► Travelling with a Disability, above)..

TRAVELLING WITH A DISABILITY

Facilities in Portugal for disabled travellers are slowly improving, but many older hotels and public buildings are still inaccessible, especially in cities where hotels are often on the upper floors of apartment blocks. You'll find dedicated, marked-out car parking spaces in most town centres, and adapted toilets at airports and train stations. It's best to discuss your particular needs before booking a holiday

CHILDREN

Hotels and restaurants tend to be child-friendly. Facilities are improving. Special attractions for kids are marked out with the logo shown above.

RESTROOMS

There are public toilets in shopping centres and by some of the larger beaches.

CUSTOMS

Duty-free allowances to the UK are 3,200 cigarettes, 3kg tobacco, 10L spirits, 90L wine and 20L fortified wine. For information for non-EU residents, see www.taxfreetravel.com

EMBASSIES & CONSULATES

 UK ☎ 213 924 000

 USA ☎ 217 273 300

 Canada ☎ 213 164 600

 Ireland ☎ 213 308 200

 Australia ☎ 213 101 500

Useful Words and Phrases

There are two distinctive Portuguese sounds. Firstly, the nasalized vowels written with a *til* (~, like the tilde on a Spanish ñ): *pão* ("bread") is pronounced "pow!" with a strong nasal twang, for example. Secondly, "s" and "z" are often pronounced as a slushy "sh" sound: *notas* ("banknotes") is pronounced "not-ersh", for instance.

SURVIVAL PHRASES

Yes/No **Sim/Não**
Please **Se faz favor**
Thank you **Obrigado (male speaker)/
    obrigada (female speaker)**
You're welcome **De nada/Foi um prazer**
Hello/Goodbye **Olá/Adeus**
Welcome **Bem vindo/a**
Good morning **Bom dia**
Good evening/night **Boa noite**
How are you? **Como está?**
Fine, thank you **Bem, obrigado/a**
Sorry **Perdão**
Excuse me, could you help me?
    Desculpe, podia ajudar-me?
My name is… **Chamo-me…**
Do you speak English? **Fala inglês?**
I don't understand **Não percebo**
I don't speak any Portuguese
    Não falo português

DIRECTIONS AND TRAVELLING

airport **aeroporto**
boat **barco**
bus station **estação de camionetas**
bus/coach **autocarro**
car **automóvel**
church **igreja**
hospital **hospital**
market **mercado**
museum **museu**
square **praça**
street **rua**
taxi rank **praça de táxis**
train **comboio**
ticket **bilhete**
    return **ida e volta**
    single **bilhete de ida**
station **estação**

I'm lost **Perdi-me**
How many kilometres to…?
    **Quantos quilómetros faltam ainda para
    chegar a…?**
here/there **aqui/ali**
left/right **à esquerda/à direita**
straight on **em frente**

EMERGENCY!

Help! **Socorro!**
Stop! **Pare!**
Stop that thief! **Apanhe o ladrão!**
Police! **Polícia!**
Fire! **Fogo!**
Leave me alone! **Deixe-me em paz!**
I've lost my purse/wallet **Perdi o meu
    porta-moedas/a minha carteira**
My passport has been stolen
    Roubaram-me o passaporte
Could you call a doctor?
    Podia chamar um médico depressa?

MONEY

bank **banco**
banknote **notas**
cash desk **caixa**
change **troco**
cheque **cheque**
coin **moeda**
credit card **cartão de crédito**
exchange office **cámbios**
exchange rate **cámbio**
foreign **estrangeiro**
mail **correio**
post office **agência do correio**
traveller's cheque **cheque de viagem**
Could you give me some small change?
    **Podia dar-me também dinheiro trocado,
    se faz favor?**

NUMBERS

0	**zero**	8	**oito**	16	**dezasseis**	50	**cinquenta**
1	**um**	9	**nove**	17	**dezassete**	60	**sessenta**
2	**dois**	10	**dez**	18	**dezoito**	70	**setenta**
3	**três**	11	**onze**	19	**dezanove**	80	**oitenta**
4	**quatro**	12	**doze**	20	**vinte**	90	**noventa**
5	**cinco**	13	**treze**	21	**vinte e um**	100	**cem**
6	**seis**	14	**catorze**	30	**trinta**	101	**cento e um**
7	**sete**	15	**quinze**	40	**quarenta**	500	**quinhentos**

Useful Words and Phrases

DAYS

Today **Hoje**
Tomorrow **Amanhã**
Yesterday **Ontem**
Tonight **Esta noite**
Last night **Ontem à noite**
In the morning **De manhã**
In the afternoon **De tarde**
Later **Logo/Mais tarde**
This week **Esta semana**
Monday **Segunda-feira**
Tuesday **Terça-feira**
Wednesday **Quarta-feira**
Thursday **Quinta-feira**
Friday **Sexta-feira**
Saturday **Sábado**
Sunday **Domingo**

ACCOMMODATION

Are there any…? **Há…?**
I'd like a room with a view of the sea
   Queria um quarto com vista para o mar
Where's the emergency exit/fire escape?
   Onde fica a saída de emergéncia/escada
   de salvação?
Does that include breakfast?
   Está incluido o pequeno almoço?
Do you have room service?
   O hotel tem serviço de quarto?
I've made a reservation
   Reservei um lugar
air-conditioning **ar condicionado**
balcony **varanda**
bathroom **casa de banho**
chambermaid **camareira**
hot water **água quente**
hotel **hotel**
key **chave**
lift **elevador**
night **noite**
room **quarto**
room service **serviço de quarto**
shower **duche**
telephone **telefone**
towel **toalha**
water **água**

SHOPPING

Shop **Loja**
Where can I get…? **Em que loja posso**
   arranjar…?
Could you help me? **Pode atender-me?**
I'm looking for… **Estou a procura de…**
I would like… **Queria…**
I'm just looking **Só estou a ver**

How much? **Quanto custa?**
It's too expensive **Acho demasiado caro**
I'll take this one/these
   Levo este(s)/esta(s)
Bigger **Maior**
Smaller **Mais pequeno**
Open/Closed **Aberto/Fechado**
Have you got a bag? **Tem um saco?**

RESTAURANT

May I book a table, please?
   Posso reservar uma mesa, se faz favor?
A table for two, please
   Uma mesa para duas pessoas, se faz favor
Could we see a menu, please?
   Poderia dar nos a ementa, se faz favor?
Where is the lavatory, please?
   Onde é o banheiro, se faz favor?
What's this? **O que é isto?**
A bottle of… **Uma garrafa de…**
breakfast **pequeno almoço**
lunch **almoço**
dinner **jantar**
bill **conta**
menu **menú/ementa**
dish of the day **prato do dia**
table **mesa**
waiter **empregado/a**

MENU READER

alcohol **alcool**
beer **cerveja**
bread **pão**
cheese **queijo**
coffee with milk **chinesa**
coffee (black) **bica**
fish **peixe**
game **caça**
meat **carne**
milk **leite**
mineral water **água mineral**
   sparkling **con gás**
   still **sem gás**
pepper **pimenta**
potatoes **batatas**
poultry **aves**
salt **sal**
scabbard fish **espada**
shellfish **mariscos**
soups **sopas**
stew **caldeirada**
tea **chá**
vegetables **legumes**
wine **vinho**
   red wine **vinho branco**
   white wine **vinho tinto**

Road Atlas

For chapters: See inside front cover

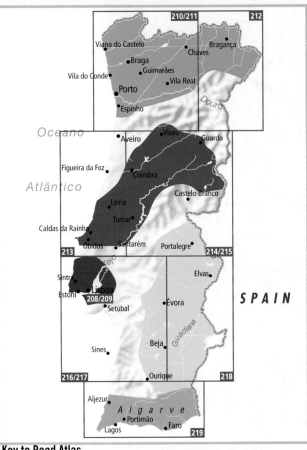

Key to Road Atlas

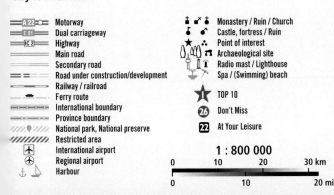

A 22 Motorway	✝ ⚔ ✠ Monastery / Ruin / Church
E 01 Dual carriageway	▲ ⚔ Castle, fortress / Ruin
IC 2 Highway	★ ⸫ Point of interest
Main road	⌂ᴪ ⛉ Archaeological site
Secondary road	⛊ 🗼 Radio mast / Lighthouse
Road under construction/development	♨ ⚓ Spa / (Swimming) beach
Railway / railroad	
Ferry route	⭐ TOP 10
International boundary	
Province boundary	26 Don't Miss
National park, National preserve	
Restricted area	22 At Your Leisure
✈ International airport	
⊕ Regional airport	**1 : 800 000**
⚓ ⚓ Harbour	

0   10   20   30 km

0   10   20 mi

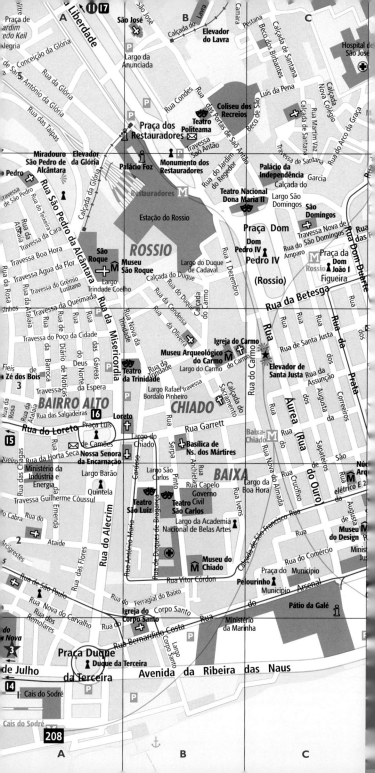

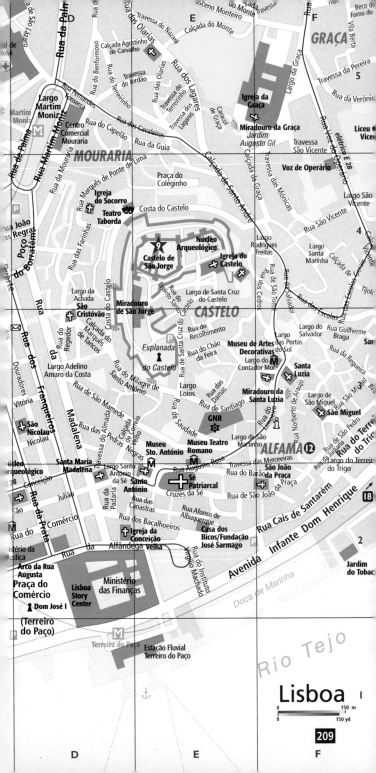

Lisboa

209

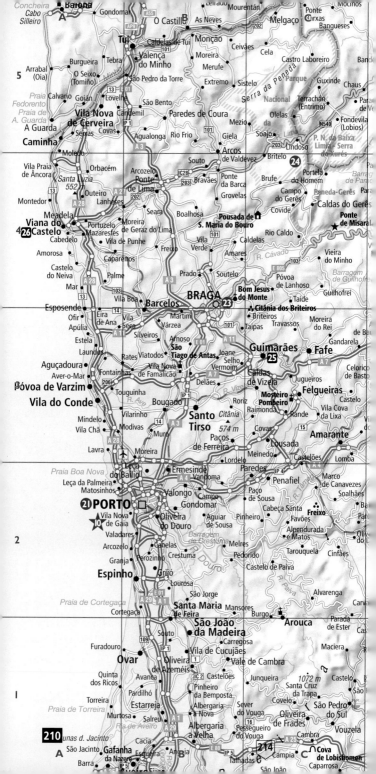

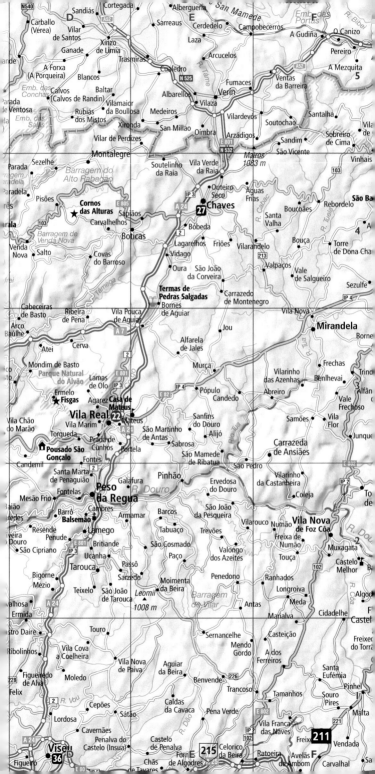

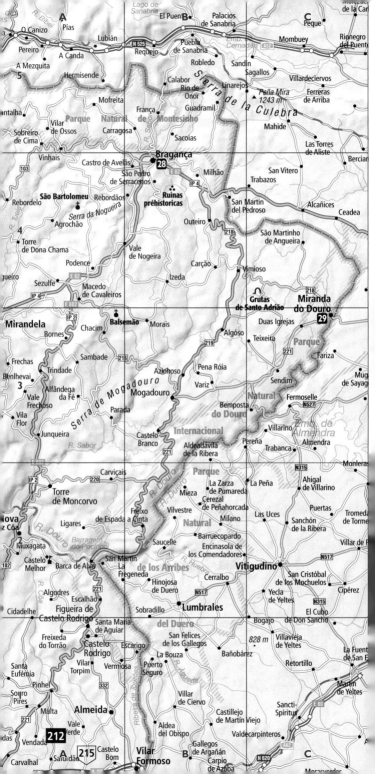

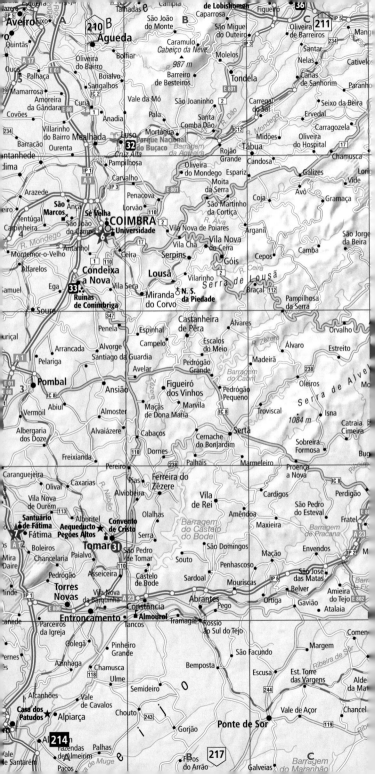

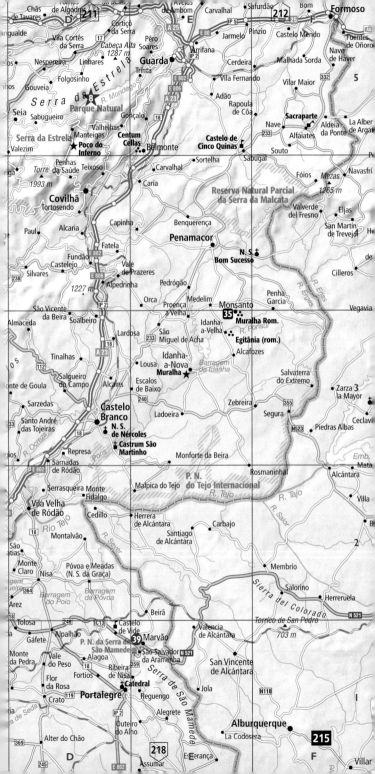

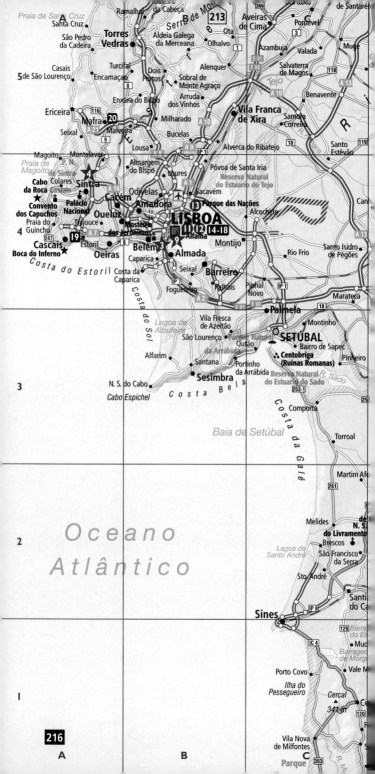

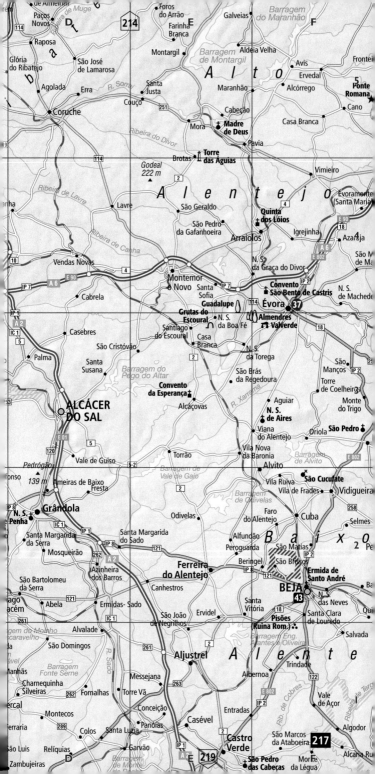

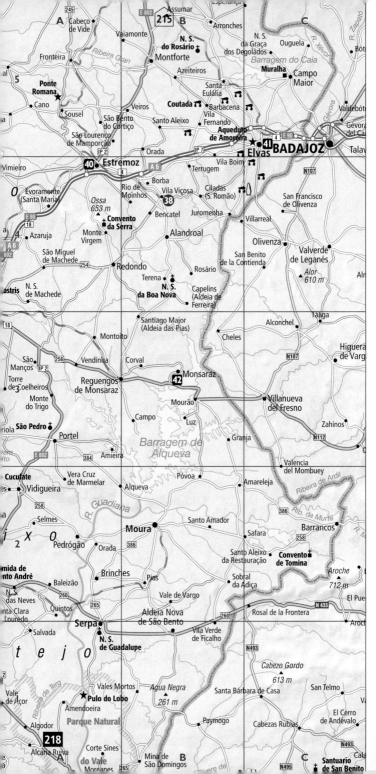

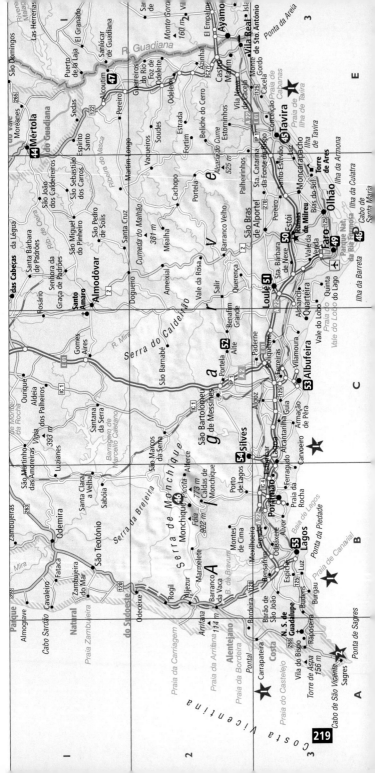

Index

Index

Index / Picture Credits

Picture Credits

Credits

1st Edition 2017

Worldwide Distribution: Marco Polo Travel Publishing Ltd
Pinewood, Chineham Business Park
Crockford Lane, Chineham
Basingstoke, Hampshire RG24 8AL, United Kingdom.
© MAIRDUMONT GmbH & Co. KG, Ostfildern

Authors: Tony Kelly, Kerry Christiani, Dr. Andreas Drouve
Revised editing and translation: Jon Andrews, jonandrews.co.uk
Program supervisor: Birgit Borowski
Chief editor: Rainer Eisenschmid

Cartography: © MAIRDUMONT GmbH & Co. KG, Ostfildern
3D-illustrations: jangled nerves, Stuttgart

Printed in China

Despite all of our authors' thorough research, errors can creep in.
The publishers do not accept any liability for this. Whether you
want to praise us, alert us to errors or give us a personal tip –
please don't hesitate to email or post to:

MARCO POLO Travel Publishing Ltd
Pinewood, Chineham Business Park
Crockford Lane, Chineham
Basingstoke, Hampshire RG24 8AL
United Kingdom
Email: sales@marcopolouk.com

FSC
www.fsc.org
MIX
Paper from
responsible sources
FSC® C124385

10 REASONS
TO COME BACK AGAIN

1. Don't miss this year's **port wine** vintage – it's the perfect drink for every occasion.

2. Lisbon's **trams** are still rattling their way through the streets of the capital city.

3. You can't fail to be impressed by the **cliffs**, **bays** and **beaches** of the mighty **Atlantic ocean**.

4. Head to **Belém** to imagine the **voyages** of the nation's chequered **Age of Discovery**.

5. Visitors never get tired of the views from Portugal's **Serra da Estrela** mountain range.

6. You'll start to miss the **local people** – they're **relaxed**, **hospitable** and **happy to help**.

7. The magnificent **sunsets at the Cabo de São Vicente** will always leave you wanting more.

8. There's plenty left to discover by **car**, **boat** or **train** in the lush green **Douro Valley**.

9. The **Alentejo's** cork oaks, meadows, vineyards and olive groves are calling you back.

10. The nation's numerous **historic landmarks** are worth visiting time and time and again.